Praise for

MESS

"A fascinating read by a hoarder about the psychology and culture of hoarding." —Melissa Clark, *New York Times*, "By the Book"

"In a memoir mixing sorrow and hilarity, self-confessed clutterer Barry Yourgrau records how he jettisoned junk and traumatic memories." —*Nature*

"Yourgrau elevates sorting through his 'curated' 'wunderkabinett' to a high art." —*Los Angeles Review of Books*

"A funny, smart, and moving memoir about the accumulation of STUFF: what it means to us, why we keep it, and how we deal with our personal 'collections.' (Great book, btw.)"
—Roz Chast, author of *Can't We Talk about Something More Pleasant?*

"My favorite bohemian unpacks his life, and his heart. I will never look at clutter the same way again. I love this book!"
—Gary Shteyngart, author of *Little Failure*

"[Yourgrau] interviews experts, researches hoarders, clutterers and collectors, and makes lively characters out of everyone in his life." —*Shelf Awareness*

"A kind of meta-memoir by a meta-hoarder." —*Bookforum*

"Compulsively readable." —Jessie Sholl, author of *Dirty Secret*

"All of us who live—or have lived—in unmentionable and unspeakable abodes owe it to ourselves to have our anti-domestic pathologies turned into something as funny and charming as *Mess*." —Lawrence Osborne, author of *The Forgiven*

"*Mess* is Barry Yourgrau's autobiography by way of neurosis, a twenty-first-century version of the *Confessions of Zeno*. Sometimes shocking and frequently self-mocking, it charts the tough negotiation between shame and fixation, between clinging to the past and moving forward, between being devoured by one's demons and facing them down."

—Andrew Solomon, author of *Far from the Tree*

"Barry Yourgrau is America's Kafka, if Kafka were hysterically funny, weirdly relatable, and had just a little bit of a hoarding problem."

—Sandra Tsing Loh, author of *The Madwoman in the Volvo*

"If Richard Pryor and Lydia Davis shared a hoarder's body, this is the memoir of that wild gorgeous being."

—Clancy Martin, author of *Love and Lies*

"This book is funny, hopeful, and true. Buy it, put in on your shelf, and be sure to dust it regularly."

—Daniel Smith, author of *Monkey Mind*

"A beautifully written examination of the pain of holding on and the agony and relief of finally letting go."

—David Adam, author of *The Man Who Couldn't Stop*

"Yourgrau, with courage and insight, transforms his most shameful secret into a gift for the reader. He's that rarest of things—the generous hoarder." —Sean Wilsey, author of *More Curious*

BARRY YOURGRAU

MESS

*One Man's Struggle
to Clean Up His House
and His Act*

W. W. NORTON & COMPANY
Independent Publishers Since 1923
New York · London

For information about permission to reproduce selections from this book, write to Permissions, W. W. Norton & Company, Inc., 500 Fifth Avenue, New York, NY 10110

For information about special discounts for bulk purchases, please contact W. W. Norton Special Sales at specialsales@wwnorton.com or 800-233-4830

Manufacturing by RR Donnelley
Book design by Ellen Cipriano
Production manager: Louise Mattarelliano

Library of Congress Cataloging-in-Publication Data

Yourgrau, Barry.
Mess : one man's struggle to clean up his house and his act / Barry Yourgrau.—First edition.
pages cm
ISBN 978-0-393-24177-8 (hardcover)
1. Yourgrau, Barry—Mental health. 2. Compulsive hoarding.
3. Yourgrau, Barry—Homes and haunts. 4. Housekeeping. 5. Storage in the home. 6. Authors—Biography. I. Title.
RC569.5.H63Y68 2015
616.85'2270092—dc23
[B]
2015009523

ISBN 978-0-393-35290-0 pbk.

W. W. Norton & Company, Inc.
500 Fifth Avenue, New York, N.Y. 10110
www.wwnorton.com

W. W. Norton & Company Ltd.
Castle House, 75/76 Wells Street, London W1T 3QT

1 2 3 4 5 6 7 8 9 0

For Cosima,
in all her variations

Contents

Prologue with Grocery Bags   1

1. The Chinese Puzzle Box   17
2. What's *Wrong* with Me?   32
3. Some Kind of Flâneur   51
4. Let the Right One In   68
5. Brothers Grim   86
6. The Cut-Glass Hand Bell   104
7. Mastering Disaster   122
8. Dodge Days, or Letting Go of L.A.   142
9. Home Comforting   156
10. The Real Stuff   175
11. The Notorious Bungalow   196
12. Freud's "Dirty" Couch   214
13. The Red Fish   227
14. Gordon's Knot   251

Postscript   269
Acknowledgments   274

MESS

Prologue with Grocery Bags

That's how it begins.

With grocery bags.

Grocery bags, and the unexpected buzz of the doorbell one afternoon, at my apartment/"writing studio" here in Jackson Heights, Queens. At that rasping blurt, my heart seizes in foreboding. It always does. Isn't one of the features of contemporary urban apartment life that the ringing of the doorbell without prior warning is a sound ripe with menace?

"Who is it?" I cry, rising uncertainly from my desk chair. The reply makes my heart dive through the floor.

"It's me!" cries my girlfriend, Cosima. "Let me in!"

I have the shock of being caught.

"What's up?" I ask, when I reach the door and open it a crack.

This is the first time in five years that Cosima has been at my threshold, though her apartment is just around the block. Her brow and upper lip are beaded with sweat. Laden grocery bags strain from both hands.

"I forgot my keys at home," she pants, irritable and short-winded. "Let me in, these bags are heavy."

I struggle to keep a wild edge out of my voice. "I can't," I reply abruptly. "Why don't you go to your mother's?" Her mother lives two flights down from me.

"My mother isn't at home," Cosima snaps. "*Why can't I come in?*" she cries, her voice rising.

"Because I don't want you to see what's in here!" I tell her savagely, through gritted teeth. "You know that—okay?"

I can see a look of horror flash in her eyes. She steps back. She's had a glimpse past me.

No, I don't have a crack pipe or a chat-room dungeon habit or a dead body. But my condition would provoke alarm, even disgust, in most people. Make that the condition of my apartment. I'm a pack rat. A clutterbug. I have something of a hoarding issue.

"*Jesus Christ,*" Cosima says. A stark pause. "Give me your keys," she says tightly.

I go and find them, my keys to her place, and bring them to the door. I offer to help her carry her groceries downstairs. "That's all right, don't bother," she answers, laboring off toward the elevator. I watch her go.

"I'm sorry," I call after her.

I shut the door, numb. I go back to my desk chair and sink down with my heart still pounding. I feel shamed and exposed. Some line has been crossed, a hidden life revealed. For a few minutes I get up again and go about lamely gathering and throwing out some of the litter of newspapers, magazines, and junk mail adrift on the floor by the entryway. But then I get overwhelmed and I go back to my laptop, back to resume half-working and half-surfing— my customary mode, the activity in which I've been interrupted. Except that a sick worm is gnawing inside me. A definition of troubled or addictive behavior I once read bubbles into my head, not for the first time, here behind my barred door: It's behavior that interferes with your intimate relationships and obligations.

■   ■   ■

No, Cosima has not been across my threshold in five years, even though this place was hers before she passed it on to me. Because I haven't wanted anyone in here. Not her. Not friends. Not the super, at first because of general concerns about him sniffing around for the over-aggressive landlord; and then, despite the place needing some usual repairs and attentions, out of paranoia that things had oozed into such a state of neglect, the landlord would immediately seek penalties. This hostility is typical for someone like me. It's about shame, but also about the hypersensitive intimacy of the things around me—however trivial and derelict they seem.

I lie: the super did come several years ago to repair the grout around the bathtub. It's long since crumbled again. And the exterminator enters, once a month: a person with a Dickensian grotty aura about him that feels oddly comradely. And speaking of God enjoying a laugh, I actually had to let in a film crew one day last year. My TV producer twin brother and I were making a video teaser for a possible reality show, featuring the two of us wandering my multicultural neighborhood, and his three-man crew needed somewhere to assemble their equipment. It was tense, on my part. The crew director is someone I've known slightly over the years. Glancing around, he said, with that quiet genial empathy that makes you grind your teeth, "Don't worry, I understand—my mother used to be like this."

Like this . . .

Cosima's lively elderly mom, Nadya, who lives downstairs from me and is the lone person I will grudgingly allow to stay overnight (when she's overrun by guests), puts "like this" like this:

"Pathological."

As she herself saw a therapist for several years for this same problem, I forgive the tone of her appraisal.

But as I'm forever fiercely reminding her—as I would you, if you were ever in here—*kindly do not touch anything*. If you want to, please ask first. But I'd rather you didn't ask, because *I'd rather you did not touch anything*.

There's a fair amount not to touch.

■   ■   ■

Pacing this lair of mine now, I make an aimless miserable survey, shaken by the encounter at my door. I actually groan at what I see (I'm given to that).

I occupy a medium-sized one-bedroom apartment. Its dim little entryway "greets" the unwelcome visitor with a dark waist-high wedged-in bookshelf, its top piled up with years-old magazines, junk mail, a few bills, some teetering empty boxes, an empty wicker basket, and a couple of long-expired calendars (from Madrid, from Brussels) which I just can't bring myself to relinquish. Down beside, ready to trip me or you, sits a box of my girlfriend's books, destined for her place for over a year now.

I drift into my small as-it-were "dining area." The dining table hosts a permanent slovenly debris, of books, mainly, plus assorted stationery, old pencil-heckled text printouts, plastic bags like an invasion of blowsy desiccated jellyfish, and a set of half-broken opera glasses. Right now this debris also boasts a dazzling white team shirt of Brazil's Corinthians soccer club, refolded in its torn grubby wrapper, bearing the signature of its rotund, recently retired superstar Ronaldo. A Brazilian friend gave it to me when Cosima and I were down in São Paulo recently. I wore it to the gala reception for visiting French grand chefs, grinning to beat the band and guzzling Champagne. I pick it up, to put it some-where more dignified, but then, at a loss, just put it back. The four chairs at the table are occupied, by books, magazines, various bags. The space from here to the side wall, one half of the dining area, is unnavigable because of heaped boxes, shopping bags.

Beyond, in the main space of my apartment, my "writing studio," the theme continues. No, I don't use "goat paths" (a grim entry in the hoarder's glossary I'll later learn) to squeeze through. But should I want to lie down widthwise, I would be blocked by more jumbled boxes and bags, and books, and pieces of luggage. The table surfaces are shale fields of miscellaneous paper clutter.

In the bedroom: the floor is thick with yet more boxes and bags, dirty laundry, more luggage. The bed, to be lain on, requires clearance of T-shirts, unwashed jeans, papers, folders. Books. A Cardio Glide exercise machine stands near the bed, hung with several sweaters, pairs of dirty pants.

The galley kitchen and the bathroom aren't so bad, though arrayed with defunct gadgets (hair trimmers, electric kettles, Brita pitchers). Actually, the fridge is awful—a morgue locker of stains and ancient grubby jars and bottles.

The four closets overall are stuffed to the gills, in good part with the unworn, the broken. Crummy mini-caves of an anti-Ali Baba.

■   ■   ■

Number of *visible* cardboard boxes in my place, empty or full: 45.

Number of shopping bags with handles, large and small, in *visible* use: 22.

Also on the premises: 11 suitcases total, more than half of them partly torn; and four laptop computers, three of them as useful as pet rocks, all of them with hard drives clogged with clutter. Also: two (or three? four?) ancient typewriters. And one baby grand piano (Cosima's), unplayed for years, used for storage on top and underneath.

And everywhere, still more plastic grocery bags. A big clumsy upright vacuum cleaner stands in the midst of things in its tangle of cord and hose, like a piece of abandoned highway equipment. It was a gift from Cosima's mother. Last used: two months ago.

■   ■   ■

"I'm sorry," I repeat at Cosima's table that evening. Apology is a domestic skill I've honed very ably; it's something I have a flair for, I'm proud of. It's one of my modes of loving. We all have our talents.

Cosima's big apartment is vivacious and airy, comfortably well-kept, with carpets that she's haggled over in Istanbul and Aleppo, and jazzy-kitschy furniture shipped back cheap from a trip to Mumbai. The upholstery is now showing happy wear and tear from our many dinner parties. Here is where we do our "living." Mornings I drift along to my pigsty while she works in her home office. In the evening I return for supper.

Cosima is a foodie, a formidable one. She travels the world writing about three-star restaurants and superstar chefs for glossy magazines. She authors cookbooks prodigiously splashed with international flavors and cultures. As a result, though I'm an "eccentric" bohemian writer and sometime performer, I live a pretty fabulous double life as Cosima's table and travel companion. I am her "plus one" at René Redzepi's Noma and Alain Ducasse at Plaza Athénée in Paris. I get to sample *pinxtos* (tapas) and multi-Michelin-starred treats in San Sebastián, bouillabaisse in Marseille, degustation menus in London, dim sum in Hong Kong, feasts of kebap and raki beside the twilit Bosphorus in Istanbul, where she owns an apartment.

The other half of the year, when we're not gadding about, Cosima cooks for us at her place. Thai lamb curry, or Valencian paella in its outsized pan? Often nightly fare to me, especially when she's testing recipes.

I lead a version of what they call "the good life." And I don't
have to work or pay for it. "You have the best setup in the world,"
people tell me. "You lucky bastard . . ."

And I come home with all sorts of fanciful cargo from our travels. That's what accounts for the merrier line of clutter swamping
my place: little mementos and artifacts from my gourmet globetrotting with Cosima.

■ ■ ■

So I'm expecting dinner this evening (if not exactly as usual)
with the foodstuffs Cosima was lugging in those ill-starred grocery bags. She'd mentioned something last night about pasta with
the anchovy essence we snuck back from the Amalfi coast.

But arriving with a double offering of red carnations (they
have a great durability-to-affordability ratio), I am informed
that she isn't hungry. We sit facing each other in somber silence,
she grim in a sea-blue dress that brings up the blue in her gray
eyes behind her glasses with their dashing leopard-spot frames,
me with a plate of rye crisps and cheese, and the very humblest
brandy from her special trove of dinner-party liquors. She has a
small pour of very good Armagnac from it. I float a light little
joke about this. I like my light little jokes. Normally she likes
them too.

But not tonight.

"That was unforgivable this afternoon," she informs me.
Meaning being turned away from my door, and the reasons for
that. Followed by:

"You, we . . . can't go on like this."

My stomach tightens, then retightens. "I'm *truly* sorry," I murmur. And more forcefully, "I will sort things out."

"You've been saying that about virtually everything for ten
years now."

I draw a deep breath. My shrink makes a similar retort, over the shorter span I've been seeing her. "I will clean up," I lie.

"But it's *more* than that—that revolting mess which appalled my soul today!" (She can talk like this.) "Every night *I* cook for us, everything on our trips *I* arrange, all the real-life work in our relationship *I* do. You don't even earn a living!"

I bow my head, fighting the urge to squirm. Yes, all true. And I'd kept from her the gory detail that two months ago I borrowed money from both my brothers, my twin and my younger one, both of whom I've only had a rapprochement with—growing but fragile—over the last year or so. This on top of the monies others had loaned me.

"I know," I murmur.

Her fork bangs on the table. "I'm sick of taking care of you!" she erupts. "You're old enough to be a grandfather—and you live like *a teenager!* Okay, that's it," she announces. "You have to clean up. And I don't mean just your house. *I mean your act.*"

"*Gee, is this what they call a life intervention?*" I quip bleakly under my breath.

"Just what do you bring to this relationship?" she keeps on, in deadly fashion. "*Tell me.*"

It's an old tack of hers, and I squirm uncontrollably. It always gets under my skin, this sudden demand for a naked reckoning up of what I take as our "understanding," our intimate fond recognition that she reminds me of my father, and even my mother too— my parents combined. And I remind her of her doting, adoring grandmother.

Instead of shrugging her off as I normally would, my domestic tactic as holder of the much weaker hand in all this, I'm about to say, goaded and raw, "I dunno—I give you lots of loving," followed by: "*I put up with you.*"

But what if she were to answer: "That's not enough"?

I stare at her. I feel the onset of panic. She speaks.

"I'm calling Dave the Declutterer."

"What? *No!*" I retort—off balance both in relief she isn't announcing the death sentence for us, and desperate again at the suggestion of intrusion.

Dave is a professional personal organizer we happen to know socially.

"*Yes!* Why not?"

"If Dave the Declutterer tries to cross my threshold," I inform her, bunching my fists, flaring with primitive (adolescent?) rage, "I will attack him physically. I will take care of cleaning myself!"

"*When?*"

"I will do it," I tell her. I blow out a long, harrowed breath.

"Do you realize how bad this is?" she says, shaking her head, doubting.

"Yes I do," I tell her. "*I realize I have a really bad problem.*"

I spend a very ugly night on the living-room couch. She wants to send me to my place, as she does when she's truly aggrieved; but I manage to get her to back off, at least on that. It would be too much on the desolation scale for one day.

But I know I have not only a problem, I have a cascading set of them. And I have to fix them. And I am in despair, yet again, because I have no idea how to do this.

■   ■   ■

In the *Inferno*, Dante consigned persons who hoard to the fourth circle of hell.

The fourth circle would get a lot more crowded if you updated it to America today. Or to England, Germany, Austria, the Netherlands, and Japan. And beyond the consumerist developed world as well.

In America between 6 and 12 million—perhaps even as many as 15 million—people, men and women equally, are estimated to

suffer from diagnosable hoarding or have severe clutter problems. Fifty cities in seventeen states have chapters of Clutterers
Anonymous; the woes of clutter rivet the boggled interest of
millions. *Hoarders* and *Hoarding: Buried Alive* have been reality TV phenoms—not to mention Oprah's visits to the topic
starting in 2007. There's a National Association of Professional
Organizers with some 4,000 members in the business of helping
sort things out. These *things*, these hoarded objects, famously
range from gum wrappers to old cars to cats and dogs—and
anything in between and around. Such as my tourist maps,
brochures, and café napkins. Or my cherished accumulation of
plastic grocery bags.

The condition is not mere bad habits. It churns deep in the
mind's mysteries and the brain's chemistries. In 1908, Freud
famously linked the hoarding of money to the anal stage of childhood development. Toilet training, he argued, is a potentially
traumatic experience that can reverberate through life if done
badly. By this theory, adults who collect or accumulate things are
unconsciously trying to gain back "possessions" they had to yield
to the potty many years before. But such "anal" types are also
characterized by excessive orderliness; opposites, in fact, of messy
characters such as myself.

There's been progress since Freud—but no real breakthroughs.
What exactly makes people hoarders and pack rats is still not
fully understood; but it's been thought for some time to involve
an anxiety pathology. Paradoxically it's been associated with elements of both OCD (obsessive-compulsive disorder), wherein the
extreme, relentlessly accumulated clutter causes distress, but can't
be parted with, and OCPD (obsessive-compulsive personality disorder), where the sufferer (your so-called "anal" type) thinks the
old worn-out stuff around him or her is fine and dandy, and won't
part with a scrap of it. There are some common traits, too, with

variants of autism and the disorganized woes of attention deficit disorder. Half of hoarders and severe clutterers are also thought to suffer from depression. In other words, a fine symptomatic mess.

Increasingly, experts have felt that hoarding deserves its own entry in the *DSM*, the all-powerful *Diagnostic and Statistical Manual of Mental Disorders*.

(And indeed, the manual's latest edition, the *DSM-5*—published in 2013, two years after my girlfriend's appearance at my door—does just that. Renamed "hoarding disorder" instead of "compulsive hoarding," it's now categorized as one of a group of distinct conditions "related" to OCD and is no longer seen as technically an anxiety problem. [OCD itself has shed its longtime anxiety disorder tag.] What's more, the new diagnosis for hoarding puts difficulty discarding things, regardless of value, as the condition's lead symptom, displacing over-acquisition and accumulation. Excess stuff is still a key characteristic, of course. But first emphasis shifts to the struggle against loss—the unwillingness and inability to let go.)

■　　■　　■

I went hectically researching on my splotchy-screened laptop, following the confrontation at Cosima's table. And almost straightaway I came across the work of Drs. Randy O. Frost and Gail Steketee, a pair of New England psychologists considered leading lights in the dark, recently emerging field of hoarding and clutter. Their book *Stuff: Compulsive Hoarding and the Meaning of Things* would become my bible of sorts. The first reading jarred me. All at once the clutter of conditions I suffered from took on some sense and shape.

Depression? Check.

Anxiety? Check.

Certain symptoms of OCD? Check—I was not a hand-washer, thank you, but I realized how ritualized, how stressfully and demandingly arranged my jumbled apartment weirdly was. Not to mention my checking—and rechecking and rechecking again—that the gas burners were off each time I left the house.

And ADD-like symptoms? Check again. People who hoard, write Frost and Steketee, "are often highly distractible . . . [Their] symptoms make it difficult for them to concentrate on a task without being diverted by other things."

That was me in spades—along with procrastination, disorganization, and indecisiveness.

A line from *Stuff*, about emotional attachment to things, struck particularly deep: "The item becomes part of the hoarder's identity—getting rid of it feels like losing part of one's self."

I recognized that, piercingly.

Immersing myself in *Stuff*, I kept ticking off more diagnostic boxes. The condition usually grows worse with age; hoarders tend to be older rather than younger. Their clutter interferes with normal socializing, prevents intended use of furnishings (read: my bed, chairs, tables) and spaces (read: my dining area, for instance), features many items still in their original wrapping (my scattered caches of postcards, still poignantly in their original packets).

Finally, emotional trauma. It was a common trigger of hoarding behavior. I ticked that box grimly.

Frost and Steketee offered an online self-test with staged photographs. The scale of clutter ran from 1 to 9. I steeled myself and took the test. I scored a 3—"mild." Maybe leaning a shade toward 4—"moderate." Temperateness in all things, I wanly congratulated myself. The photo sample for 9—"extreme"—suggested a Guinness World Record stunt for most junk in a confined space. I figured my score gave me a hopeful enough prognosis.

But then again . . . how truly *clinical* was my problem? When (cautiously!) I began to describe my situation to friends, I kept striking a chord. Someone said how she had notebooks lying around everywhere. Another, moodily, that the storage bill for her husband's memorabilia going back to his childhood ran to $3,000 a month. A third, darker still, that his mother kept *every envelope she had ever received* for possible reuse. The glamorous editor-in-chief of a lifestyle magazine, celebrated for her well-organized office adorned with expensive flowers, launched a torrent of confession about her inability to discard any item of clothing she had ever owned, and her grief, anxiety, and turmoil when forced to do so. A film critic admitted to saving every email he'd ever received—including many he needed to reply to but simply didn't. A cyber-hoarder.

■   ■   ■

I pondered all this, and more, in the wake of Cosima's riot act. Of which I'd heard variants before—and always counted on the strength of our affection to override them. But this time, after that messy shock at my door, felt different. Cosima long had had a problem with how I led my life—my finances, my Internet surfing, my "irresponsible work ethic." But now she'd had the first glimpse in years, as I say, of my housekeeping. Poor Cosima actually thought I was neat. Sure, I was a guy who loaded up on postcards and brochures when we traveled. But I was also a bloke who meticulously folded his T-shirt and hung up his clothes at night, who carefully washed dishes after our dinner parties. Why, I'd even occasionally snapped at *her* messy kitchen counters.

But I had become increasingly at wit's end myself, frightened even, over the state that I was living in, there where I spent my days.

From the mid-1980s I rented a storage unit in Manhattan, where I stuffed most of my things away, unsorted. Unsorted but not unfretted over. I would close the Yale lock, walk off twenty feet, then feel compelled by anxiety to go back and check the lock, then reopen it and reclose it, then walk off again—and repeat three, four, five times even. I would laugh in horror lest someone see me and call the men in white. I'd given the unit up when I moved in here, my very own place at long last. Except I hadn't given it up. I'd just transferred my jumbled storage to this new address. I was *living* in it, as it accumulated.

While I brooded, a pair of cockroaches went skittering by a leg of my writing table. I cursed and stomped them. A few days later, for the first time, I saw and had to kill a mouse—smaller than my thumb, but I was shouting in disgust and outrage while I flailed with a rolled-up glossy art magazine. (*Artforum*: I had stacks of unread issues on the floor.)

As a writer I'm a fan of wretched farce, but not as the world I really want to live in.

A desperate idea began to take root, as the days slid into weeks after Cosima's ultimatum. I must engage my clutter, in *all* its aspects, as an all-encompassing project. That was the only way out for me. As sufferer and as writer.

Meaning I would chronicle my ordeal, too—an ordeal was what lay ahead, I had no doubt. I would descend into the existential bowels of my beleaguered self. (The metaphor flared up one particularly bleak pre-dawn.) I would be a questing pilgrim slob, on a twelve-stations-of-the-Cross trail of transformation. (Another pre-dawn simile.)

Part of my ordeal would be this very act of chronicling. I wrote about myself all the time, it was my beloved topic—always in the disguise of fantastical fiction. Now I would bare my existential soul without benefit of costume. My existential soul was very scared at the prospect. Scared and then some by what lay hidden under dusty drapings beneath Cosima's piano, and crammed into closets: the boxed possessions from my late parents. Among them: a cut-glass hand bell from my mother's last illness, achingly swaddled in tissue paper. Among them: my neurotic, domineering father's books, his initials stark on the flyleaves.

For so many years, these had remained too charged for me to deal with.

My apartment and my mind: veritable root cellars of the undead. I was long, *long* overdue for resolving pain-frozen unresolved things . . . somehow.

So the idea of this project was born.

Midwifed in part by two bugs and a mouse.

1

The Chinese Puzzle Box

From a portrait of the artist as a young clutterbug-in-the-making: Something that broke.

It happened in South Africa, where I was born and where we lived until I was ten, and my family boarded a ship for America. I and my twin brother, Tuggy, and my younger brother, Palle, entered the world in Johannesburg, but by the time of the incident we were living in hills of Natal Province in Pietermaritzburg, Maritzburg for short, the drowsy red-brick-Victorian provincial capital.

A fifteen-minute walk along the road from our house stood Scottsville Government School. For school meals my mother would pack us each a lunchbox. Included was a flat round-shouldered glass Dettol bottle filled with orange juice. An odd-ball choice of vessel, this bottle: Dettol was a popular household cleaner and disinfectant. My thrifty mother had washed it out and removed its green label for repurposing. One day in third grade—on Scottsville Government School's dusty playground? on the walk home along King Edward Avenue, stubby fields of maize here and there below in the distance?—I dropped the Dettol bottle. It broke into pieces.

The stab of intimate loss that went through me at that moment still traverses the decades, crosses the oceans. More than loss; it was somehow wounding, humiliating—as if something acutely private and poignant between my mother and me had been forcibly exposed; violated and shamed.

All this over a Dettol bottle?

Yes. Because that silly rinsed-out bottle felt like an intimate talisman of my mother's love and concern, of the security and comfort of home in the alien universe of school. My universe overall was pretty alien. Scottsville was my third school; Maritzburg my third city, fourth if you counted the farm outside Jo'burg where we'd spent part of a year. The house on King Edward Avenue was the sixth I'd by then called home.

In such an uprooted environment the Dettol bottle must have been, I now think, some kind of equivalent of what the English psychoanalyst D. W. Winnicott called a transitional object—a thing adopted by a child as a comforting presence between mother and the outer world. I'd poked around in Winnicott's writing in the late eighties, after suffering a harrowing depression during which I desperately tried to "reform" myself so an ex-girlfriend would take me back (no luck). A blanket or a fluffy toy are common such transitional objects, soft and huggable usually, for very young children. But the category serves well on into later life, even psychologically evolves, according to Winnicott, into the zones of culture and art. And my variant of such an object fell and shattered.

Even at the time I was aware of the bottle's goofiness. Who'd use a container of household cleaner for juice? My mother, that's who—the same woman who, after we'd moved to Denver later, would march regally along the sun-blasted sidewalks wearing an inverted shallow fruit basket as a "Chinese" summer hat, on her way to the Albertson's supermarket. Or would sport a leopardskin pillbox hat jauntily modified with a clinking-clanking brooch, for a march to visit, and charm, our family doctor. It was

the Dettol bottle's tender screwiness, combining with the fact
that it broke in public, that charged the moment of breakage with
an almost lurid, voluptuous pathos. I felt a weird surge of pleasure
too, I confess. My Dettol bottle's destruction was my own private
sentimental showstopper—a heart-tugging spectacle of self-pity,
one to which I felt myself an admiring audience as well as a participant. I was starring under the 1950s' Maritzburg sun in my
personalized revamp of Oliver Twist and his orphan bowl.

Did I bear the broken bottle pieces home? Was I supplied a
replacement, freshly rinsed out?

I must have been, though the exact aftermath I don't recall.
But from then on the word "Dettol" acted like a glassware madeleine, summoning a desecrated intimacy involving an object.

■   ■   ■

And then there were my marbles.

Also in third grade, an age when many children start collecting things, I developed a yen for marbles. Their jewel-like candy
store colors thrilled me; their perfect spheres, their weight and
clink when I jostled some in my hand.

During recess, the playground of Scottsville school under the
purple jacaranda trees became a hubbub of marble games. Boys sat
legs wide on the bare ground, nesting over their target pyramids
of glassy cat's eyes and nougaty, swirly regulars. You shot from
a distance. Hit the pyramid and it was all yours. Miss and your
marble was lost to the host. Shyly I got up the nerve to try my luck
once or twice—not just risking but exposing to a collective reality,
to public transaction, a marble of mine. *A Barry marble.* One of
the cache I hefted and savored and kept in a jar by my bed in our
latest house, our eccentric Yourgrau world a mile back down King
Edward Avenue. I lost, of course. I was a timid, precious-minded
visitor—a transient dabbler—so very private and identity-involved

with my marbles. My heart hammered when I stepped up to shoot, there in my dark blue Scottsville cap, blazer, and tie, with gray shorts and long socks. Maybe on the blazer's school badge I should have worn a personalized Latin caption: *Futurus Neuroticus de Obiecta* (future object-neurotic) or *Factorem Turbamentum in Factione* (maker of clutter in the making).

Or maybe all my troubles to come sprang from the existential realization that struck me all at once on that playground one afternoon during recess: the epiphany that I and my family were transients. *Foreigners.* I might have been born in South Africa. But it wasn't my, or our, home.

What was?

The answer was clear: us Yourgraus. Our unit of five—my dad, Dr. Wolfgang Yourgrau, with his German accent from being raised in Berlin, who'd only come to South Africa with my mother from the turmoil of just-born Israel a year before I myself was born; Thella, my mother, who hailed from South Africa; and us boys— this was my only true home. What's more, no other persons in the whole world shared our Yourgrau name. We were unique, distinct, unrooted—a neologism. We were a special mini-species of our own. More than that: we were a cult, with my father as the cult's chief propagandist and booster. "We have only us Yourgraus to count on, no one else!" my father would repeat, on through the years whenever Tuggy and I felt snubbed by the outside world or by classmates at yet another new school. He seemed to derive satisfaction from this state of affairs. It was his constant theme and credo: us the wandering grand Yourgraus, led by him, versus the world.

"You should be grateful," he'd remind us for most of his life, "for having such a wonderful family *compared to what your school-mates have.*"

Which meant a family with a father from Europe who was a student, friend, and colleague of Nobel Prize-winning scientists (not to mention knowing Herman Hesse), and a mother who'd been a trained violinist with a degree from the London Licentiate of Music and had played with the Palestine Orchestra. We were a mini-Noah's Ark peering down at the flood from on high. Our little itinerant closed sect—with him at the heroic head.

This became the rooting sense of myself in life, sustaining and bolstering me as I grew up. It also became an awful oppression. My full name, for instance, courtesy of my old man, inspired by philosophers he admired, was Bertrand Robin Baruch. "Barry" came from Baruch (Spinoza). It was like walking around with a Louis XIV wig tucked under my haircut. Come high school, I hid from sight the photo my father had presented to me, signed by the great man himself: "*To Bertrand Yourgrau from Bertrand Russell.*" I hid it so well I eventually couldn't find it.

■   ■   ■

But to return to my marbles.

The South Africa I knew was the land of apartheid. Official discrimination had been instituted the year before I was born—only a few taunting months after the publication of *Cry the Beloved Country*, the international bestselling lament over the country's racial iniquity by Alan Paton. Paton was from Pietermaritzburg. He'd gone to primary school two miles from where I went at Scottsville, and he graduated from the university where my father now taught. Maritzburg had another famous connection in the country's racial history: it was where Gandhi was thrown off a train in 1893, inspiring his dedication to *satyagraha*, the non-violent struggle for justice.

Like most whites or "Europeans" (as the parlance of the day went), my family had black servants. Our King Edward Avenue house counted a cook and a maid, a handyman and a gardener. Their quarters were a primitive cement structure in the bushy backyard where my brothers and I groped about for blackberries. We three boys had been tended early on by black nannies, but my memory is blank about them. I never got to know any of our servants. My parents dealt with them, my mother for the kitchen and house, my dad for the yard, where a snake—a dread black mamba once—might rise up like a dragon. A couple of times I overheard my parents conversing low about firing someone, my mother's tone jarringly hard.

Then starker images: our lamplit kitchen table one dark night where a grizzled older servant, still in his bulky overcoat, is having the gashed-open flesh on his knuckles tended by my father after *tsotsis* (thugs) have beaten him; my father answering the phone, then hurrying away to intervene for a servant who'd been seized by police for being without his passbook. Out behind our dark red *stoep* (veranda) there on King Edward Avenue, the cement lodgings are another alien world to me. I keep diffidently wide of them when I go past out the back gate, glancing over uncertainly to see if anyone is about. I'm awkward about my status, uncertain how I should behave if I encounter any of the servants here in their domain.

Then one afternoon I stand beside my father at the threshold of a murky room in those backyard quarters. A stocky, spottily-bearded middle-aged man I don't quite recognize—one of the servant's relatives?—gazes up at us stolidly from the packed dirt floor. He's Zulu, no doubt; that's the dominant tribe here in our house and in Natal Province. The miserably furnished room around him reeks of sweat and ashy smoke and *mielie pap* (cornmeal mush). It's shocking, peering for the very first time into this shabby other privacy existing steps away from our airy house. And more shocking: on the dark floor by the man lies a mattress, on whose grubby disheveled plaid blanket glimmer, faintly, two of my marbles. They're cat's eyes: glassy with a twisting flake of color inside, like a trapped bit of brown or blue leaf. I must have forgotten them somewhere, haven't really missed them. Until this moment when I'm suddenly almost paralyzed, choked by the shock of seeing marbles of mine—*my marbles*—here.

A considerate if patriarchal employer, my father sternly instructs the man to give them back. The man surrenders the marbles without protest. Then he rests stiffly against the mattress on his elbow, stolid, stoic. Perhaps he'd wanted the cat's eyes' bland prettiness for decoration. Perhaps he'd wanted them as a gift for his kids back wherever he came from (where that might be I had no idea). And again, a gust of poignant shame sweeps me—this time that an *adult* is being forced to return some stray little things overlooked by the careless kid of the master of the house. The white master in the land of apartheid. I still squirm, years on, thinking of the scene's racial colonial undercurrent.

And through it all, like the twisted leaf in a glassy cat's eye, that upheaval of disquiet and violation that something of mine—no matter how trivial—appears in someone else's possession. In *their* intimacy and privacy. This sense of certain objects of mine as sacral to me and non-sharable is the deep pulse beating through my childhood way with *things*. In adulthood this sense will spread to include my emotions, even my opinions until I'm ready to make them public, properly fashioned. I'll be secretive not just about what I'm thinking, but even what I'm reading. When other writers share personal chitchat about how they write, I'll get up and leave the table. Half a century after those cat's eyes, here I am, still cringing when Cosima blithely wants to borrow a favorite pen, or—God forbid—a friend asks to use it.

■   ■   ■

Right before I turned ten we left for America, and I left marbles and Dettol bottles behind. (History would amuse itself in 1988 by turning my clutterer-to-be King Edward Avenue bedroom into a storage room for Alan Paton's archives.) Departing Pietermaritz-burg station, where Gandhi and his luggage had been tossed out, we took a slow looping train all the way south to Cape Town. From there we set out to England, the first leg of the journey, on the *Winchester Castle*, a small lumbering vessel with a very large hole in a ladies' room that required pumping the whole way. To mark the crossing of the equator, a costume contest was held. We three boys prepared for the judges and prizes with our parents pitching in. Finally I was ready: my father's baggy pants rolled up to my knees, his dapper black shoes flopping on my feet, his big pin-dot tie around my thin young neck above his slack waistcoat. My blue Scottsville cap sat on my head; rouge shone in pink cir-cles on my cheeks; thick dark lipstick distorted my mouth into a garish, doleful sag. For buckteeth, I had an orange rind inside out under my lips, cut jack-o'-lantern style. My helpers appraised me from a cabin bunk: my father, that portly unshaven gent with his thinning hair flying up and his front false tooth out, wearing a food-stained shirt and, at mid-afternoon, pajama bottoms with a frayed belt cinched over his potbelly to back up the elastic waist-band; my mother beside him, laughing in movie-star sunglasses, cigarette holder in hand.

So appropriately, so achingly to my grown mind, this was how I crossed my first equator—as a sad young homespun clown wear-ing his parents' makeup and clothes. An award-winning clown, please note. I was voted first prize in the judging and received a gift as resonant as my outfit: a cheap Chinese puzzle box of check-ered blond wood, with slats you moved in a complex sequence to reveal a tinkling secret little drawer at its heart. With my name, as I recall, grandly engraved on the bottom. This trophy from my crossing into our new life—garbed as a woeful young clown— was here in my Jackson Heights sprawl, somewhere, buried out of sight inside another box, one of the cardboard boxes under Cosima's piano.

Decades after the equator crossing, I wrote a story about it, featuring a little model replica of us on the *Winchester Castle*—an object meant to be a good-luck talisman but which turns out dismally. Decades now after writing the story, I reread it. My heart capsized and sank at the familiarity of the ending.

I pack the whole thing (the model replica) *up in a box. I do what I always do. I find a storage place in the neighborhood and lock away the dismal boat and its half-rendered occupants, and get a ticket for the lot. I throw this in with the disorder of my papers, onto the little heap of all the other tickets just like it.*

Yes, I thought. Here I am: *living* in that storage place.

■   ■   ■

In January 1959 we steamed into New York harbor from England, more grandly, on the *Queen Elizabeth*. In our new country my sensitivity about *my things* almost immediately got another echoing jolt. One snowy Sunday in St. Paul, Minnesota, a university colleague of my father's dropped by to visit. Two sons my age were along. Without asking a word of permission, my old man went upstairs to Tuggy's and my bedroom, came down with *our* teddy bears, and with a grandiloquent show of hospitality gave them as presents to our visitors. Both Tuggy (from Tuggelin, a pseudonym my father had invented for his political writing in Germany and Palestine) and I were too generally cowed to protest on the spot. But when we plaintively squawked afterward—I was privately stunned, wounded, outraged—my father replied dismissively that we'd been ignoring the teddy bears, obviously we didn't care about them, what was the big deal?

So maybe I'd pretty much forgotten the teddy bears, as I had the cat's eyes in the servants' quarters. So maybe they were lackluster specimens, with pale stringy fur the color of weak honey. Transitional objects they weren't, despite being in a classic category; I'd never showered cuddles on mine. *But it belonged to me!* And what child-rearing IQ did it require to know you don't give away a kid's possession without asking? A birthday present to boot, from my parents!

I never forgave my father for this. It infected how I felt about him—and about objects, directly and then by association. It fed my emerging hatred of my old man and his usurping and domineering manner. Embarrassing as a longtime adult to admit it—to blurt out in shrinks' offices how much I still seethed over this teddy bear injustice.

█   █   █

In America we kept up our transient ways. My father ever the wandering "visiting professor," candid with his exalted opinions about academics (*he* trained under Einstein and Schrödinger in Berlin) and his fellow academicians. Our initial six months in St. Paul (Univ. of Minn.) were followed by a year in nearby Northfield (Carlton College), then three years—at three different houses—in Northampton, Mass. (Smith College), until finally my father settled in at Denver University for the rest of his career. By the time Tuggy and I left for college near Philadelphia at age seventeen, we'd logged five different schools in our seven and a half years in America—eight schools all told if you counted South Africa. Counting South Africa, our Yourgrau family cult had kept house at thirteen different addresses.

So I became all too familiar with moving vans, and new classrooms, accents, walks to school, and temporary friends. And always, cardboard boxes. For the move to Denver, my brothers and I were roped into helping pack up my father's big library at Smith College. What a tribulation, that book-packing! I can still recall the gooey stench of brown paper tape in my father's clubby college office suite, as Tuggy and Palle and I labored among the stacks of boxes and books day after day. I remember the tedious, archaic, demanding artisanship of fitting the big books in solidly— the heavy volumes on Greek philosophy, quantum mechanics, logic, gravity, general and special relativity—solidly and deftly secure from squashing or pinching in transit, the tape wetted with a slimy sponge but not too sodden, so it would grip just right. The durability of the boxes under Cosima's dusty Steinway was a testament to my hard-learned packing skills.

And how all the more grueling and obnoxious the experience was made by my old man's glower and punctiliousness, his domineering ways. "It's not enough," he'd say, looking over from his office blackboard thick with equations. "Come!" And I'd have to carry over my perfectly well-wrapped box, across which he'd smear another anxious soaked layer of tape, like plaster of Paris on top of plaster of Paris.

His overbearing style featured at home too, of course.

"If you don't know—*ask*," he'd scowl over his Liebfraumilch during conversation at the dinner table. Meaning he the Doctor Professor *knew*. We boys didn't.

And always, his edge of agitated anxiety.

My father's anxiety . . . Forever in my mind's eye I saw this image: my old man's plump face straining bug-eyed and sweating over his shoulder as he backed our secondhand lumbering gray Buick out our narrow driveway—at our first house in Northampton—and we'd hold our breath in the back lest he sheer off the hedge (he did) or gouge the car door (he did), or plow backward into an oncoming vehicle in the street (somehow he didn't). I was always holding my breath around my father. Or clumping after him, such as later, on our journey out to Denver, my heart in my mouth, struggling with baggage, as he barged, ever frantic, ever bug-eyed, ever sweating, through the Chicago train station to lead us strung behind him to the hair's-breadth connection westward.

And yet my old man had a different side. Which was confus-

ing. There were his thrilling tales of his Berlin Weimar days brawling with Nazis and riding in race cars, of his dashing uncles with
their racehorses and saber duels; of his Belgian father who was an
ambidextrous pistol-shooting champion. And even as late as my
high school in Denver, he'd stand in the doorway of our darkened
bedrooms as we lay ready for sleep, and softly croon Nat King
Cole's "Mona Lisa" in his German accent, inserting our names into
the lyrics. *"You are my sweetest Tuggy, Barry, Palle-pie . . ."* The
hall light's glow tinted his short, burly silhouette. It was a lullaby
I never tired of.

To be followed by the noise of him at the back door, wrenching the doorknob back and forth, back and forth, in a singsong of
anxiety to make sure it was locked.

Anxiety, anxiety. It rubbed off early. Stock internal photo of
my young self: I'm lying in my pajamas and terrycloth bathrobe
on the couch in our living room in Northfield, Minnesota. The
sun streams in the windows, it's late morning, I'm ten years old,
home vaguely sick (again) from school. The small rented house is
empty; everyone's out. And for an hour, two hours, I lie paralyzed
with dread in the sunlight, not daring to move. *Because I'm alone.*
Because any little sound from me might alert some potential evil
presence to my location—like a prey giving away its hiding place.
Or any blithe moving about by me—ignorantly assuming things
were normal—would trigger a shock ambush out of a horror movie.

When my mother returns from her errands, I'm fine. The
house resumes its placid everyday reality.

Here in Jackson Heights these days, I'd sometimes look around
at my boxes, bags, and drifts of knickknacks and I'd feel like that
frozen boy on the couch again—not daring to move or act or touch
anything, lest the full chaos of my situation be unleashed.

■   ■   ■

It was in Denver, when my old man began traveling to eastern Europe for his work in the sixties, that a new category of objects entered my life. Not only the presents he brought back—cheesy East German rock and roll records in the flimsiest of cardboard sleeves; garish catalogs of Romanian frescoes. There were also the little foreign "daily" things he'd gotten for himself—the small beaked white bottle of stinging Odol mouthwash; the quad-ruled notepads.

Anything associated with Europe and travel became infected for me with my father's aura. I might have liked something, but couldn't bear its presence because of its poisonous connection to him. But couldn't bring myself to throw it away. So the object got frozen—that word again—in a limbo zone of ambivalence. This zone expanded through the years, extending to anything with any connection I felt unsympathetic or intrusive. Objects became the genies of their affiliations—invasive spell-casters. Whenever I wore the yellow and green rugby cap that my twin brought me a couple of years ago from South Africa, I felt a twinge of disquiet. I kept almost anything from him shoved away in the filing cabinet in my bedroom. We had long-rocky relations, and I found him oppressive. But even friends' artworks I stashed in a closet. So they couldn't impact me with their vibes, their connections.

Classic ambivalent item, father-related: a small gift metal penknife, dating from his sixties' return to Berlin. Silvery, flat, and oblong, hardly thick as a wafer, barely two and a half inches in length and half an inch wide, with two thin blades and a nail file like a short crosshatched straw. A streamlined modernist tid-bit, its sides thinly grooved in decoration. I'd kept it over all the years—most of the time hidden away. Because it so reeked of him. And because it radiated from its petit knife-self the memory of *another* knife as well, one I no longer had, lost somewhere. *That* knife was a cherry-red Swiss Army penknife my old man brought back from Einstein's old stomping ground of Bern. I was delighted, touched by his spot-on thoughtfulness as I unfolded the knife's clutch of handy features.

Until he offhandedly displayed the knife he'd bought for himself—a gleaming deluxe version, bulging with extra features. A veritable royal yacht of a Swiss Army knife; a display model of his weird, astounding self-centeredness.

A few years ago I'd come across the silvery little penknife from Berlin while making a quick foray into a taped box. On the spur of the moment I'd decided to keep it out. It was a fine aesthetic morsel and the passage of time seemed to have dimmed its intrusive paternal glare.

But not quite. I'd pick up the knife to handle now and then, but only quickly. I couldn't have it regularly visible around me, part of my ambience. I kept tucking it out of sight in the papery mulch on a counter shelf, where I'd have to hunt to find it.

I couldn't just toss it, of course; or give it away.

Those books of Wolfgang Yourgrau's under Cosima's piano were symptoms of this same ambivalence. This limbo of hate and clinging and admiration.

Internally and externally I was a man haunted by his old man . . .

In fact, a paternal specter lurked in what I brought back from my own European travels with Cosima—if not in the very travels themselves. I felt a quiver of unease about our glorious, gluttonous trips, an anxious reluctance to absorb them fully into my psychic world.

So back in Queens the mementos just sprawled around me . . . limbo material. Notebooks in quadrilateral squares I'd eagerly bought, then couldn't bring myself to write in. Or throw out.

The shrink I was seeing once said: "It's the things we hate that we can't let go of, more than the things we love."

She also astounded me by declaring that in fact I loved my old man—*too much*.

"Most people get over their father hero worship," she said. "You still don't seem to have. The question is, *why?*"

"You do ask probing and confusing questions," I told her.

2

What's *Wrong* with Me?

Every week following her ultimatum, Cosima would announce she was coming over for inspection.

No, I would insist. I wasn't ready.

"You mean you haven't started cleaning yet?" she protested.

No, I'd explain, I had not. My project needed doing in proper order. I was still in the researching phase. "I found this great encyclopedic guide to cleaning," I informed her, chuckling. "It's called *Home Comforts: The Art and Science of Housekeeping.* It weighs almost three pounds! I weighed it on the bathroom scale."

"Why are you weighing books when you should be vacuuming and throwing out all your crap!" she demanded.

"Jesus, why don't you get a job harassing orphans?" I muttered.

"Why don't you get a *job.*"

It was a long-scoring touché.

Now, I did have arguable reasons for slow going. But in my heart I recognized an all-too-familiar, mushy, cowardly specter in my life: procrastination. Frost and Steketee, *Stuff*'s authors, recognized it too, so I've noted. It was a standard feature of clutterbug and hoarder behavior.

But then again: having been inspired to cast this whole business as a Project (capital P) to be eventually written up as a book, I couldn't very well go rushing headlong into things any old way, could I? I needed to lay the groundwork. My efforts to meet Cosima's challenge would require an appropriate dramatic tack, an unfolding shape, a structure.

A schedule.

It got to the point where I would consciously resist disturbing any dust or wiping any grime, or throwing anything out, because I was saving those grueling experiences for when my Project was formally launched—whenever that might be. I began to think of my clutter as a film set waiting in suspension for the camera to roll, which would only commence once all "preparations" were in place. Actually, the camera had begun rolling. I'd had an extra inspiration to make photographic portraits of my mess, as arty documentation. Fiddling with color values on my laptop, I achieved a garish lonesomeness that was pretty cool. A scuzz-shadowed kitchen corner looked luminously ghoulish. I thought it wisest, though, not to share these images with Cosima just yet.

Then, drifting around my premises, it would hit me that I'd be exposing all these shambles to the eyes of the world. In turmoil I'd scuttle over to a notebook and scribble out little absurdist fantasies thrumming with anxiety at the prospect of exposure. Such writing was an avoidance twofer: it avoided work both on my cleaning memoir and on the cleaning itself.

"But if you're really going to do it as a project, we need to see your experience of—you know—*cleaning*," protested Cosima.

She'd supported my inspiration of an "all-encompassing" approach; she thought the chronicle aspect would offer the chance for a wider appeal, for me as a writer, than my oddball minifictions. But now she was baffled and alarmed by how long it was taking me to assemble a book pitch. She herself was already well into a new opus, not a cookbook this time but instead a complicated historical lollapalooza she was tackling with characteristic focus and vim.

Me, I was making a sprawling mess of chronicling my sprawling mess. Literally so. My laptop with its absent *j* keypad like a missing tooth held a mega-scraggle of versions of MESS.doc, hundreds of them at various stages, practically unnavigable, multiple versions bearing only the minutest of changes. Copies of various of these multiple versions were helter-skeltered among my email accounts, as security backups. Backups against what—my laptop's dust spontaneously combusting? The photo portraits I'd fashioned of my mess were stashed about under a motley of clever but misremembered pseudonyms in the uncharted hinterlands of overrun photo folders. Indecision had met digitally powered disarray. They'd mated like rabbits, at first sight.

■   ■   ■

"You need to *start cleaning*," Cosima repeated. It was almost June. An early-strawberry gazpacho she'd whipped up sat glossily on the dinner table between us. She's a seasonal cook, Cosima. Her ultimatum to me had come far back in the days of fava bean stew with pecorino Romano—early March.

"All right, okay," I muttered. I held out my bowl. "Tomorrow."

"And another thing," she said. She didn't like the name I'd given her for my Project. She didn't like being Cosima.

"But it's for *my* book," I pointed out. "*I* like Cosima, and *I* get to assign names."

"Says who? I'm the one being referred to."

This casual disdain of supposedly self-evident norms was a common and maddening experience with her.

She had a selection of new potential monikers already drawn up. "Something with an ancient Greek or maybe Byzantine tinge," she said. "Ariadne, Xenia. Theodora?"

"Theodora? Are you crazy? No no no no! Why not . . . Agrippina?"

"But wasn't she some awful harridan?"

"Exactly."

We made a truce. She would remain Cosima for the time being, until we mutually agreed on a replacement.

"But really, when are you starting cleaning?"

"*Tomorrow*," I repeated, gritting gazpacho-pink teeth.

Tomorrow arrived.

And departed.

But two days later I finally launched into it. Some actual cleaning. As an inspirational slogan, I summoned a cliché from my complexly Lacanian shrink: aim to clean a little at a time, not all in one go. *For this wisdom I need a shrink?* had been my response at the time. But now I chose a modest target: the small overwhelmed bookcase in my front entryway, which was the first cache of clutter to greet me every day, like a mangy whiny runt fixing its eyes on me when I came in my door.

I decided to keep a brief journal of my experience.

Unsurprisingly, my first entry read: "*Started cleaning 2pm. After 4 hours of . . .*" Of need I say what?

Much of this "need I say what" again involved my splotchy-screened laptop, where, after morning calisthenics in my crowded bedroom while the latest goodie from Netflix squawked and blasted—a seventies Japanese yakuza classic—I found myself sucked into a familiar death spiral of checking and sending email, then rechecking, and then rechecking again—I have four uncoordinated email addresses—all the while Web surfing like a hopped-up lab rat.

An all-too-familiar cry blurted from my lips, as in the cheesiest horror flick:

"*What's WRONG with me?*"

Part of an hour I burned selecting a new screensaver from my mushrooming accretion of digital photos from our travels. I was angling for an exact Proustian signifier of "calm and neutral." I settled at last on some trucks in profile on a highway near São Paulo. Why? Something about the quality of color and light, and the scene's anonymity . . . But it wasn't *exactly* right.

I kept returning, trying out alternatives.

At two o'clock at last I tore myself away. Wrenching around I seized hold of the huge office chair with dismal brown fabric parked nearby, the one Cosima's mom had left as a surprise gift for me while Cosima and I escaped briefly to Miami in early May. I bumped and banged this monstrosity right out the door and down to the basement, where I left it with the startled building porter, Sammy.

I was pumped. Back upstairs, I seized and wheeled out a chewed-up trolley with wire mesh shelves, an eyesore in which I'd been stuffing the plastic supermarket bags I brought in daily. Every week I had the impulse to heave the crummy thing. But then I'd hesitate. Moth-eaten as it was (I'd rescued it from Cosima when she was throwing it out from her bathroom), the trolley might still be useful someday . . . *you never knew*. What if a situation came up exactly suited to the trolley's storage properties, and I'd foolishly gotten rid of it?

This concern was so characteristic of the clutterbug and pack rat mind-set that it approached parody.

"*Decided I could live w/consequences w/o trolley,*" I noted emphatically in my cleaning journal. "*Freed space feels* good!!"

Inspired, maybe too far, I decided on bigger game than the small bookshelf. I turned to the beast of the upright vacuum cleaner—another unsought unwieldy gift from Cosima's mom. She had given it a couple of years before, when she squandered a fortune on a scandalously expensive dust-sucking contraption for herself called Rainbow Cleaning Technology from some Odessa gangsters in Brooklyn. Cosima was furious. How could an elderly woman living alone in a modest one-bedroom need a souped-up deluxe vacuum cleaner *costing several thousands of dollars*? But her mother dug in her heels and refused to return it. Cosima refused to speak to her. There was an epic stony silence lasting four days, the worst fight I remember them ever having. In the midst of it, Cosima's mom called me down and presented me with the Kenmore "PROGRESSIVE Direct Drive," which she'd received as a bonus for her appalling purchase. I immediately saw this for what it was: a crude attempt to finesse me into acquiescence to her recklessness. And the vacuum, though brand-new, was completely ill-suited to the cramped nooks and crannies of my spaces. But how do you call out an embattled septuagenarian?

So this gift from her stood there in my main room, mainly gathering dust. I had jerry-rigged a hose and brush head to the back of it from a broken old canister model I kept in my front closet. (It might be fixable—*you never knew*.) But vacuuming with this was like using the grafted-on trunk of a tranquilized elephant you had to drag around. It made my nerves seethe any time I could force myself to turn it on.

"*Tension + anxiety + irritability,*" I wrote. "*Kneeling awkwardly with big backwards vacuum + knocking CD's over.*"

The CDs were on a nearby crowded armchair by my overrun dining area, and they came clattering down as I bumped about with the PROGRESSIVE Direct Drive. I looked around hastily for a box to stow them in for the time being. There were lots of empty cardboard boxes to choose from; but the decision was not straightforward. I became stalled in peevish deliberations over the right box exactly calibrated for a) housing these particular CDs (my hip mix for our dinner parties, such as Mel Torme classics and Xavier Cugat nuggets) and b) for housing these CD's *temporarily* while I vacuumed (they would go elsewhere *permanently*). With much snorting and various tryings-out, I settled on a box.

I resumed vacuuming.

Until I paused, in agitation.

"*Brush head keeps falling off,*" I wrote. "*Work 4–5 minutes + go onto Internet.*"

The familiar loop was taking hold: some kind of work leading to rising agitation, leading to email-checking and online diddling, which led to their own agitation, from which I turned back to work, which kicked off the loop again. It all blended into an intense, interknit, exhausting ordeal.

It was as if I slogged eternally in an undrained marsh of anxiety and agitation.

"*Stress of decisions . . .*" I wrote. That was the main culprit. Decisions gnawed at me—everywhere. Even the color of ink I wrote in represented a decision—or a curatorial ordering. Years ago I had decided that all my handwriting not in service of my fiction could only be in black ink. Beats me why. I just found myself fixing on that internal rule. If I got a pen with blue ink, I wouldn't use it, even if it was a great, cool pen (from Claridge's in London, say). Eventually using blue ink at all unsettled me, represented a betrayal of a private order I'd staked out.

In the crowded universe of my apartment, the number of decisions I confronted was overwhelming. At worst, it seemed a version of Zeno's paradox. Each decision seemed to involve a subset of prefatory decisions, on and on to the scale of infinity. Put another way: I had lost the capacity to untie Gordian knots.

The first day of cleaning kind of petered out.

I retook a grip the second day. I refocused the "a little at a time" angle on my original target: the small overloaded bookcase in my entryway. Finally getting going after noon, I made real headway, tossing some junk mail, some long unread magazines; doing some tidying. But then I stalled. Should I keep a glitzy lifestyle publication for doctors, years old but still containing enticing-looking articles worth possibly checking out later, about St. Moritz hotel lobbies and director Robert Wilson's personal collection of over 6,000 art objects? And what about this clunky Brussels tourism brochure, outdated but offering several nice black and white snapshots of Jacques Brel? Not that I'm a big Brel fan; but the photos were atmospheric. Where to put them? Just leave them there? Decisions. Anxiety kept driving me over to my laptop, as if cowboyed by a spell. The dusty air quavered with my plaint:

"*What's WRONG with me?*"

Well, at least I hadn't torched most of the day surfing politics and porn, as was known to happen in the bleakest depths of the Bush years.

The bookcase did get more presentable, for all that. But it was back almost as before by the end of the week, clumped with new additions.

Now Cosima's attitude took a dark turn. Mentions of Dave the Declutterer disappeared. Instead I caught the dread name of Zinaida being invoked, when Cosima and her mom prattled in their cacophonous native tongue on the phone.

This was disturbing.

Zinaida was a Soviet-style battle-ax for whom housework was an urgent heavy-industry operation. Demolition and purging were her favored methods. Cosima had to fire her after she tossed half of Cosima's cosmetics (seeing as they weren't Chanel). But Cosima and especially her mom remained fond of Zinaida's screwball vehemence and kept in touch.

I thought my suspicions must be paranoid. Surely they wouldn't dare sic Zinaida on me. From the get-go, I'd been lecturing Cosima on how hoarders generally, and me particularly, resented interventions. There'd famously been suicides in Nantucket. But then one afternoon, while I was in the bathroom, I heard a knock on my front door. When I finally got to the door, there was no one there.

But there had been. Zinaida! Cosima's mom had sent her up on an ambush mission. Apparently she'd come back down in a huff.

"She said she could hear you—in there—with a mistress!" roared Cosima, quaking with laughter when I went over early that evening just to confront her. "Isn't that hysterical? She refuses to have anything to do with you!"

"You ever try that stunt again, I'll call the police," I snarled, not seeing the humor one bit.

"Oh, c'mon," said Cosima. She was taken aback. "She really helped Mom clean up her clutter. Mom was only trying to help!" But she saw she might have crossed a line. "So when are you going to Clutterers Anonymous, then, sweetie?" she asked, turning gentle and concerned as I simmered on the couch. "Didn't you say you were going?"

"I will go," I snapped. "I will go!"

I sighed, much besieged. A procrastinator, cornered.

There was a dinner party that night at Nadya's place back at my building. Nadya was an obsessive *salonnière* and hostess herself. Twelve of us sat crammed around her table as vast platters of food emerged relentlessly from her tiny overcrowded kitchen. We downed toast after toast (no imbibing without a toast) under shelves of books adorned with family photos and literary postcards and topped with a motley of dolls collected on Nadya's own travels. On the walls hung drawings and photos of Cosima through the years, alongside various gifts from Nadya's artist friends. Her apartment was still a stuffed, even cluttered, environment, but it was well-tended: a sociable welcoming place. In major contrast to my writing studio two flights above.

This was the émigré salon world I'd entered thanks to Cosima. Tonight's guest of honor was a corpulent old theater comedy actor from Moscow, who stood up to read a flowery, raucous poem in praise of the hostess. Amid the laughter Cosima translated for me. She obviously still meant to soothe my ruffled feathers, because sometimes I'd be imperiously left to fend for myself at such evenings so that she and the others could savor their native jokes unimpeded. I'd gotten accustomed to it: it was like boozing agreeably at an opera lacking subtitles. I never read opera subtitles anyway.

Cosima would turn back into a very young girl at these gatherings—a feisty bright-eyed kid who still belonged to some distant long-vanished world. I always felt pangs of tenderness at this around Nadya's table. Now I stroked Cosima's knee under the table as she took a huge menacing slicing knife to her mother's sour cream cake.

Nadya did not mention Zinaida all evening. But I'd detected a glint of amusement in her welcoming smile when we arrived.

A procrastinator, well and affectionately fed. And besieged.

■   ■   ■

I had come across Clutterers Anonymous early in my researches. Effectively, it was AA for pack rats and hoarders. Doubtless there exists such a program for every human affliction under the sun and moon. Now, I knew a few people whose lives had been rescued by AA. I had come to approve of its approach, based on what I understood in a sketchy general way, not just for drink or gambling addictions but for pretty much any problem short of rampant psychosis. Group sharing, hardnosed truths aired, and actions committed to by a community of supportive sufferers, one proverbial day at a time . . . How wasn't that treatment to commend to anyone and his storm-tossed brother?

For myself, however—a different matter. I'd always been staunchly anti-group when it came to intimate me. I tended to view groups of any kind as either an audience or a gang of antagonists, to be charmed silly or crushed to pulp, probably both. I saw them, regardless of avowed mission, as presumptive deniers of my uniqueness. That included the uniqueness of my personal problems.

But still. I appreciated that admitting one's shared human frailty—a cornerstone of the twelve-step approach—was a big, a crucial . . . well, step. It was a rite of passage. An acknowledgment of existential modesty, that any specialness you laid claim to didn't exempt you from the common laws of demons. In fact, your clinging to uniqueness probably largely got you into your mess in the first place.

"What have I in common with these people?" was the question, to which the raw answer would be forthcoming pretty quickly.

At least that was the supposed scenario.

In this spirit I had announced to Cosima several weeks earlier my intention to brave a local Clutterers Anonymous meeting. It would be my way, discreetly yet publicly, of copping to a genuine problem, whatever exactly it was. Possibly CLA could teach me something about my bags and boxes. Maybe I'd get a little "scared straight."

Also, it was free. And you could keep your mouth shut if you wanted and just listen.

And yet I kept stalling. I feared discomfort, awkwardness, drudgery—maybe even real pack rat squalor, right beside me. Poor souls who did require "goat paths," who lived in seas of old newspapers and cat food tins. Secretly I'd counted on Cosima losing track of Clutterers Anonymous in the jumble of my other plans. As I had.

But she hadn't.

It was to get her off my back finally, and to simultaneously show my resolve to her—and to myself—that one Friday evening I went trudging past a blowsy mid-Queens shopping mall, off along a drab boulevard, and on through the graffitied dimness beneath an expressway overpass. It being Friday had factored in my foot-dragging. Who wants to spend TGIF fessing miseries with a huddle of strangers? And who would these strangers be, given this particular nowhere section of Queens?

I cut across a playground undergoing bedraggled renovations. Opposite on the side street stood a funeral home—a poky specimen, in modest white brick. What a proper Dantean landmark, I thought, for my expedition to the fourth circle for hoarders. I paused a moment, steadying myself before heading on to a low clapboard building further down the street, where I could see a small group clustered at a side door. I drifted up. We waited for the key to be brought over—me and my companions in the fourth circle.

■   ■   ■

So here I sat: a lone, balding male at a conference table in a basement room in mid-Queens with five, and then eight, late-middle-aged women. (To respect Twelve Steps' fundamental policy of anonymity, I've disguised certain details.) All of them looked more presentable, actually, than I did. Except, perhaps, for a mother-and-daughter pair, daughter in her mid-thirties, both glum, mushroom-pale, and spindly, with short, blunt hairdos. They wore corduroy shirts, ironed but faded, one brown, one maroon.

So it'll be a learning experience, the voice in my head bucked up dismally. *Learn from it!*

We began by reading aloud bits of the program protocols. Mirroring AA, CLA lays out a sequence of healing actions you progress through at your own pace: the venerable twelve steps.

Step one: "We admit we are powerless over clutter—that our lives have become unmanageable." ("Clutter" standing in for "alcohol.") All right, fair enough, I thought, if a touch purple for my case. But the overall formulaic codifying didn't sit well. Rules and regulations—of any sort—instantly inflame me. Please, God, get me out of here!, I start thinking.

God indeed appeared in step three: we were called to make "a decision to turn our will and our lives over to the care of God as we understood God." Meaning, what, I could substitute "fate" for "God"? But still: it said "God." That infinitely resounding word has always struck me as cheesy and medieval if bandied with anything like seriousness.

Then step four: "Make a searching and fearless moral inventory of ourselves."

"Sure, no *prob*," I wanted to quip. Instead I thought: *What a genuinely terrifying proposition.*

The person we'd voted evening leader was a moodily can-do, late-fiftyish lady who'd gotten hold of the basement key. She kept being interrupted by a somewhat younger woman at the other end of the table. This interrupter, a librarian, objected to how things were being conducted. Our leader kept explaining that she was conducting things this way because of all the newcomers (like me)—so please stop the interrupting. The librarian just shook her tight-coiffed head. You could feel her muscular tension keeping her mouth shut. Until she couldn't anymore and burst out with yet another protest.

So the meeting blew up.

"I will end the evening here and now," our leader astonishingly announced.

Yes, she could. *She* had signed for the key. *She* would simply lock up and leave. She called for a vote: no more interruptions. With the air of visitors made to judge a domestic dispute, we timidly raised our hands in favor.

Comic glee surged through me at this fracas. There was even another Dantean echo: the howling souls of the *Inferno*'s fourth circle forever go slamming into one another with big weights they push with their chests. But my ironic fun was blunted by shock—

at such a breakdown of the legendarily supportive twelve-step spirit. Plus it would have been a drag, an honest drag, returning to my bag-infested lair and to Cosima's interrogations with only a weird bust-up to show for the emotional effort required for my being here.

The librarian smiled and shrugged, seemingly nonchalant at the ad-hominem vote. Maybe it wasn't a big deal for her. Maybe it happened all the time.

Order achieved, we proceeded to personal testimonies. This was where I was looking for CLA, if it was going to, to connect with me.

The rebuked librarian volunteered first. Displaying an "I-am-a-clutterer" confessional briskness, she recounted a personal "triumph"—how with a cousin's help she had packed and heaved from her house one hundred (!) boxes of acquired stuff, including expensive and never-worn clothing. But who cared about the money—because *she could now open her front door.* Her son could visit. Her voice trembled as she said this. I softened toward her, maybe half a centimeter. But it was hard; already she'd begun backsliding. I softened another half-centimeter, thinking of my re-cluttered entryway bookshelf.

At heart, though, her account didn't touch me. She was the real hoarding deal, all right, struggling with her mountainsides of clutter. But she offered no ruminative intimacy about any of her possessions, their pull on her. Just the tonnage. And if I had to spend *every Friday evening* with her spoke-in-the-wheel act, I'd quickly go to shouting and throwing things at her.

Which is a big no-no at twelve-step meetings. There's no slagging on others' confessions or their personal style, no interactive fireworks like what we'd just witnessed. You're asked to tend to your own crooked plot, and bring but quiet sunshine to those of your crooked neighbors.

Much general gazing at the carpet now followed. Meetings

have no preset talking order. People volunteer. A woman who'd arrived late and perspiring in a sequined T-shirt finally shrugged and picked up the gauntlet. After another CLA-style intro, she commenced vehemently that her *possessions* weren't in control, *she* was! It was a self-pep talk essentially. Her jargon ached with cliché; but she had a game ruefulness about her all the same. Again, lots about lots of boxes; the Salvation Army had her address on file because she threw out such vast amounts periodically. She mentioned being able to glimpse her dining room table now, first time in years. My mind flashed to my own such table, tablecloth unviewable for months. Or was it years?

Time's up, announced the librarian, who was managing the timer.

I shifted around in my chair, trying to subdue a fresh wave of non-sunshine toward her.

Then I perked up. The meeting's secretary, keeper of our log, went next. She was a breezily trim redhead, and I thought I detected the slightly daffy, plummy manner of a former actress. A grin of collegial approval formed on my lips. But her story drifted off into a long hazy muddle, something about forgetting where she'd parked her car, and people's kindness.

I tried hard not to show my disappointment.

About everything, really.

All the clutter talk so far had been about *quantity*. My tablemates expressed their struggles via the conventional elements of consumer commodity culture. This culture preached shopping and buying, the joys of acquiring—and then stigmatized the over-converted, the fragile suckers, the commodityholics who couldn't handle their consumption. But I was almost a teetotaler about consumerism. I hated shopping per se. I did have this thing for postcards, and tourist calendars, and cheap old tacky paperbacks (not forgetting plastic bags, though in a different way). But never by the yard, credit card whoopily flashing. All my clutter probably would be gaveled for less than $500—were dollars the index.

Clutterers Anonymous was helping the participants here, I could believe that. But it didn't feel right for me. What did I share culturally with this group? Where was a sense of that intimate power of objects, their fetishistic spell, the almost sacramental *personalness* they could possess, for me at least, even—or perhaps *particularly*—the most trivial ones? Though maybe I was harboring a scenario in which I would show up here, polite but deep-down skeptical, only to be surprised by a jolt of recognition—an ambush of shared emotion. A twelve-step Hollywood ending?

Suddenly I had a disorienting thought. Perhaps I didn't like shopping because I cared *too much* about objects: every choice for purchase overwhelmed me with its vibrations.

I was wandering these interior hallways when the mother of the mushroom-pale duo in corduroy began speaking.

"*I'm a hoarder,*" she blurted.

Her voice was quiet, blunt, lurching.

"*Like you see on Oprah!*"

She spoke plainly, starkly. There was no practiced twelve-step ease to her.

I thought later of comparing her to a kind of a homespun mystic. But that would be a reach. She just blurted things out with this quiet awkward urgency, this naked, forlorn dignity.

She told us she'd filled the tiny condo where she lived with her daughter and a nephew to bursting with, lately, packing materials and saved pizza takeout boxes. The stuff was even spilling out into the common hallway. She couldn't stop herself. "I'm the child of hoarders," she lamented, "my mother and father were hoarders." An enraged neighbor had sprayed her car one night with noxious chemicals. When she and her daughter complained to the police, the cops found their story so screwy the two of them were committed for psychiatric observation. (It can happen like *that*? I thought, aghast.)

That's where they'd come from to here—*from three weeks in a mental ward*.

I felt shamed, being in their presence in the guise I was in. It was as if we were at a clinic and they had spinal meningitis and I'd trudged in for post-nasal drip—and mainly because my girlfriend was pressuring me to quit coughing already.

She had never heard of Clutterers Anonymous until that afternoon, the mother told us. She had come over in desperation for any kind of help. The social worker assigned to her was hostile. She wondered if her life was worth living. ("Time," murmured the librarian. Nobody paid attention.) Her car was unusable because of the neighbor's chemicals, she said. She and her daughter had to take a taxi they could little afford to get to the meeting.

We were somber and chastened when she finished. The daughter was coaxed into talking as well.

She had the same quiet, lurching way, but with bleats of exhausted despair. She wasn't a hoarder. She was forever pleading with her mother to let her handle the household money so it wouldn't be squandered. But her mother refused. She said this directly and plaintively to her mother, who shrugged forlornly.

"And I can never have friends over to the house," she went on, "because of my mother's hoarding." Her cousin, the nephew, was a manic-depressive who beat the two of them. "He calls us vile names," she told us, shaking her sad quiet head.

Tears prickled my eyes. She was actually quite beautiful, I realized, despite her pasty gangliness and awkward hair. She had luminous, strikingly tender eyes behind the grandma glasses she wore. I found myself gazing openly at her, not just heart-wrenched but a little smitten. She caught my look and blinked back. I scrambled together a crumpled empathetic half-smile.

Our leader waited me out for the closing spot. She had a three-minute pat on her own back to deliver, about how she was finally standing up for herself.

For myself, I'd had half a notion not to speak. But that would brand me as a basement-confession tourist, especially now after the mother and daughter's harrowing tale. So I just stayed in the moment. I felt the rule-breaking urge to address the mother directly—and I did, after introducing myself as one with "a clutter problem." (I couldn't bring myself to mouth "I am a clutterer.") I asked if she was on medication. She was: Celexa, one of the five (six?) antidepressants I'd been on myself over the years. I told her to look into cognitive behavioral therapy (it was the most recommended approach I'd come across in my researches). She nodded—probably wondering who this droopy man was, playing psychiatrist.

I thought of a cartoon from the old *National Lampoon*. A thickset fellow is aiding someone who's collapsed on the street. "Don't worry," he assures passersby, "I'm a sheet-metal worker!"

Then I found myself talking in subdued tones about depression, about boxes piling up from a loss of will (our leader grunted in wise, irritating recognition). Suddenly I was painfully aware of my oddly English accent, the curious (as some people describe it) relic of my South African childhood.

I talked on, feeling dissembler and confessor at the same time. I noted the enormous effort just to turn on the vacuum cleaner. I described my recent frazzled cleaning attempt. I promised to switch the vacuum on again, when my turn came to make a commitment to take home with me. This was a piece of fine hedging, though, against any real commitment involving CLA. I could observe the strict letter by simply turning the switch on.

Then I could turn it off.

Meeting done, everyone collected around the tragic mother and daughter. Our leader sidled over and said I should hang around a minute, there was something "interesting" she wanted to tell me about. This sounded like an opening social gambit, and with a hasty "Good luck" to the desperate pair, I slipped away from my visit to the fourth circle, back out past the funeral home, back across the playground, and on trudging through the dark underpass.

3

Some Kind of Flâneur

Back behind my door next day, I felt a somber relief as I surveyed the familiar sprawls and slurries around me.

In the tranquil morning sunlight, my chaos seemed innocent, cheerful even. It possessed a plush, raffish coziness. "Pathological," Nadya had slagged it? "Appalling," according to Cosima? They should spend time with poor souls in basement rooms.

True, my dining area was hard to negotiate for the piled boxes. And any actual dining around my, er, dining table was a bit of a pipe dream. But my apartment was simply a *mess*—that was the scale of it, surely, after what I'd heard the previous night. And despite the dusty disorder and excess of plastic bags, there was a certain verve to the chaos I'd created.

Or might I even say "curated"?

Yes, why not: considered from a certain angle, a freewheeling aesthetic, wasn't my whole space a kind of private untidy display case? A wunderkabinett, as such, if you will? Or perhaps, rather, a reliquary? An archival site, one forever mushrooming?

Or maybe (I was warming to the theme) an archeological dig that was evolving into an organic museum—something vaguely sci-fi? Or, indeed, an art installation? Was I a species of naïf artist, working with interiors and cute fetishes in my own inimitable style of piles and sprawls?

These were appealing notions; even insightful, perhaps.

I pulled loose a book from the dining table. It was a collection of essays by Walter Benjamin, from Cosima's grad school days. She had an M.A. in Slavic lit, to go along with an M.A. from Juilliard in her earlier incarnation as a budding concert pianist. For cultural gravitas for my Project, she'd urged me—she was an indefatigable urger—to read Benjamin's canonical rumination about unpacking his library. To be honest, from the great cultural critic's musings on opening the crates of his beloved collection of 2,000 volumes, I'd gotten little. But one passage had caught my eye:

"For what else is this collection but a disorder to which habit has accommodated itself to such an extent that it can appear as order?"

At first I'd had in mind just the rich (cheap) laugh of comparing Benjamin the Book Collector's vision of "disorder" with my well-gone book-scattered shambles. But now I thought, No: more than *habit* was the source of order in my disorder.

I cast a museful glance at the black Steinway at the rear of my main room. Cosima's sheet music sat open on the music rack—pages of Scriabin and Schubert, exactly as they'd been when she moved out. She herself hadn't touched them since the early nineties, after a wrist problem forced her to make a new career, which turned out to be food writing. And I hadn't touched them since I'd moved in! But not solely from habit. Instead, because they reminded me of Cosima in our swoony early romantic days, when we first met fifteen years ago. When I still had my storage space in Manhattan.

Call me sentimental.

While my apartment was hers, it was cozy, even a little crowded, I thought at the time. Zany folkloric hats from her earlier travels hung in the small dining area and primitive ceramic Russian toys perched on the shelves.

Many of the folkloric hats remained behind after Cosima's move. They still hung on their original nails. They reminded me of her, these hats. Especially the brown bowler from Lake Titicaca, where women sported such eccentric chapeaus. A satin-banded charmer, the bowler was a fine avatar of Cosima for me. I would notice it and smile. And blow a bit of the dust off it. The bright colors of all her hats here had softly dimmed from dust and neglect. There were still some of her ceramic Russian toys around too, and all of her old sheet music, and cartons of her cookbooks. So I was not just living in my storage but in part of hers, really, as well. Helping keep *her* place uncluttered.

This state of affairs aggrieved me sometimes. But I liked it too, for sentimental reasons.

Cosima, for her part, had practically zero material sentimentality. I was astonished at first that she kept not a single childhood photo of herself anywhere, and still doesn't to this day. Later I learned that her mother kept them all, right there available nearby. She was sentimental for the both of them. She'd haul the photos out, doting and boastful, and Cosima would squawk in embarrassment. Myself, I'd select with tenderest calculation cards for Cosima's birthday, for Valentine's Day, for Christmas. She'd be touched; she'd plant kisses on them; next morning, out with them. I still displayed an old postcard I'd given her of a lovingly rosy Renoir dancing couple, which I'd had to rescue from her trash bin one February 15. No doubt the gang at CLA would have shaken their heads at Cosima in incomprehension. Or shrunk back perhaps, in awe and wariness?

My appraising eye now turned to the rest of the piano top. It was a shipwreck, of course—but draped strikingly with red-and-gold-striped fabric. This red and gold striping sounded an oddly merry note in the room's disorderly music. Actually though, the quirky pep of color and pattern lay all about, if you looked. A once-sunny Provençal oilcloth, half-obscured, covered the dining table. The wall counter opposite me, by my desk, revealed, after some squinting, an embroidered Kurdish fabric with dancing girls, and an opulent burnt-tangerine tartan cloth.

Over here, on the counter by the piano, merriness and grunge mingled again: a beleaguered fabric of Uzbek design underlay things, floral with pink and aquamarine. Behind the piano, by the window, propped in splendor on a frail armchair, sat a kitschy throw pillow I'd acquired at the Covered Bazaar in Istanbul. The pillow's printed front touted a lascivious daydream from a French orientalist painting: a hot-eyed flowing-robed Bedouin licking his lips over a diaphanously veiled cutie, as his gaudily tasseled camel smirks behind them.

So that's who decorated this place, I suddenly grinned: *a clutter-mad wannabe camel driver!*

Over on the side window above my writing table, the wannabe camel driver had dangled a pair of multihued Mexican plastic mesh shopping bags with blue handles.

The overall effect of all this now struck me as, well, quasi-orientalist. My mess: a hodgepodge swamp festooned with touristic knickknackery amid the flotsam. As if someone were constructing miniature travel-themed picnic spots in a rubble world of boxes and litter.

I thought of another essay in Cosima's Benjamin book. The one about Baudelaire's notion of the flâneur—the idle roamer of the streets of nineteenth-century Paris. Wasn't I—now, and generally—the flâneur of my own flat? Like one of those nineteenth-century Parisian poets rambling the *rues* of the vast jumbled disorderly city, aimless and open to random aesthetic and emotional encounters?

Except I just wandered the messcape inside my apartment.

I took a break and made myself tea in my kitchen, trying to

ignore the flecks of vintage grease on the walls. The mug with blue swirly flowers I used was a souvenir from an Andalusian sojourn with Cosima. Its white inside had long gone tannic brown. But I still couldn't bring myself to part with it. I sipped. Sentimentally.

Souvenirs and artifacts from my globetrotting with Cosima: that was what accounted for the merrier line of mess in my apartment, the stuff lovingly on display. What did I bring back? Oh, little things.

Cosima had a naval officer's organizational attitude. At some inevitable point in all our trips she would blow up as my luggage swelled with mini-clutters of postcards, calendars, brochures, tourist maps, copies of local newspapers. I was worse than her mother, she'd snort. Always collecting "silly rubbish!" (As noted earlier, her mother had her own, if lesser, clutter habits.) It's the universal plaint of any sort of pack rat's nearest and dearest, this silly rubbish. Cosima just didn't understand. She'd never even been near a shrink in her life.

I flâneured over past a mid-floor jumble of boxes, to one of the prides of my silly rubbish: my collection of hotel stationery from around the world. Or should I say: *From Around the World!* It was clumped in halfhearted tidiness in an open Excelsior tub I'd saved from the trash man.

I murmured in my head some of the atmospheric grand names. "*Cipriani, Venice* . . . *Claridge's, London* . . . *Hotel Astoria* ("In Residence"!), *St. Petersburg* . . ." And flavorsome sub-grandees: "*Hilltop Hotel, Tokyo* . . . *Hotel Borg, Reykjavik* . . ." (the latter from my very first foreign trip with Cosima).

Sure, I was namedropping with these letterheads—to myself. I sunned my moods in the aura of such travel junk(et) mementos, even as they sat on my gritty floor vainly awaiting a proper home. Naturally I rarely wasted them on actual correspondence.

I stepped over to the glutted nearby counter, and adjusted a favorite from another of my "prides"—my small clutch of hotel shopping bags. This one was from five-star Le Meurice in Paris. I propped it against the green wall there.

■   ■   ■

I first saw this green wall, admiring its apple-y hue, on my first date with Cosima, in 1994. This was her place then, out in the wilds of Jackson Heights. I was a longtime downtowner, recently back from L.A., still with my old sublet walkup by Little Italy. We met at a literary cocktail party in Tribeca. She scribbled her phone number on a matchbook at the end of the evening, after our group went for burgers at the Odeon. (I still have the matchbook, naturally.) The old pal who introduced us warned me that Cosima was already spoken for, if in some complicated long-term long-distance way. But I trusted what I sensed, and hoped. "Complicated" suggested possibilities, a not quite locked door. I'd caught glimpses of her around town a few times, and she thrilled me.

To Jackson Heights I brought as discreet wooing gifts a big blob of mozzarella from Little Italy, a tape of me guest-DJ'ing an L.A. radio show, a book of my stories, and my deeply smitten heart. We ate at a neighborhood Indian restaurant along with a friend of hers—Jackson Heights is Indian central—after Cosima announced, with a giggle, that the tuna she'd prepared for dinner had spoiled. We climbed over snow banks down into the restaurant. There'd been a big March storm a couple of days earlier. "You're *old!*" she exclaimed, when we somehow got onto the topic of our ages. She was nearing thirty, I'd just passed forty. "Cosima, that's so *rude!*" cried her friend.

Living and traveling with Cosima in the years since, I'd remained delighted but often shocked by what comes out of her mouth (I've repeated her friend's words many times)—and

amazed by her talent for languages (she speaks four) and her inge-
nuity with the maddening practicalities of our journeys.

And since our initial date, I'd let the apple-green wall blister
and peel.

Poor Cosima! When we kissed at a salsa club up in Harlem,
she had no idea she would be tying her life, in her words, to the
"only male person I know who collects hotel shopping bags."

But really: how could you fault a specimen like this one from
Le Meurice? Just consider it: an on-the-go debonair lad "starred"
on it, illustrated in cool retro-fifties style, his trench coat and
tousled hair snappy against a background of palest creamy mint
above the hotel's crest with its twin sleek, seated greyhounds. A
gray cord handle draped gracefully over the bag's side. I'd had it
for five years—a talisman of breezy chic and worldly-wise luxury
in my plastic-bag-blown lair. It neutralized its surroundings: not
an air freshener but an atmosphere freshener for my shabby, if
colorful, messcape. It was a winsome signifier that I had access to
another sort of life than this one behind my unwashed windows.
Someone else, I suppose, might have considered it just a bathetic
irony, a lite version of a homeless person sporting a Caesar's
Palace cap (a cap, in fact, I owned). But that someone probably
wasn't a poet of clutter at all. They wouldn't understand how
just the right little object—be it trivial, disposable—can work on
heart and memory like a line from a song.

A visual song: my Le Meurice bag also summoned to my mind's
eye the gravel and tulips and statuary of the Tuileries across Rue
de Rivoli from the hotel—staffers once scrambled there to catch
flies for Salvador Dalí—and one of my favorite stretches of the
Seine—where Cosima and I had our first real fight about clutter.
Yes, there'd been some minor blowups before; but no full-throttle
onslaught. On this night in Paris, we dined, so-so, on the Île Saint-
Louis. Things had already gotten ruffled earlier over my lack of
planning for our cultural docket. I was a flâneur. (Baudelaire, fit-

tingly, lived for a time near where we had dinner.) Cosima, on the other hand, insisted on a program: *TimeOut* guide consulted, museum hours coordinated. Attending to this was my responsibility, she insisted. My slackness about planning piqued her; not undeservedly, she felt she carried a disproportionate burden for our trips.

Now she tried to shove a copy of the restaurant's big menu into my shoulder bag, where I carried the ill-consulted guidebook. I snapped at her that she was crushing stuff inside.

"What's in there?" She was suddenly suspicious. "I want to see!"

What was inside, of course, was "silly rubbish" accumulated over several days.

"No—" I told her.

"Yes—" she insisted.

We were on the Louis-Philippe bridge over the Seine, idling after the meal. We engaged in a brief moonlit tug of war over the bag. Whereupon she furiously stamped her foot—she's someone who actually performs this cartoonish action; she also flings things to the ground—and went storming off, just like that, toward the distant Le Meurice. I watched her diminishing figure in shock. Then dolefully I trailed after her—three kilometers along the eloquent quays of one of the loveliest stretches of riverside in the world, where only two evenings before we'd come ambling hand in hand and she kept halting in gales of laughter at my freeform parodies of the Parisians. "Paris is fine, if you don't have to talk to the locals," she liked to declare, adding, to scandalize any Francophiles on hand, "or eat the food." It was another beautiful, dreamy night out now. I trudged through it alone, past kissing couples, seething and sighing at my girlfriend's flamboyant tempestuousness, and sheepish about my clutterbug habit—me and my shoulder bag of "archival-quality" souvenirs.

What's more, because of Cosima's spectacularly hopeless sense of direction, I needed to keep a protective eye on her, despite things, lest she get lost and the night turn really disastrous.

■   ■   ■

Paris didn't make me change my ways, though. Well, slightly. Afterward I took care to be more cagey in my accumulating. I became wary of Cosima's probing eye. I played guileless, uninterested, until her back was turned and I could snatch up whatever interesting bits and pieces were at hand. My habit made me half-ashamed—because of its fatuousness. Other men got scolded for running up gambling debts. I got rebuked for, among other things, a yen for mementos. I thought Cosima was being outrageously domineering, actually, about a quirk of mine that was essentially harmless, whimsical, verging on the poetic. But as our travels were courtesy of her assignments, I felt I had to make the concessions. Her traveling was for work, mainly; mine, to enfume an idyll. A callow, puppyish idyll, as of a boy on a family holiday abroad.

Souvenirs, wrote Susan Pearce, an English academic theorist on collecting (and another commentator suggested by Cosima), are "intimate and bittersweet, with roots in nostalgic longing for a past which is seen as better and fuller than the difficult present." Even if, or particularly because, that past dates from recent gourmandizing tourism. Even if the souvenirs are contributing to the difficulty of the present!

At any rate, I came back from Paris with the Le Meurice shopping bag. Along with postcards of troops gaudily parading under the Arc de Triomphe, church brochures, napkins unstained by jam or yolk from late breakfasts at Café de Flore, and several carefully folded copies of *L'Équipe*, the sporting paper, featuring apocalyptic headlines about *"le rugby."* After the savors of selecting them, I kept most of the postcards in the wrapping or bag I bought them in, amid or on top of my home slush piles. Withholding their full pleasures for later tapping. This storage mode constructed its own appeal: another aesthetic layer, another form of object created. It tickled at a psychological nerve, for sure—as of Christmas presents left unopened under the tree long past 12/25, to keep that happy tension going. Pushing the tension theme even deeper: like bonsai-scale memory orgasms, forever delayed? Accent on forever.

Surrealists like Dalí and the poet Paul Éluard, I'd discovered, were major-league deltiologists, the formal term for collectors of PPCs (picture postcards). The word derives from the Greek for "little tablet or letter." After the collecting of stamps and coins, it's the third most popular of the acquisitive hobbies. For the bourgeois-baiting surrealists, postcards came from the universe of "found" art—unintended art, those stains of the unconscious seeping through cracks in the veneer of mass-produced culture. Éluard traded a Dalí artwork for two hundred postcards. Dalí himself merrily specialized in PPCs of porn and of art nouveau architecture (the "official popular" high culture of his Barcelona). Myself, I went for Kodachromy vistas of the *plaza de toros* in Seville or the harbor at Capri, seen through frames of orange blossoms and lemons. Icons of travel holidays in campy miniature. The campiness operated as an intellectual sarong over the stark flesh of my sentimentality.

Dalí and company traded postcards, employed them in exhibits, wrote essays about them. I was a miser of mine. They were for my eyes alone, my touch, nobody else's. They were for the opposite of sharing.

(Though I must note that Susan Pearce also said, somewhat harshly: "no one is interested in other people's souvenirs." Meaning, the wonderful version of the past evoked is only in the eye of the souvenirist.)

■   ▦   ▧

It was six years after we met and fell in love that Cosima and I began traveling together openly. This was because until then she was still publicly allied with that "complicated" longtime boy-friend. Exactly how involved was an ongoing dispute between us, since they mainly lived on different coasts. Nevertheless, he was her partner when she went on magazine assignments. This wasn't easy for me. But I had settled on a long strategy of patience and wily resilience, having faith in our fate. There was a poignant romantic thrill, too, I admit. My heart flared afresh at each postcard from her, each testament that I was her true beloved behind the public façade. We'd have our rapturous furtive lovers' reunions. And of course, I kept the postcards.

After a couple of years, I started accompanying her on trips every now and then, discreetly. Finally not so discreetly. Our first time together in Rome, I turned up a slim hour after the long-timer's exit, after cooling my just-off-the-plane heels in the Villa Borghese. He had exited for good this time; my love and tenderness had won out over the security and energy he brought Cosima. She was waiting in emotional tears on a sumptuous bed at the St. Regis as I came in with a calendar of the highlights of the Eternal City I'd already picked up on the way. We were just steps from Bernini's *Ecstasy of Saint Teresa*, it turned out—that most cluttered piece of sculpture in art history. I snagged a calendar with her in it too.

I kept a laundry bag from the St. Regis from that trip. I wandered into my untidy bedroom now and found it in a closet, among others of its monogrammed fellows from around the globe. I refolded it. It was a trophy, I guess, representing my great victory over "the Landlord," as we referred to her ex (for his periodic lordly sojourns at her place). Cosima hadn't spoken to him in ten years now. But, strange to admit, some of his old clothes, rumpled shoes, a tennis racket, were still there in my closet, along with a few of Cosima's old things. Why on earth hadn't I thrown them away?

Was it partly to preserve a tinge of the romantic poignancy of our early days? Was I still clinging to that, somehow? Putting the "mental" in "sentimental"? I grinned in sudden embarrassment, of a slightly creepy order. The Oedipal implications were pretty ripe, weren't they? I had after all written a book called *Wearing Dad's Head*. I was a guy with father issues, who'd taken his lover away from her "landlord"—and was hanging on to his clothes. Was I secretly longing to dress up in them at some point?

Or were the Landlord's belongings more props to sustain a sense that the apartment wasn't really mine—that it still somehow belonged to Cosima? That I was only camping out in it. That even now, a decade on, I hadn't committed to it, not deep down. Because I obviously had commitment issues overall, in my indecisive way. And because I loved sunlight, and the place was dim, in the back of the building. So this was another layer of embarrassment: years of squatting in noncommitment.

The brief morning sun had long passed my windows as I left the bedroom. The day after the CLA meeting had turned cloudy. The dimness was settling in; it would too soon give way to shadows. My spirits had started to sink.

■ · ■ · ■

After Rome, Cosima and I were a public couple and I became a full-time travel partner. For a third to half the year I traveled anywhere from San Sebastián to Hong Kong, accumulating aprons from celeb chefs and olive oil producers, menus from cool Basque food counters, drink coasters from beer-soaked *botecos* in Rio, cups from sake bars in Tokyo. I brought the savor of our trav-

els back home, again in miniature. But I didn't really *do* anything
on our jaunts. I accompanied Cosima to table, I drove the rental
cars (either anxiously or *extremely* anxiously); I carried the bags,
and halfheartedly I concocted sightseeing agendas which Cosima's hyper-organized brain would revise. I took lots of pictures.
Once in a while I wrote a blog post or drummed up an article. But
I didn't want to become a travel journalist; certainly not a food
one, that was Cosima's domain. I was a *fiction* writer. If we did
go somewhere for a stretch of time, I could work on my stories:
in an apartment in Barcelona looking out on the Sagrada Familia;
at the Biblioteca Nacional in Madrid, where I'd wink up at the
portrait of Borges; at a leafy tea garden in Istanbul with a view to
the Bosphorus.

I'd return carrying extra pounds around my waist, and a haul
of souvenirs to strew around my premises—new trim for my
flâneur's messcape.

I was back at my station again by Cosima's piano. Out the
window curtains beyond, a dour overcast had settled in, this
day following the CLA meeting. A gloomy thought struck me:
Baudelaire—the champion of flâneurism—was also the great
champion of Poe. And people were always getting buried alive in
Poe's tales, weren't they?

Almost against my will, my eyes drifted to the shadows under
the piano. The gritty Mexican blanket below the Steinway hid
boxes of my father's books I couldn't bear to touch after thirty
years, but couldn't relinquish. There were caches of photos and
torturous letters from a couple of romances that had ended
wretchedly, decades before. I still had them. One was with someone who chased me in rage down Houston Street in SoHo in her
panties and T-shirt. All we did was drink and screw, and scream at
each other till the cops came. The other concluded with a doctor
friend asking with an uncertain grin, "Barry, are you having a nervous breakdown?" She guessed right.

From under the tasseled skirt of the Mexican blanket the edge of a certain pale oversized envelope caught my eye. Yes, I in my turn, I thought: I buried things away, too. Things that caused me anguish to confront or experience. Almost literally I swept them under the rug. Crammed them into closets. Stuffed them beneath the piano. I gave them the Poe treatment.

But I couldn't get rid of them.

The pale envelope under the blanket held a CAT scan we brought back from Istanbul at the turn of 2007.

■   ■   ■

While I was scribbling away in my tea garden near the Bosphorus, Cosima had been complaining—not eating much, frightened by what she felt when she touched her abdomen. I finally persuaded her to see a local doctor, to reassure her there were surely no grounds for her alarm. Given our food-happy life, her discomfort could be from anything. The genial doctor seemed to feel likewise—until he examined her and gravely murmured two words: "abdominal mass."

He hurried us scrambling on foot to a nearby hospital. We sat waiting for a CAT scan, trying not to let shock turn to panic. Beside us a family were wringing their hands, conversing in agitated Turkish. Cosima didn't want to talk with the radiologist. It was me he showed (I was trembling) the large ominous image at her mid-abdomen. And two spots "of some kind" on her liver.

We reeled back to New York. We shuttled between doctors' offices with that CAT scan, turning more ashen each time. Major surgery was scheduled for two months hence at Sloan Kettering. We lived out the weeks in stunned dread, trying to embargo the truth from Cosima's mother. Every night I sat across the dinner table from Cosima, struggling with my composure as she talked about graveyards and ignored the food Nadya had sent over. By

her hospital bed the unsentimental, antireligious Cosima kept
a figurine of the Virgin of the Macarena and a little plaque of
another Virgin. Nadya sank into a chair white as a sheet when
she saw them. They said all that we didn't want her to know.

Then the surgery was done. I called in for the biopsy result.

"You mean you want me to walk all the way down the hall to
check it?" said the surgeon's assistant. It was negative.

Benign.

It was like being smashed upright by a truck that had smashed
you down. Or realizing your execution was mock, after the roar of
the rifles. It was relief in the form of a mind-warping blow.

And all throughout, echoes of my mother's desperate last
days had kept besieging me. I couldn't mention them to Cosima.
I also got a royalty statement from my publisher. My series of
"provocative" kids' books to which my editor tied such wild
ambitions had come out—and tanked. My career seemed just
a series of dashed hopes. The indie film I'd starred in, based on
my book *The Sadness of Sex*, had fizzled ingloriously. Ditto the
workshop of my would-be one-man show at a prestigious theater lab in Utah. My short stories, though nicely received, were
barely in print. ("I'm biggish in Japan," I'd note with a crooked
smile.) I was pretty much broke again. Credit cards kept me
afloat. I had five.

■   ■   ■

It was in the aftermath of those two gothic months—without
fanfare, I had decided on suicide if Cosima didn't survive—that
conditions in my place had really gotten out of hand. The full
force of the whirlwind we'd gone through hit me. Habits—the
effort—of order and tidiness—never all that robust anyway—slid
into outright neglect, into powerlessness. My will melted away.
Not just hotel shopping bags and cute tourist calendars were on

display around me: so was my depressed and post-traumatic self. My apartment had turned into a stage set of my internal condition. I became too down to even turn on the vacuum cleaner, or keep up with my cargos from abroad—or deal with the plastic bags full of dirty T-shirts and socks clumped around the bedroom, and the dusty books, not to mention the unwashed towels and greasy shower curtain in the bathroom. Flâneur? I was a guy slumped in a slightly decorated ditch. My knickknacks—and all the physical things around me—had swollen in psychic scale, into a monumental terrain that dwarfed my power to shape or tend.

Decisions paralyzed me. If I was fond of something, anything, I couldn't seem to part with it, or find a proper place for it. The same even went for what I wasn't "fond of," but felt I might need or could possibly use—such as those infernal plastic supermarket bags. Or anything for that matter that was just *there*. My rubble and junk filled me with corrosive dismay; but I couldn't bring myself, couldn't *bear*, to make changes to them. I had boundary issues—with everything, material and emotional.

I had left it all undigested (to tease my gourmandizing life).

I sighed a long hopeless sigh. I looked at my cold and hulking upright vacuum. At Clutterers Anonymous I'd promised to turn it on again. I slogged over and did that, as a gesture of Dantean co-humanity, bumping around with it roaring away for a few minutes in the awkward undergrowth of chair legs and bags and boxes under and around the dining table.

But that was enough. I turned it off.

I went into the bedroom, past the calendars on the wall either side of the bathroom door. One calendar, from Istanbul and five years out of date, showed the father of his country Atatürk dandied up like a silent movie star. The other, from Brighton Beach, local but Russian, two years old, celebrated the pleasures of vodka in little engraved glasses.

The encyclopedic *Home Comforts* housecleaning tome lay on

the bedroom floor by the bookshelf. A fine film of dust had gathered on its cover. In the book I'd marked a random passage, chuckling as I did so:

"It is your housekeeping that makes your home . . . a vital place with its own ways and rhythms, the place where you can be more yourself than you can be anywhere else."

It seemed funny, a good butt for a joke . . . a couple of months ago.

Back in my main room, I found one of the pamphlets I'd brought from the CLA basement. "Am I A Clutterer?" it asked. I eyed the list of questions again:

1. Did I have more possessions than I could comfortably handle?
2. Was I embarrassed to invite family, friends, health care providers or maintenance workers into my home because it was not presentable?

I put the pamphlet down. The questions went on in their similar ad-hominem way.

11. Did I have difficulty making decisions about what to do with my possessions, daily living, or life in general?

And lucky 13:

Did cleaning, organizing, follow through, upkeep, and maintenance all become daunting tasks, making the simplest of chores insurmountable?

That's where I'd quit rereading. My mess lay all around me. Who was I kidding? I was in the fourth circle.

But Clutterers Anonymous wasn't the path out for me.

So what was?

4

Let the Right One In

"**Y**ou're talking *clutter*, right?" said Dave the Declutterer. "Hoarders, man, they are kooks—they relapse on you." It was a fine placid Sunday afternoon in mid-September. We sat on a bench in Central Park, discussing mess in general and, to a limited extent, mine in particular.

It had been a couple of months of zigzags on the pilgrim's trail to bring me to this bench.

When I'd informed Cosima of my thinking about Clutterers Anonymous, she protested that I'd only been once. So how was I sure it wasn't for me? I needed to go at least another time.

No, I protested back: I was *telling* her. "They're on a different wavelength about their stuff."

"That's good—another perspective. Maybe you'll learn something. Go interview the poor mother and daughter whose neighbor attacked their car!"

"Are you crazy? No!"

So inevitably (in about a month), I found myself tramping along again, jaw clenched, under the dim overpass a second time, on beyond the Dantean white brick funeral home to the low clapboard building. I had a brief flare of hope: there was no one by the side door. But the door, it turned out, was open.

"Hello," said the CLA librarian, regarding me warily as she came up the stairs from the basement. She showed no signs of recognition. "Do you know which group you're here for?"

"The same group you are!" I replied, bristling visibly on several counts.

■　　■　　■

"Well?" asked eager Cosima when I returned later that evening. "How'd it go? Why the strange look on your face?"

"Because it was *fantastic*," I said. "Fantastic! First the librarian didn't recognize me, which made me feel A-1 special. Then the lights didn't work, so we had the meeting with the door open to the hall for illumination. There were just four of us, me and three women. Ms. Pushy Librarian insisted we read long excerpts from the twelve-step protocols—in half-darkness, squinting and using cell phones as lighting aid. Okay, to be fair, there *were* a couple of moments. The librarian, God bless her, told us she'd thrown a party to celebrate her progress—and then her will just fizzled out in the cleanup phase."

"The fizzling of will," Cosima quipped. "Bet you could relate to that. What was the other moment?"

"Whatever," I said, with a shrug.

In fact, another of the clutterers had spoken of how, on vacations, her husband was forever complaining about her things spreading like weeds all over their hotel room. I figured Cosima was self-righteous enough without hearing this.

"Anyway, the third woman was a more somber case. She lives with her grandparents, can't bring herself to make her bed or clean a dish. She was dressed really conservatively and spoke with a slight Southern accent of some kind. During our closing group hand-holding, she declined to take my hand for 'religious reasons.'"

"Maybe she thought you were snooty," said Cosima.

"That's it. I was being snooty!" (Had I been snooty?)

I added the kicker: they had passed around a sheet for phone numbers. "So God knows who's going to be calling me now, thanks for forcing me to go."

"The mother and daughter weren't there?"

"No they weren't! Okay? Happy? I'm *not* going back. And now don't say anything, I will get in touch with Dave the Declutterer." I cut her off further. "*Very soon.*"

■   ■   ■

Over the weekend we went to a garden party at the house of friends in Brooklyn. Who was sitting in the kitchen among the partygoers, chopping vegetables for the salad: the by-now semi-mythical man himself, Dave the Declutterer.

Cosima gripped my arm. "Now's your chance!" she whispered hotly. "Talk to him! Set up a meeting!"

"In a sec," I hissed back, wrenching loose. "Let me say hello first to the people outside."

I ambled past Dave with a wave and a nod. Out in the backyard, I got a beer from the zinc tub and fell into conversation with a publishing pal, McCoy. I confided to him the gory details: the vivid wretchedness of my place, my planned interviews with experts, my CLA experiences, my upcoming hobnob with Dave the Declutterer. McCoy grinned along, approving. "The Professa of Messa," he chanted, in the hip-hop tones he likes to adopt.

I must have lost track of time because I had my third bottle of boutique "smoked" lager in hand when Cosima stormed into the garden. Eyes flashing.

"It's *your* project, but *I'm* the one writing down cleaning tips from Dave the Declutterer!" she declared. "And you're out here guzzling beer!"

I told her to relax. I was going inside right now to talk to him.

"That's too bad," she said. "Because he just left."

It was true.

I came back out to the yard crestfallen. I had a sudden shocked sense that the humor of my position as a procrastinator, as a pilgrim full of fine pronouncements and grudging action, had gone too far. I was screwing things up, for real.

"I'll email him," I muttered.

I did. Days went by. No reply.

"You probably insulted him by not talking to him at the party," said Cosima.

But then he wrote back. He'd been out of town. He'd be happy to meet me and talk.

■   ■   ■

So here we sat on a bench in Central Park.

Dave, doleful of mien and around forty, eyed the needful world through stylish horn-rimmed glasses. He sipped from his takeout vat of coffee while I took notes. My notepad was the one I'd been employing, after intricate calculation, as Notepad 1.0 for my Project. I'd bought it at the Nabokov museum in St. Petersburg, on a trip with Cosima in 2007. It seemed the right pairing of signifiers: chronicling clutter in a memento of multiple elegances, literary and domestic (the museum was in the old Nabokov family mansion). A tiny man sailed charmingly through the air with his umbrella and briefcase on the notepad's cover.

Dave had formerly worked in commercials at some very hip ad agencies, East Coast and West. He was a great believer in twelve-step programs. He'd come to decluttering as a specialty he had a knack for: part organizer, part psychologist. He wasn't a member of the National Association of Professional Organizers. (The profession isn't officially regulated.) He advertised on Craigslist and by word of mouth, and his clients took him from the Dakota apartment building behind us out to the Hamptons, even to lowly Queens. Who were his clients mostly? I asked. Married couples and "busy people." Gay men never required his services, he joked. (He was gay himself.) He said most of the job was "editing," and helping people let go.

And he no longer worked with hoarders!

That's when he suddenly inquired pointedly as to my situation, to which I'd only referred in general terms:

"We're talking *clutter*, right?"

I reassured him, trying not to sound the least defensive, staring into my finely calibrated Nabokovian notepad, that I wasn't an extreme hoarder. I half-thought to cite my online hoarding self-test. Roller-bladers whizzed past through the Sunday sunshine.

Dave's beef with hoarders was this: they were just too unreliable and frustrating to work with. They'd be 75 percent finished with the cleanup and then they'd just disappear. Sometimes he found them replacing what they had just thrown out. He said he could always spot a hoarder by their initial emails. "If it's a *looong* email, full of enormous complications and details," he said, "that's a hoarder." But hoarders did always show a sense of humor, for that.

"They're kooks," he said, speaking as a self-employed professional, not a selfless angel of succor.

While he talked, a central question took shape in my mind: Could I imagine this *specific* person beside me here, who knew about clutter—his hoarder remarks being part of his knowledge —could I imagine him going through my intimate things with me? I being one for whom almost any *thing* was an intimate thing. Was I willing to open my privacy up to Dave the Declut-

terer? Or would I resist his presence? Would I always be wary
that he was sizing me up as a kook?

My answer, soberly considered, was no. No Dave the Declutterer to stand alongside me.

When our conversation inevitably came around to my mess,
I hedged on the specifics. I stayed private. Dave declared he was
pretty sure he could help. I told him I had to be honest: I wasn't
ready yet for anyone to come in yet. He nodded. He understood,
he said. He offered a free piece of advice: clean up one small place
where I spent a lot of my time. He called it "the Hurdle." Clear
that Hurdle, more would follow. I laughed. I said that sounded like
what my shrink had told me. I'd tried it, and backslid.

"So try again," he said. "It takes patience, decluttering. It's all
about self-love, really."

I left him and wandered in the park, full of thoughts, wary of
bladers and bicyclists, the Sunday enemy of the pensive. The question I'd just posed to myself about Dave rose from a dawning sense
that I would have to allow other human beings into my apartment
at *some* point. That I didn't want to turn into some poetical goofball stewing behind his slovenly door. But the condition of my lair,
as is, was too shaming and too intimate for any "civilian" visitors.
Jolted by Cosima's ultimatum, and fashioning my response to it
as a Project, I'd forced myself to reach out about my condition
(okay, with a bit of a push). I'd slogged to CLA—twice—and met
up now with Dave the Declutterer. These hadn't panned out. But
I realized, by dint of all this airing of my existential situation, and
my research, too—recognizing myself in books and articles—that
I was feeling less freaked out at the notion that a *right* sympathetic
person on site might be of help. Because I sure hadn't had much
luck on my own.

But the question, again: who might that person be—other
than a mental health professional? Certainly not a CLA would-be
buddy. And not my shrink, either; she didn't make house calls. I

bet she was even theoretically opposed to them. She wanted to deal with my linguistic representations of my troubled universe there in the bright-lit cubbyhole of her office.

Who could I invite in to share, in a controlled way, my situation? Someone sympathetic, a fellow sufferer. Someone with whom I could maybe kibitz about another attempt at clearing the Hurdle.

I realized I knew such a person. Right in my building.

■　　■　　■

My buzzer rang. I opened my door and welcomed the ringer inside, into my chaos.

"You're the first person I've personally greeted and invited across my threshold in years," I announced, a smile splitting my face. "Other than the exterminator!"

"I'm honored," said Cosima's mom, Nadya. "But do you have a chair I can sit in? I'm seventy-eight years old, I don't want to stand if we're gonna talk."

I cleared the bags off a chair at the heaped, clutter-infested dining table. She settled in, a plump gray-haired elf in a tie-dyed brown housedress. For a second I had a horror that the chair might be unstable and she'd go crashing to the floor. But there were no ominous splintering noises, so I assumed we were okay.

How did I feel? Not exposed, or shamed, or in turmoil. My emotions were the opposite: a feeling of liberation, of tender reassurance. I was actually sitting in my mess with another person without having to negotiate any initial gasp of horror or involuntary swiveling of saucer eyes. It helped that Nadya had known my place in this condition for years now (though never while I was on the premises). Yes, she'd thrown around the term "pathological" to Cosima; but since I almost never ever slept here, she'd in fact spent more nights in my "diseased" flâneurscape than I had. (I would semi-tidy at least the bedroom and bathroom, grumbling, when she was due owing to an excess of overnight guests. My tidying would revert to weed quickly.) I had dinner at Nadya's place almost every week; she traveled with Cosima and me sometimes. I loved her.

And she was a fellow clutterbug.

I brought out my Nabokov notebook.

Interviewing Nadya about her clutter history amidst my own sprawls would be a rich prelude to taking her into my kitchen to look at the area I'd chosen for my new Hurdle. An opening gesture of clutter fellowship.

■   ■   ■

Nadya and Cosima emigrated to America from behind the Iron Curtain in the early seventies, when Cosima was eleven. Just the two of them with two tiny suitcases. Although they came from a culture where every scrap and shred was recycled for lack of commodities, Nadya left all her possessions behind and didn't look back. Her hoarding issues only truly began after Cosima moved out of the apartment downstairs, where she'd lived with Nadya, into this place she'd passed on to me. With bossy Cosima and her restraining presence gone, Nadya's premises, the same 700 square feet as mine, became a shipwreck of papers from work (before retirement she was an elementary school teacher), of food spoiling because she overstocked and forgot what she had. Overstocking food was a longtime habit—an emotional legacy of a culture where you were never certain when you'd next be able to buy anything. Nadya was also a World War II survivor with memories of relentless shortages and near-starvation. The paper mess—that was an excess of her chronic disorganization.

At her low point she had to cancel a long-scheduled visit from her best friend from Chicago because her place was simply unfit for guests, no matter how close. Her bedroom resembled a live-in tomb of teaching materials and useless books. Her closets were jammed.

"It was embarrassing. *So* embarrassing."

But now, for years, Nadya's apartment, though more crowded than spare, had been pleasant and welcoming, the site of almost nonstop dinner parties and visitor stayovers. What had improved her: therapy? I wondered. Cosima always mentioned that.

Nadya shook her head. Though she'd seen a therapist for a time and had talked a bit about clutter, what cured her was the fearsome Zinaida. Cosima had hired the Russian housecleaning tyrant, and just to make Zinaida's long haul from Brooklyn worthwhile, Nadya with characteristic excessive compassion hired her to vacuum and dust *her* place. She'd never had a cleaning lady before. To prepare for Zinaida's arrival, she tidied up.

Cleaning up for the cleaning lady: that's how Zinaida had helped Nadya declutter! The dread of someone barging around in her shame.

Zinaida no longer came; what kept Nadya on the right road was hosting her endless dinner parties. Preparing for guests sent her into a tornado of purging and cleaning.

"But I struggle," she sighed. Her closets were still packed, her fridge an overcrowded graveyard of wilted vegetables.

I nodded, wondering what might work the trick for me. Since I didn't plan on having tyrants hoovering around, or on throwing banquets.

What went through Nadya's mind when she hung on to stuff— she paused at my question—was the sense of a possible future being crushed if she gave a thing up. She confessed this almost shyly. Her address book was thick with slips of paper, scribbled tear-offs of envelopes. If she lost a paper with a phone number on it, even one without a name, she felt as if somebody or something had died.

But also, she said: she just liked to collect brochures and give-aways at the theater or the opera or when traveling. She brought these home, intending to go through them of an evening "cozily"(as she put it), reliving rich memories. But she never found time. So they just piled up.

This last was not just a page out of my playbook—it was half the chapters. No wonder Cosima threw up her hands at the sce-nario. I was grinning. This was like my own private support group.

"You're the first person together with me in here in years," I repeated, amazed. "Not counting the exterminator."

"Yes," said Nadya. "You said that."

"So what d'you make of all this?" I asked, emboldened, indi-cating the bag-blown table before us, the jumbled acreage beyond. "Are you *shocked* still?"

"It's far beyond my own capacities for clutter," she answered. "The boxes! Why so many? For years! And most of them empty."

Because I held on to them for packing use—at some future point.

"'But just go to the liquor store if you need some."

"Know how hard it is to get *good* boxes?" I said.

"We have very different styles of clutter," she mused. "You exhibit everything, I hide things away." Every messy person was messy in their own manner, she went on, quoting Tolstoy, as she was prone to.

"Oh I hide things away," I murmured. I glanced over toward the piano.

Then I led us on into my galley kitchen and showed her my Hurdle.

I had decided on the wooden kitchen counter—a purple-painted, seven-foot length of piled clutter. It presented a mod-est, clearly defined target, and one I trafficked with throughout the day. So it was an influential zone. One I had not addressed in cleaning terms since the first *Iron Man* movie was in theaters. Opposite stood the sink and drain board, with cabinets above them and the stove alongside. The ancient microwave Cosima had bequeathed to me sat on a murky shelf in front of the window at the end.

"Those plastic tubs piled up there are useful, no?" I said, hopefully.

"Not if you don't use them," said Nadya.

Sweetly, patiently, she pointed out that I could store things in the tall standing cabinet beside the shelf—the one on which she had made an unauthorized guerrilla cleaning raid several years ago.

I went for the bonus: my beloved floral-decorated mugs soured with tannin.

"What d'you think"? I asked, awaiting the obvious.

"They're lovely," said Nadya.

I could have hugged her. "You think so? But look how brown they are inside!"

"Baking soda," she said.

I thanked Nadya and saluted her, and escorted her to the door, pulling her away from the bathroom where she suddenly headed to comment on the state of my shower curtain.

■   ■   ■

"So how'd it go?" asked Cosima when we met up at Lincoln Center for the opera that evening. The plaza looked gorgeous, matching my mood.

Really great, I told her. "Your mom speak to you?"

"Yes. She said it went great." Pause. "She couldn't believe all the boxes you have."

I blew out a long breath. "Your treacherous mother, I thought we had a real rapport!"

"You do, you do," said Cosima. "Mom loves you."

Indeed. The seat I was making my way to behind Cosima, overlooking the stage far below, was a gift from Nadya.

The lights began to dim; Cosima reached back for my hand. Darkness always prompts her affection.

"Interesting," I whispered as the chandeliers rose past us into the ceiling, "how after immigrating the way you did, your mom has clutter inclinations and you the opposite."

"Because I saw her give up all her life," Cosima whispered, "husband, parents, friends, and I felt really proud she only took two tiny suitcases. The other émigrés all had refugee parcels and loads of crap. I still remember that lightness we felt, it affected me deeply, moving into another life without anything." A storm of applause burst out as the conductor, William Christie, prince of baroque music, appeared. "But Mom went through the war and then the deprivations. Back home everyone hoarded in some way. She just can't let go."

At intermission, while we munched surreptitiously on the curried chicken sandwiches she'd made, she continued. "I like things but only useful things, ones I can display. I never shop randomly."

I told her this was straight out of all the anti-clutter tips I'd read.

"And I hate presents that don't fit in with the décor of my house," she went on. "That's why I always tell you and Mom what to get me for Christmas."

These gift lists of hers, they rankled me still. Where was the surprise, the giver's role? Even if the "gifts" were greeted with effusions and appreciation.

"And I thought it was just 'cause you're bossy," I snorted. "An eleven-year-old's idea of a harridan. An eleven-year-old with two tiny suitcases. Go back to the Iron Curtain. Except though, wait, I'll miss your cooking."

I leaned and kissed her on the soft of her shoulder.

"Awful man," murmured Cosima. "*Hoarder.*"

■   ■   ■

But enough emotional sharing and byplay with mother and daughter. Now for actual cleaning.

I didn't need the almost three pounds of *Home Comforts* for this. I took my camera into my kitchen and snapped a "before" photo of the Hurdle as documentation. Then I snapped on a pair of new 99-cent store rubber gloves—and went to work. Wait, I misspeak. First I brought in the iPad which Cosima had recently purchased in a fit of keeping up with the times and handed over to me to figure out how to use. This figuring-out principally involved my streaming movies on Netflix. I leaned the iPad screen against my quarter-century-old espresso maker on the stove and found a cheesy film noir about a boozy, possibly homicidal, struggling artist.

Then I snapped on the gloves and went to work.

There were three of Cosima's old colored plastic chopping boards stacked on the purple shelf against the wall. I kept them because of their vivid colors: orange and yellow. Call me a magpie. They were knife-scored and worn, though. Decisively I decided to dump them.

But in what?

A box.

I stepped into the dining area and scanned around for a suitable box. And a familiar pang of anxiety stabbed through me. Or more like the sharp, ringing ache of smacking a deep, never-healing bruise. Which box was the *right* box from my stock, not just for size, but symbolically suited to the occasion; and also one that didn't deplete the reserve of importantly and valuably useful boxes for the future? What to an outsider resembled a trash heap was to me not just a zone for flâneuring but a site governed by protocols worthy of the court of Versailles. Okay, a mini-Versailles. Protocols that were intense but shifting. Almost designed, it seemed, to snare and hinder.

All at once I realized I could avoid the whole suffocating business by just detouring around this part of my mini-Versailles. Forget a box! I snatched a supermarket plastic bag and shoved the boards into it. I gave a little fist pump. Just like that I'd cleared a hurdle in my Hurdle.

Why had I come up with this bit of freed and clever thinking and action, now, when on an earlier day I would not have? I would have spent minutes and minutes agonizing over my box choice. I can't say why. Probably the side effect of Nadya's visit, and the momentum of the thinking that went into inviting her. And partly just because it was a lovely sunny day out my windows.

In another plastic bag I stuffed the empty Lavazza coffee cans I'd ordinarily set aside (they were maroon, Italian, and could be handy) and two glass jars that once contained gefilte fish. *Gefilte fish?* Ah, probably something from Nadya. (But how long ago?)

On the stove behind me, a woman's voice suddenly started shrieking: "*He tried to kill me! He tried to kill! He was a crazy man!*" I turned and stood watching in my rubber gloves. This wasn't good—I mean, my watching. Gritting my teeth, I turned off the iPad and pastured it out to the welter on the dining table. Then I snatched up the stacks of plastic tubs and lids on the counter and dumped them into the sink to clean and deal with later. There were some fifteen of them (I counted, for documentation). Some were in pristine shape. Perhaps I should hang on to these? The stab of indecision seared again.

I found myself back at my laptop, Web surfing. It was all sinkingly familiar. I was suckling on the cyber teat in the face of gnashing anxiety. I realized (not for the first time) that thanks to new technology I'd harmed my capacity to press on through such anxiety. The same way computers had affected my handwriting. My muscles for sustaining focus had turned twitchy and flaccid.

I decided to challenge myself. I would not check my laptop for a solid hour of Hurdle-cleaning. I set an online timer and marched back into the kitchen to face the plastic tub decision. Whereupon I had another Versailles-detour epiphany (can you repeat an epiphany?) and grabbed a bag and stuffed every tub into it—the whole lot. I took a photo of the clutter-filled bags I'd assembled and marched out into the hall and dumped them into the recycling bin. I strode back inside, cleared the purple counter of its cloudy glasses into the sink, and removed the wretched naked emblem of clutterbugging and hoarding, the electric kettle which I'd kept for years despite its being kaput. Into a bag and out the door.

I photographed the cleared counter. Cleared but oh not cleaned. I photographed it again after I'd roared at it with Nadya's PROGRESSIVE Direct Drive vacuum. While roaring underneath, I discovered hooks for hanging pots and pans. My God, for how many years hadn't I noticed them? I took my beleaguered stove items piled on the microwave and hung them there. In the cleared space I trimly set three petit boxes of teabags—red, green, yellow—which formerly sat any old place on the counter.

Finally I went at the counter, and nearby wall areas, with Fantastik "All-Purpose Heavy Duty" cleaner. My discount rubber gloves showed their value. By breaking. Never mind. I soldiered on—harried now and then by flits of anxiety and frustration, by the siren's call of the laptop, which I converted into angry energy for climbing my Hurdle. The cock crowed an hour gone by on my laptop, and I was almost done.

Then I was done. For the first time in years, I could see it: my kitchen counter. I needn't grimace when I made my workday coffee and tea here, fixed my primitive lunch. I decided to get some flowers the next day, and take an "after" picture. The purple could use a fresh coat, of course. And the cabinets now holding the counter's once-cloudy glasses needed a cleaning. Not to mention that unhearth of unhearths, my fridge. And the sorely tested linoleum floor.

But I'd cleared my Hurdle. Held up against distraction and anxiety. Invited a human being who wasn't the exterminator into my place without her wearing a blindfold. I felt a silly sense of accomplishment. The light was gold in the windows.

And yet.

Something deep down nagged that I hadn't yet cleared the Hurdle.

I hadn't tackled emotional loss. I had not let go of an object dear to me which had long outstayed its proper tenure.

I took a long breath and picked up the shallow serving bowl sitting in the dish drainer by the sink.

■　　■　　■

If you looked at this bowl, you'd see a banal item of ceramic dishware some ten inches wide and three inches deep, its bottom painted with three red tomatoes dangling from green stems, its sides white and sloping, a green line around its rim. You'd see, too, the dark crack that for the last couple of years has run from the rim line down through the tomatoes, ending in a perpendicular smaller crack on the opposite slope.

Me, I saw those tomatoes as red clappers of the great ringing bell of harvest time. And I saw the tackiest of tourist gift shops in Little Italy where I purchased the bowl in the mid-eighties, when I was supplementing the kitchenware at a friend's cubbyhole of a walk-up on Lafayette Street nearby. I'd just sublet it now that I was on my own. Now that I had money from my parents' inheritance. I looked at the bowl here in my hands and saw those days and that neighborhood—saw the final night of my endless breakup with my longtime girlfriend S. (I still had her leather coat from college in my storage when I got ready to take over Cosima's place.) Saw the Smith-Corona electric on which I thundered out the manuscript of my book *Wearing Dad's Head*. Saw myself strolling home up Mulberry Street, noticing a slick-suited cliché bozo lounging at a sidewalk table ahead with a bottle of Sambuca—and realizing, drawing near, that it was John Gotti. And going pitter-patting past, eyes staring fixedly into the distance, desperately avoiding eye contact, holding my breath lest I somehow knock over the Sambuca.

And I saw the salumeria across the street from that same Little Italy gift shop, where a decade later, in the nineties, after moving back from L.A., I selected the mozzarella that I brought along to Cosima on our first date.

That's the Proustian lode I held in my hands; why I'd hung on to this old bowl. But the crack was so bad I could with little effort begin splaying it in half. The crack was a dark fracture line—no, not at all sanitary. Repairing it would be a waste of time and effort, it didn't cost much. I could go back to Little Italy and replace it.

I needed to let go. Part of the Hurdle.

I was talking myself into it. Three or four years before I'd broken a cereal bowl (colorful and cheap, what else?) that I'd bought myself when I was living out in L.A. on the beach at the end of the eighties. The bowl was what I ate from mornings in the flat Pacific light, gazing out at the tireless surf and the Santa Monica Pier, the gray Malibu headlands beyond. At first it was emotional, the loss of that cereal bowl, like losing a literal part of my past, a past where I'd walk out at sunset and watch dolphins roll in the dying Technicolor waves. But then my past recovered. It lived on.

Thinking this way, I emphatically yanked the serving bowl in half. It broke with a snap. I wrapped the pieces in several plastic bags. If I could have, I might very well have burned the busted-up bowl and kept the ashes. But I made do with wrecking and then tossing. I always wrecked objects I threw out—cutting clothing apart, tearing up books, smashing CD players. The thought of anyone using anything of mine that I'd disposed of was intimately violating. If I couldn't have it, then no one could.

I went out into the hall and opened the garbage chute. I let go of my package. I listened to it clanging down away from me.

5

Brothers Grim

"*Good evening, Mr. Collyer. The neighbors tell me . . .*" The New York Public Library's main research division on Fifth Avenue in mid-Manhattan is all lofty marble halls and echoes. Pondering my problems, I'd refocused my attention on research. I wanted some perspective on hoarding's history—human and natural. Mainly, though, I wanted to get out of my lair. And who wouldn't trade used plastic bags for the grandeur of this library? Besides, it had air-conditioning.

And so, on a humid midsummer day while Cosima was off at a beach barbecue in honor of a visiting grill master, I slumped on a wooden chair in the library—deep into a long-out-of-print 1953 book titled *Out of This World*, by Helen Worden.

"Good evening, Mr. Collyer. The neighbors tell me you keep a rowboat in the attic and a Model T in the basement."

With this perky halloo fit for a screwball comedy, the two Olympian figures in the cosmos of hoarding were launched into the public spotlight. Being recluses as well as pack rats, the Collyer brothers weren't happy about it. Which was too bad: Homer and Langley Collyer would become the lurid poster boys of mess and clutter gone haywire, the embodiments of hoarding in twentieth-century popular culture, depraved creatures from some ultimately gruesome fairytale.

The "rowboat in the attic" line was originally aired one midnight in August 1938 by Worden, a crime reporter at the time for the *New York World-Telegram*. "I collect hermits," she declared in *Out of This World*'s preface. Springing from a taxi by a derelict-looking brownstone she'd been staking out at 128th Street in Harlem, she accosted a wraithlike figure emerging from the basement.

The ambushed specter was Langley Collyer, fifty-two years of age, with a droopy mandarin moustache and an operatically aquiline nose. Right then he was clad in janitor's overalls and a bulky cap with his uncut lengths of gray hair tucked up in it. One of a pair of scions of a well-to-do, grand-lineaged New York family, he was dragging a wooden box by a rope for his nocturnal rambles far and wide to forage for food and all sorts of things— newspapers, bits and pieces of furniture—to haul home. Behind him in the dilapidated mansion—gas, electricity, and water cut off for years—waited Homer, his older brother, blind like his Greek namesake since 1934, and two years hence, in 1940, an invalid. Langley was Homer's devoted nurse. Contemptuous of doctors, he fed Homer a special diet of oranges (100 per week), peanut butter, and black bread. And he was saving newspapers for his brother to read when he regained his sight. Thousands upon thousands of newspapers.

In her opening *World-Telegram* story, Worden rolled out with gusto the wild rumors about this "Harlem house of mystery"— that it was haunted, that behind its decrepit shutters lay an Ali Baba's trove of miser's valuables. In fact, by its end it was something more fantastical and bizarre: a fortress of dust, rot, rats, and rubbish—all maniacally tunneled and booby-trapped against intruders by Langley, who'd studied engineering at Columbia.

Langley's other preoccupation had formerly been musical; he'd given a piano recital at Carnegie Hall. Homer, meanwhile,

trained in property law at Columbia. The siblings were cultured gents of independent means, born to Susie Gage Frost
Collyer, a former opera singer, and her cousin Dr. Herman Livingston Collyer, a well-to-do gynecologist and someone quirky
enough himself to have paddled a canoe daily from Harlem to
a hospital job on what's now Roosevelt Island. The canoe was
the "rowboat" indeed there inside the brownstone—as was the
late doctor's Model T, in pieces. Langley had tried to rig it to
generate electricity.

A gothic Peter Pan air flickered around the brothers, courtly
and shy, given to the cravats and celluloid collars of the Gilded
Age. They moved into the brownstone with their parents in 1909,
when Harlem was fancy real estate and all white, and stayed on
after their parents' deaths in the later 1920s, as Harlem around
them turned increasingly poor and nasty and non-white. Only
Homer ever held a job—as a deed researcher at two law firms in
lower Manhattan. He walked the eight miles each way to work
and back.

The ongoing saga of these "ghosty" men (a neighbor's term)
became Helen Worden's prize baby. It also became nonstop freak
fodder for New York's newspapers—a preview of reality TV's
hoarding shock fests. The mansion lured the curious, the throwers
of rocks at windows, the would-be larcenous. Worden, however,
didn't get past the door that August, not for years still. Just one
reporter ever got invited inside—so I learned now in the library
research division's antediluvian microfilm room, where I peered
at the blurs on an ancient hand-cranked machine. Someone from
the competing *New York Journal-American* talked his way in right
after Worden's initial article. Langley dismissed all the rumors of
hidden wealth as "tommyrot." He held forth in the brownstone's
gloom surrounded by "17 pianos, an organ, four violins, two flutes,
a violoncello, a French horn, a cornet, a trombone, three radios
and a phonograph."

After this intrusion the beleaguered siblings just wanted the world to stay out, go away. Even so Langley, the pair's public face, retained his odd courtliness. "Forgive me but I can't invite you in," he told another, stunned reporter who was camped on his doorstep. "The house is too upset . . ."

There were two aborted forced entries by the authorities over unpaid bills, in 1939 and 1942. These yielded brief chaotic glimpses of the monstrous "upset" growing—and growing—within. Another reporter described a "ceiling-high barrier of garbage cans, trunks, crates, great pieces of rusty iron."

A teaser for what was to come in the spring of 1947.

■   ■   ■

Hoarding does of course have its role in the nature of things.

In the animal world, the caching of food (mainly) represents sound evolutionary behavior against scarcity and poaching. Birds from chickadees to crows bury and hide edibles; magpies are prodigies at remembering where they've secreted multiple, small, usually short-term caches. (Their famous attraction to shiny objects apparently only applies to tamed, not wild, magpies.)

I was back again researching in my own grubby lair. I say "lair" but why not, instead—I was musing fresh from the library—why not my own ramshackle version of an *archive*? A "raw" version, lacking the attentions of a proper archivist (an important distinction, admitted). But still, sharing a similar instinct: to preserve documents and artifacts. "The Yourgrau Archive Center." I liked the sound of it. Suppose all this slush in my apartment was put into handsome folders: what would I have? An art installation, at the least.

Helen Worden's words of Collyer empathy in *Out of This World* flashed through my mind:

"Let the maid or cleaning lady stay away a week and I'd

be caught in a tidal wave of debris . . . cowering behind my possessions."

On this cowering note I moved on to rodents. There was the squirrel hoarding caches of acorns, and hamsters with their prodigious cheek pouches for loading up. But appropriately, it was the pack rat (also known as the wood rat) that particularly echoed the Collyers' barricading. Packrats cache food *inside* their constructed habitat—a habitat, called a midden, that extends around the intimate nest up to two meters, built up from their nocturnal hauling in of materials, including bright shiny things to go along with the pack rats' own droppings. In the American Southwest, spiny yucca needles in the mix help ward off predators.

I thought of blind Homer Collyer's last known appearance in public. A cop saw him helping his brother ferry a tree limb into the mansion at a late-night hour in 1940.

The pack rat's accumulations result in a kind of live-in garbage pile ("midden" derives from a Scandinavian term meaning dung hill), which its denizens cement by constantly urinating on it. Highly viscous stuff, this pack rat pee; it dries into a fossil-like substance called amberat. In dry climes (say, Utah's), middens last for multiple generations— even for tens of thousands of years. They display their own quirky courtesies, too, these original pack rats. If, while carrying something, they spot something else more desirable, they'll leave the first item in its place. So they aren't really like me, or the Collyers or other hoarders that way.

They're able to let go.

The word "hoard" derives from the proto-Germanic term for "hidden or secret treasure." Hoards are well known to archeologists, dating back over 10,000 years to the hunter-gatherers of the Stone Age. Foodstuffs such as joints of meat were common early deposits, ditto ornaments, weapons, and human remains— all buried for safekeeping and intended for retrieval. The hoards of the later Bronze and Iron Ages got more elaborate: sumptuous weapons (lots of axes), tools, jewelry, coins. Votive hoards, or ritual offerings, though, were interred permanently. Often in watery areas, and after being rendered useless, I noticed: many broken swords flung into rivers. I couldn't help think of myself destroying my old bowl before sending it down the garbage chute.

But here was the thing: those caches of bangles and weaponry and joints of meat—and later the hoardings of jewels and gold—they all involved objects that were *valuable*, for prestige or for use, according to the norms of the time. (No trans-historical plastic bags or travel knickknacks.) And such hoarding of valuables eventually came to be looked down on by society. Ancient Greeks philosophized against personal greed. Socrates chided his fellow Athenians for caring more for wealth and personal possessions than for the welfare of their souls. (Though, a man after my own heart, he didn't refuse fine wine and food if they were offered.) In the New Testament, Jesus launched one of the most familiar tropes of Western civilization, decrying "covetousness" and "the abundance of things" as the aim of life (Luke). The audience on the Mount were beseeched to not "lay up for yourselves treasures upon earth," but instead "lay up treasures in heaven" (Matthew).

And then it suddenly dawned on me: those famous tormented souls in Dante's fourth circle? They weren't the grand avatars of pathological hoarding at all. No! Because their torments in the *Inferno* took place (hurriedly I double-checked the canto) under the guard-dog scowl of Plutus—the god of *wealth*. The poet crowded this sub-basement of hell with clerics, why? Because the Catholic Church of his day was aswarm with greed and corruption. Indeed, money loomed large in Dante's late-medieval Florence—home of the golden florin. Banking families dominated local life. Whom did the hook-nosed poet's beloved Beatrice, his guide to Paradise, marry in real life? A banker, one of the Bardi family. Not surprising, since Beatrice was the daughter of a banker herself.

All of this was a far cry from that woebegone mother at Clutterers Anonymous with old pizza takeout boxes piled up in her condo. A far cry from me, here in my "work chair"—my un-let-go-able art deco relic of once-polished wood, its once-crimson vinyl seat now blotched and flaking with an ever-expanding gash down the middle. A beloved living ruin of a chair I'd hung on to for well over a decade, having snitched it from a sculptor's tiny ninth-floor loft apartment I'd been subletting by the darkened canyons of Wall Street. Or a farther cry from my "waste basket"—a torn-lipped, badly rumpled, black-and-gold paper shopping bag from the Mandarin Oriental Hotel in San Francisco, souvenir of my furtive first rendezvous in that city with Cosima.

Or behind me, the most regularly valuable thing in my place, Cosima's Steinway. Filmy with grit, unplayed and ignored, my ancient boxes underneath jamming its pedals.

I ran a fingertip through the dust on the sheet music, still in place from my girlfriend's time here. Schubert, Chopin.

"What do you think of Chopin?" Langley had asked Helen Worden at their first encounter. "He's my favorite composer."

At least my premises held only a single morose piano, compared to the Collyers' multiples.

But speaking of Chopin: various commentators hold that it was his Parisian friend Balzac, master of nineteenth-century realism, who produced the first real portrait of the properly pathological hoarder. The term "realism" aptly derives from the Latin *res*, meaning thing or material, and Balzac's sprawling pages are stuffed to the gills with physical description. He himself was an obsessive collector (a borderline hoarder?), to the point where his lover, Hanska, thought him insane. As part of his multi-novel sequence *The Human Comedy* (title in contrast to Dante's *Divine Comedy*), the great novelist gave us Sylvain Pons, the elderly bachelor in *Le Cousin Pons*, a poor musician who, like the author, was an insatiable collector—of bric-a-brac. That term, a neologism for "at random or any old way," from the original nonsense phrase *à bric et à brac*, had entered the French language a few years before.

Okay, *voilà*! I thought.

But no dice again. Because in Balzac's day, bric-a-brac didn't yet mean junk, it meant miscellaneous objets d'art. Poor, shabby Pons was a connoisseur, in fact—passionately hunting art bargains with his fine eye. In his humble quarters he'd amassed, on the cheap, a collection featuring works by Dürer and Bruegel!

Balzac wrote during the rise of industrial capitalism in France. It was the era when more goods and commodities became readily available, and when collecting became democratized and accessible to the non-noble classes. It was the age of *bibelots* (little decorative objects), of mass-produced items meant as collectibles. It was also the time of the decline of an aristocracy that had been the great collectors of aesthetic treasures. Enabling Cousin Pons to go around snapping up the art they'd had to let go of.

"And what led Pons to grief at the end?" I said to Cosima later at dinner. "His other passion. *Gluttony*."

For it was when his access to his bourgeois relatives' fine dinners was threatened that the old connoisseur cooked up the scheme that brought his collection disastrously to the wrong attention.

"Balzac was a celebrated glutton himself," I observed, scraping up the last pink bits of my girlfriend's radicchio and red wine risotto. "He could eat a hundred oysters at a sitting! He was famously toothless and fat at thirty-two. *Unlike* Pons, who was thin. And *unlike* me."

Cosima's eyes narrowed shrewdly "Meaning there's a connection between Balzac's gluttony and his famously excessive descriptions in his books, his *verbal* hoarding?"

"Yeah, something like that," I allowed, having missed that specific parallel. "Gluttony and uncontrollable acquisition. Balzac was a huge collector. And Dave the Declutterer said there's a well-known saying, Get rid of the clutter and you get rid of the pounds. Though like I said, Pons was thin. As am I . . ." My voice trailed off at this contradiction.

"Wait," said Cosima, looking off in thought. "Wasn't there a hoarder in Dickens?"

Supposedly there was. Right across the Channel from Pons: Krook in Dickens's *Bleak House* (1852–53).

According to Mario Praz, the singular Italian cultural critic and historian of interior decoration—and a man infamous for possessing the evil eye—claustrophobic clutter was the ruling aesthetic of furnishing during Victorian times. "Horror vacui," Praz called it—the dread of empty space. And this dread seemed to have found an over-the-top fan in Krook, the gin-soaked proprietor of a jumbled shop that's a rusty, musty, cobwebby chaos of old documents, keys, bottles, and whatever.

"And I can't bear," old Krook declares, "to part with anything I once lay hold of it . . . or to alter anything, or to have any sweeping, nor scouring, nor repairing going on about me."

Straight from the pages, at last, of Frost and Steketee's *Stuff* . . . if not from my premises?

Again, not quite.

"Because Krook isn't really a character portrait," I reported back to Cosima. He was Dickens's human embodiment of the Court of Chancery—Britain's monstrously interminable, document-clogged legal system for property disputes. His name was a blatant pun. And he was illiterate. I described to her the gin-sodden Krook's fantastic demise: spontaneously combusting, leaving only a splatter of oily soot!

"Ah, noooo," she protested, "is that all we're going to talk about now? *Hoarding?*"

"Huh? But you're the one who brought up Dickens!" Flummoxed, as so often, by her whiplashes of logic.

"Whatever," she shrugged.

And then a minute or two later, she proceeded to lecture me animatedly about Plyushkin.

■   ■   ■

The first real McCoy of a fictional hoarder turns out to have emerged a couple of years before *Bleak House* and *Le Cousin Pons*, in what is often called the Russian answer to the *Inferno* (Dante, again): Nikolai Gogol's *Dead Souls*. Specifically in the squalid, elderly country serf-owner Plyushkin, a character whose name has become synonymous in Russian for a miser who hoards.

As in . . . hoards *trash*.

An unappetizing genius, scrawny and dank with a prodigious beak of a nose, Gogol was yet another glutton, like me and Balzac and Pons (for what that was worth). With authorial lip-smacking, he dove into overflowing accumulations of detail—his own version of writerly hoarding—about the shambles of this Plyushkin's abode. On Plyushkin's table stood "a ragged chair, with, beside it, a clock minus a pendulum and covered all over with cobwebs. Against a wall leant a cupboard, full of old silver . . . On a writing table . . . lay a pile of finely written manuscript . . . a lemon dried and shrunken to the dimensions of a hazelnut, the broken arm of a chair, a tumbler containing the dregs of some liquid . . . a pile of rags, two ink-encrusted pens, and a yellow toothpick with which the master of the house had picked his teeth (apparently) . . ."

But it is Plyushkin's "treasure-hunting" in his village streets that captures the modern hoarder's reality.

"[E]verything he came across," wrote Gogol, "an old sole, a bit of peasant's rag, an iron rail, a piece of broken earthenware, he carried them all to his room and put them . . . in the corner."

Syllogomania, such collecting of rubbish is called, according to Frost and Steketee in *Stuff*. The Collyer brothers would have clapped their dusty hands in solidarity.

■   ■   ■

Cosima grew up reading *Dead Souls* in the original. As she served me Turkish green beans with tomatoey ground lamb next evening, she giggled, recalling how miserly Plyushkin offered a guest a piece of old Easter cake with the mold scraped off.

"Actually, the book is *full* of hoarders," she marveled. "There's that lady landowner Korobochka, her name means 'little box.'"

"Yeah, I know, Korobochka," I replied breezily, busy with my fork. "But she was always stuffing money—i.e. *valuables*, not *rubbish*—into socks and things. Note the distinction?"

"I think she also hung on to old dresses forever," said Cosima. "Also in Gogol's 'The Overcoat,' the protagonist is a petty clerk who actually hoards letters and words! Odd."

"Well, that's Russian lit for you."

"I mean that your place is such a miserable mess and your fiction stories are so, well, lucid and concise."

"Oh," I said. "Thank you."

"And of course," said Cosima, "unlike in Balzac and Dickens, Gogol was describing an economy of a Russian countryside that was still almost medieval. Though Chichikov, the grifter protagonist of *Dead Souls*, is a proto-capitalist—since his childhood he always sold and bought and bartered. And now he's buying up dead serfs for gain."

"Cool," I said. "Except I'm not really writing a study guide to *Dead Souls*."

"Plyushkin was a model landowner," she replied. "Who destroyed *everything* he had by his hoarding. So let that be a warning to you!" She wagged a finger.

"Is that for dessert?" I said. "My doom?"

To which she informed me that "Plyushkin syndrome" was the current Russian term for pathological hoarding.

I told her that, unbelievable as it might seem, *I already knew that.*

■　　■　　■

The Collyer brothers gave rise to a term too. "Collyer Mansion" is still the New York Fire Department's code for a hoard-filled house. On a sultry afternoon I rode the subway an hour from Queens up into Harlem. I hadn't been up there in years.

"Collyer Brothers Park," read the plaque. It was the very site where the end came, gruesome and squalid, for Homer and Langley.

On March 21, 1947, police received a mysterious phone tip about a dead man in the Collyer mansion at 2078 Fifth Avenue, on the corner of 128th Street. As a large crowd gathered, cops bashed and belly-crawled in through the blockaded windows. They found the beggarly emaciated corpse of Homer, his bony knees drawn up, stiff in a universe of debris. But where was Langley? A sensational manhunt began, and ran for a week—and then a second week. At the same time, searching and clearing of the brownstone laboriously commenced. Helen Worden finally got inside the brothers' hermit kingdom, thanks to her official connections. At one point she went slogging up a slope of rubbish near where Homer was found. Underneath that very pile Langley was discovered on April 8. She'd literally walked over his body. He'd been crushed in one of his booby traps, leaving Homer, blind and immobilized, to die of starvation a few days later less than ten feet away. The rats had gnawed away a good deal of him.

Some 130 tons of stuff—estimates range up to 180 (!)—were extracted from the brownstone's twelve dust-choked rooms and three rotting floors. Besides Herman's canoe and Model T, the hoard included, in part:

14 pianos (one, a Steinway—same number as in my
   place; another, a gift to Susie Collyer from Queen
   Victoria)
various gramophones
Susie's hope chests
25,000 or more books, including works by one of
   Balzac's favorites, James Fenimore Cooper
an early X-ray machine (likely Herman's)
six toy trains
a two-headed baby under glass
baby carriages
multiple crates, barrels, boxes, cartons, suitcases
thousands upon thousands of newspapers in bundles
a pair of decades-old tickets to a social event for
   Trinity Church near Wall Street, where the brothers
   once taught Sunday school

Workmen lit up stinky cigars against the stench which assaulted them early on "like a mailed fist." It rose from Langley's undiscovered body, though the brothers' decades without plumbing surely contributed. Shades of a pack rat midden, indeed.

The rumored misers' wealth turned out to be all of $4,000 from the sale of salvageable items, $2,000 in savings, and $60,000 in real estate. The taxes that followed took much of this.

2078 Fifth Ave. was quickly declared a hazard and torn down.

Now I stood in the middle of that historic ground. I felt moved, truly a pilgrim. Had I really developed an intimate connection to those mythic, hyperbolic, genteel pack rats of yore? I made an inventory. Where once 130 tons of stuff had been piled, I now counted eleven plane trees. Also seventeen bushes, three benches, three large wooden planters of flowers, eight small planters and pots on a ledge by the adjoining brownstone wall, and two plastic trash bins.

On one of the benches sat a slim young black woman, sleek and casually model-like in her jogging outfit and a black baseball cap. A kindergarten-age boy and girl played on the barely grassy ground beside her. The woman told me that she was from Ghana originally, lived in the neighborhood, and was in fact a model. She didn't know who the Collyers were. So while her young son harassed one of the pots by the wall, I told her Langley and Homer's story in excited detail. I told her about "Collyer Mansion" being Fire Department code, the department whose cap she was wearing.

"Wow," said the model. "Like that show *Buried Alive* my friend's always trying to get me to watch!"

In more homage, I walked four blocks south on Fifth Avenue to the shaggy acreage of Marcus Garvey Park. It was known as Mount Morris Park back when Langley would creep along after dark to draw water. Something was nagging at me about the Collyers as the paragons of hoarding. Of conventional pathological hoarding. It was the booby traps and barricades. Yes, hoarders' dwellings famously can wind up packed to the very ceilings, like giant nests with only narrow paths to squirm through. But the interior at 2078 Fifth Avenue seemed deliberately *constructed* and *fortified*. It wasn't just a matter of excess accumulation. Quite literally, the brownstone was a defensive fortress, composed of massively piled and tunneled booby traps. It was one giant rabbit-warren booby trap, built supposedly because of the diceyness and hostility of the Harlem neighborhood by a cracked, eternally schoolboy mind. Since Homer was blind for his last thirteen years, that meant Langley the engineer's mind.

A question unsettled me: were those neighborhood dangers in fact *brought on* by the rabid attentions of the newspapers?

A 1999 article in the now defunct *New York Press* argued as much. Though "gloomy," it claimed, the Collyer mansion hadn't been "messy" until Helen Worden turned up in 1938 to "smoke out" (her phrase) some hermits. By 1942, declared the writer William Bryk, "Langley had single-handedly accumulated vast quantities of newspaper, cartons, tin cans and other refuse, transforming the mansion into a fortress."

William Bryk, I was pleased to discover, was by day a bankruptcy lawyer and a former part-time administrative law judge with New York's Housing Authority. In other words, a man who knew the nuts and bolts of city living. I emailed him.

"I found that an unknown person," he wrote back, "had assembled a microfilm collection of articles on the Collyers, going back to the 1930s . . . I read everything, word for word . . .

"I believe that, before the Worden article, folks simply didn't know anything about the occupants of the house . . . After the Worden piece . . . folks began trying to break into the house to find the hidden treasure and punk kids began throwing rocks . . . Langley responded as one might expect a timid recluse to respond: close the shutters against the rocks and begin fortifying the house against burglars."

Bryk summed up with an understatement: "It is simply that his response was more paranoid and spectacular than most."

In other words, the appalling evolution of the Collyers' mansion wasn't the natural progress of a hoarding condition. It was more like a freaked-out haywire hoarder's defense against ongoing intrusion—brought on by the era's forerunner of a Michael Jackson-style paparazzi blitz.

Helen Worden and her smoke-'em-out ilk had a lot to answer for.

■   ■   ■

The day after my visit to Collyer Brothers Park I went up to Columbia University. As fate nicely had it, Helen Worden's archives and papers are at Homer and Langley's alma mater.

I was of two minds about this Worden. On the one hand, there was her pivotal role in the hounding of a couple of recluses, which arguably led to the Poe-worthy awfulness of their end. On the other hand, she was a dashing, eclectic figure in a bygone newspaper style—a society reporter who turned to the crime beat, author of several books about the carnival that is New York, which she illustrated with her own suave Paris-trained drawings.

Now, in the windowless sleek hush of Columbia's rare book library, I pawed gingerly through folders of Worden's crumbling brown newspaper clips on the Collyers. There was a letter to Barbara Stanwyck, suggesting *Out of This World* would make a great TV series and Stanwyck would be the perfect choice to play Worden. There were heated communiqués back and forth regarding Worden's demand for extra credit and money from playwright Howard Teichman for *The Girls in 509*, his 1958 stage adaptation of *Out of This World*.

Then my heart leapt. I held apparently the original draft of Worden's fateful first *World-Telegram* story about the Collyers, typed in bygone reporter style, triple-spaced on cheap newsprint paper. Then my heart really jumped. I held an old photocopy of a 1933 letter addressed to Inspector James J. Wall of the 123rd Street Police Precinct.

It was from Langley.

"Dear Friend," wrote Langley. "Dire necessity compels me again to seek your kind assistance and cooperation." He then proceeded to complain about twenty-four years' worth (!) of police inaction at "young ruffians . . . demolishing my windows, railings, front door . . . in an attempt to destroy my property." His tone was indignant but excessively courtly—a meandering, unparagraphed, single-space-typed courtliness. The kind of letter you'd immediately regard as from someone unhinged.

But what then of William Bryk's accusatory thesis? That the Collyers' tribulations with the neighbors only began after Worden turned up. When Langley wrote to Inspector Wall, Worden wouldn't come leaping from her taxi for five years yet.

But Bryk's larger point still felt right. The competing reporter who actually got inside the mansion in 1938 reported gloom and clutter, but not demented barricading. Come the next year, however, when authorities tried to force their way in, their access was blocked by "a solid wall of rubble." Langley complained to the press in attendance that his "troubles" had begun when "a newspaper article . . . described [me] as a wealthy hermit who kept his money hidden around the house." He and Homer had been "annoyed by rowdies and others" ever since.

Worden's *Out of This World* would be just the start of the deepening voyeuristic obsession with the Collyers specifically and then hoarders generally. The siblings' gothic story has inspired novels ranging from 1954's bug-eyed potboiler *My Brother's Keeper* to E. L. Doctorow's speculative 2009 reworking, *Homer and Langley*. *Ghosty Men*, a tart nonfiction portrayal, came out in 2003 from Franz Lidz, whose uncle was a hoarder. There've been plays about the benighted brothers: *The Dazzle* (2000), which the inventive playwright Richard Greenberg prefaced by declaring he knew almost nothing about them; and *Stuff* by Michael McIver, more recent (2011) and closer to the facts. On TV over the years you could have watched Art tell Ralph on *The Honeymooners* that with Alice gone, the Kramdens' place looked like the Collyers lived there. Or you could have seen the episode of *The Streets of San Francisco* entitled "The House on Hyde Street," featuring hoarder brothers with an ancient automobile in an upstairs room.

■   ■   ■

At the Columbia library I browsed on some more through Worden's papers, leaving a crumble of browned archival newsprint bits—a mouse mess—on the table. A 1946 photo of Langley I hadn't noticed before peered up at me from a clip. There, drawn out into daylight by a legal subpoena, the younger Collyer brother looked dapper, even rascally, in a turn-of-the-century bow tie and dark jacket. I gaped at him. Notwithstanding his bushy swept-back hair (who'd cut it?) and bristly handlebar moustache, in this particular photo, with the expression around his mouth and the angling of his eye, Langley startlingly resembled—no, it couldn't be.

I snapped a picture with my cell phone, making a thunderous CLICK in the archival silence.

In Queens that evening Cosima leaned close to the cell phone screen, which I held up to her breathlessly.

"Yeah," she allowed. "I guess." She shrugged.

"*You guess?*" I hooted. "*Are you kidding?*"

There on my cell phone Langley Collyer, engineering hoarder, peered out, and, startlingly, he resembled—

Me.

As for Helen Worden, she turned out to be buried in Fairmount Cemetery in Denver. Her grave lies a couple of hundred yards away from the graves of my parents.

6

The Cut-Glass Hand Bell

"So what does Dr. Equis say about you and your childhood marbles?" asked Cosima idly as we browsed the Sunday *Times* an early November weekend. We were back from an extended trip, highlighted by a month in Moscow for *her* book project, now well advanced.

Her question was a good one. In fact, I hadn't ever brought up my marbles at my sessions with my shrink, Dr. Equis.

"But why not?" Cosima raised her head from the travel section. "What do you talk about, then?"

I told her that her query showed a profound incomprehension of a fundamental element of the therapeutic process—namely, its privacy.

"*This*," I sniffed. "That's what we talk about: *this* and *that*."

"But your marbles were part of your early way with objects!" protested Cosima. "Definitely you should ask your therapist what she thinks!"

"Do not," I replied, "*tell me what I should ask my therapist!*"

■   ■   ■

At our next session, I asked Dr. Equis about my marbles.

Any symbolic significance to my boyish attachment to those *little round colorful things*, I wanted to know.

She shrugged. "Every kid likes to play with feces . . ."

But was it a sign of something deeper and troubled, I pressed, if I couldn't bear to have my things touched or even viewed by others? If, when someone asked to borrow a pen I'd classified to myself as "special" or "private," I'd break the pen in half right afterward and throw it away?

Another shrug. "Could be anything, neurotic, psychotic. Normal."

"You think I might be *normal?*" I couldn't hide a note of disappointment. "Just quote unquote *quirky?*"

To which she replied, "Obviously you're not just *quirky.*"

"Dr. Equis," I sputtered, "I can't believe you just said that!"

And my shrink who, when I first met her, had seemed so somber and staid, gave yet another little shrug and grinned, pleased with herself.

■   ■   ■

I'd been seeing her for a couple of years. Schizoid years of a schizoid life. Either I was overeating with Cosima at the hot spots of London or Barcelona or Japan—or Moscow—or we were back and I'd go plodding along once a week to the Behavioral Health Clinic at Sunnywood Hospital Center. Sunnywood is our city-owned neighborhood facility. It boasts that it serves the most immigrant-dense locality on the planet. A prospectus for the hospital's psychiatric internships touts the neighborhood's "feeling of dining in a foreign country, with great meals . . . from Thailand, China, India, Korea, Japan, Cuba, Colombia, Argentina, Mexico, and interesting hybrids of these."

On arrival at the block-long Sunnywood complex—one of those insipid modernist hodgepodges indistinguishable from its adjacent parking garages—I'd first line up to pay my discounted $15 fee at a cashier window with signs in Spanish, Russian, Chinese, Hindi, and Korean. Then I'd edge into an elevator among elaborately headscarved women, baby buggies, and wheelchairs. The waiting room of the third-floor Behavioral Health Clinic did not, unfortunately, recall the gracious tranquility of an Alpine lakeside spa. Dr. Phil might be blathering on a pair of old overhead TVs as you and your bundle of woes joined the company of the gloom-ridden or spacey from across the tattered globe. Recently there had been a vastly dreadlocked dude sitting by me pondering a book titled *Don't Beat Your Children Or They'll Turn Out Like Me*. Then there was the old Asian-Hispanic señora costumed like an elegant ghoulish gypsy, who turned slowly as I sighed up behind her in line to the nurse's desk and stared at me—a wild, soul-piercing, bone-chilling stare, like a close-up from *Dracula*.

Other times I've seen there the big guy who shambles around our neighborhood in all weathers in a hand-drawn clown T-shirt with a rubber nose stuck on it.

Dr. Equis, on the other hand, had a large fur coat of some kind hanging on the door hook in her office. Middle-aged and grave, she was stylish in a bourgeois Gallic way, given to scarves and Prada glasses and substantial jewelry. Once, when I was moaning on and on about procrastination, she offered the didactic tale of how she finished writing her dissertation. Holed up at the family château of a French friend.

Initially I found her somber, almost dour. Then one day I noticed the half-rolled-up poster on her filing cabinet.

"*Che Guevara?*"

So it was. One of those Andy Warhol multi-portraits. The next week Che was up on the wall on the other side of Michelangelo's Adam and God touching fingers, across from the poster of the great gods of psychoanalysis: Freud and Lacan.

Che warmed things up between Dr. Equis and me. I was tickled to find his dashing radical visage at a public clinic crowded with toiling immigrant clients. Then again, it made sense. Whatever Che eventually became, I mused aloud, as we both gazed up at him, he was galvanized to fight poverty and suffering.

"There you go," said Dr. Equis, and left any politics at that. But she would smile at times now.

■   ■   ■

There was something else truly jarring about Dr. Equis amid Sunnywood's multicultural hurly-burly.

She was a Lacanian.

From my days as a hanger-on hanging out in the New York downtown art scene of the eighties, I'd had a vague, hostile awareness of Jacques Lacan, the cult French psychoanalyst and supposed successor to Freud, who decreed that the unconscious operates like a language. The trendy art criticism of the day was all edgy Lacanian theory—an invading fog of complexities I found preposterously cerebral and impenetrable. What's more, around then I'd become obsessed with the psychologist Alice Miller and her iconoclastic work on the prevalence and toxicity of child abuse. I took as my credo her pronouncement that our most powerful weapon against mental illness was discovering the emotional truth of our childhood, as we'd lived it. And *reliving*—not just *describing* —primal hurts and injuries was Miller's fervid therapy model. I embraced it as mine. I visualized tears and cathartic anguish as the royal road to emotional growth. The jargon-puffed abstractions of Lacanian psychoanalysis (Miller rejected all psychoanalysis) seemed to me so much pishposh—the stifling enemy.

And now, owing to the discounted-fee options at the Sunny-wood Behavioral Health Clinic, here I was, decades on—in therapy with someone who'd trained under Lacan's major disciples in Paris.

"See it as a cosmic joke," Cosima had suggested. "Try it as an experiment."

To help me out, she'd bought me a book of comics: *Introducing Lacan: A Graphic Guide*. The text bits were by Darian Leader, a hip London psychoanalyst and art critic. Grudgingly I'd puzzled over the cartoons about Lacan's foundational "mirror stage"— when we as infants supposedly develop our ever-to-be-frail egos by identifying with our image in the mirror. But then what confusions awaited me? I was a twin. My image had been in the mirror but also again right beside me *in the flesh* in the baby carriage!

I'd flipped on. Here they came, in graphics and text balloons— those dreaded Lacanisms of yore: "the registers of the symbolic, imaginary, and real," "the phenomenon of the phallus" (not to be confused with any actual penis), and my old semiotic bugaboos, "the signifier and the signified." I broke into a sweat. Abstract concepts have that effect on me.

Then the mighty *jouissance*—which meant something like sexual orgasm or ecstatic pleasure. A very postcoital female face was pictured. "Jouissance is felt 99% of the time as unbearable suffering," contended Darian Leader's text, bewilderingly.

Or maybe not *so* bewilderingly, I'd thought, come to think of it (God, the double entendres would hatch like bunnies). I'd written a book called *The Sadness of Sex*. Had I the makings of a half-baked Lacanian?

To her credit Dr. Equis mostly avoided technical jargon. Except once, early on, when I asked her what healing role she was supposed to play in my unconscious. Another version of my mother? A better model of my father?

"Actually," she'd replied, "I'm the *objet petit a* ['object little-a']." Then she'd laughed and waved the question away.

I'd looked up this "object little a." It meant something like "object of desire." But in a nurturing, not sexual, sense. It was part of Lacan's schematic diagram of the mind. And how strange—how psychoanalysts of all kinds employed the term "object" to mean people or parts of people.

I scratched my head object.

■   ■   ■

The awful state of my place I mentioned for the first time when I announced my Project to Dr. Equis. It was at this point that she'd offered the tip about cleaning up a little at a time. Such banal advice, I'd scoffed. I'd decided that for the practicalities of decluttering I needed to look elsewhere, somewhere specialized. Dr. Equis I'd consult for the emotional further resonances, the deep reverberations.

"So describe your clutter," said my Lacanian. As I talked, she sat up slowly in her chair, eyes wide.

"Wait a minute," she exclaimed. "You bring back all these things from your *gourmet* trips with Cosima . . . and they sit around, you say . . . *'undigested'*?"

Lacanians. They do pick at the carefree worms of your language.

How had my toilet training gone? she asked another time, when my lair's conditions came up again. I practically hooted at her raising this musty antique from antiquated Freud. To my astonishment, after I left her office the question provoked an onset of unsettling memories and images: in particular, how as an infant I became dangerously constipated and my father—I only knew the story through his telling it—had dramatically saved the situation by unblocking me with his bare fingers. I had a sudden mental picture of my tiny self struggling and squealing in his hands. Was I unconsciously struggling still against this forced "giving up of things"? It was all too gross and I shuddered. I stepped around in my dusty litter very creeped out for a while.

A bigger jolt awaited a couple of sessions later. Dr. Equis all at once asked me to read aloud from *Wearing Dad's Head*, the stories I'd written years before about my parents after they died. I snorted. What a hokey idea, I thought, reading your fiction aloud to your shrink! Almost dismissively I chose "Flood," a very short piece about an imaginary flood deluging my family home. I read, from a Xeroxed page I had given her some months before:

> The lamplight is green and dimmish under water, and the
> house around us a sad and unrecognizable place of disarray.

I started to sob. That was my cluttered apartment: a sad and unrecognizable place of disarray! I continued on, to the "greasy silt pressed into the corners," the "clammy" chairs, the "spongy" stairs. I wept like an orphaned child. The hokum, I guess, was on me.

■   ■   ■

Dr. Equis wasn't the only one ministering to my mental state at the Behavioral Health Clinic. I first turned up there in 2008, a year before Cosima buzzed my doorbell. My place was a mess, to be sure. But what brought me to Sunnywood was the generalized mess of my life: depression, anxiety, poverty, unproductiveness.

Initially I was assigned a psychiatrist, who then fixed me up with Dr. Equis for counseling apart from medication. This separation of roles—between M.D. psychiatrists to manage the drugs, and non-M.D. psychologists or social workers to conduct talk therapy—had dramatically widened in recent years. Psychiatry

used to provide talk as an essential part of its practice. But the
increasing trend was toward focusing on psychopharmacology.
A national survey from a few years before found that barely 11
percent of psychiatrists offered talk therapy to all their patients,
down by almost half from the previous decade. The percentage
has gone on shrinking since. No pun intended.

My first psychiatrist at Sunnywood was a suave young M.D.
from Sri Lanka. Who noted the alcohol use I'd filled out on the
intake questionnaire and announced that actually AA was my best
treatment option. I counter-announced that half my life with my
girlfriend involved delightful bars and gloriously aged wines—so
I had no intention of quitting. In frustration Dr. Sri Lanka passed
me on to a chubby junior resident psychiatrist from Guadaloupe.
When I mentioned AA, Dr. Guadaloupe pulled a face ("that whole
religious thing"). Whereupon I found myself actually defending
AA. When his residency ended, I was referred for meds to a boyish but senior psychiatrist from Bangladesh.

Dr. Nandy resembled a petite Steve Buscemi, the actor, in
a homey sweater. At first, I liked his amiable sleepy-eyed quiet
manner.

Then things turned weird.

"Because Dr. Nandy doesn't believe in the unconscious," Dr.
Equis informed me, sitting in her small windowless office with
Lacan and Freud peering down at us.

"Sure—I believe in the unconscious!" declared Dr. Nandy
when I coyly asked, next visit. But his awkward little giggle didn't
convince me.

Dr. Nandy often seemed awkward with me. Even wary—
there in *his* windowless small office. Perhaps that was because I'd
assumed any mental health professional would welcome my richly
shaded evocations of the internal ditch I was stuck in. Would be as
a shepherd to a troubled lamb, bending an ever-curious ear.

"Wait, don't *unload* on me! Don't deluge me with detail!" Dr.

Nandy protested at our second session. "You people who've been in a lot of therapy think you should just dump everything out there!"

"But Dr. Nandy," I replied, fairly stunned, "people coming in here do regard someone in your position like a father or mother figure."

"That depends on your school of thought," he replied.

"Well," I said, another time, "whatever the type of treatment, they say it's the relationship that heals."

"That depends," he said, "on your school of thought."

And yet another time, on my way out his door, I'd sighed that I'd never learned independence, thanks to how my father—both my parents, really—treated me as a child.

"But you're *not* a child now," exclaimed Dr. Nandy. He looked genuinely bewildered.

"Good for him!" said Cosima when I complained to her. She gave an enthusiastic thumbs-up.

Dr. Nandy's straightforwardness toward my problems continued to rankle me. He wanted to just go ahead and address my "issues" directly, without any ceremonial delicacy. Regarding depression, for instance—I'd been on Zoloft with Dr. Guadaloupe but had discontinued—he emailed me a link where I could monitor my mood online.

"I don't consult websites about my psychic life," I huffed to myself, and never followed the link.

And then there was the Prozac and Ritalin business. I read in an article that a leading neuropsychiatry researcher, Dr. Sanjaya Saxena at the University of California–San Diego, recommended for hoarders a cocktail of Prozac (an antidepressant) and Ritalin (a stimulant used for ADD). I pushed Dr. Nandy to prescribe them. Initially he resisted my pharmacological kibitzing, but my persistence prevailed. He wrote the prescription. But then I got cold feet. I read that Prozac could cause mania in some people.

"What? You still haven't started? But it's a very small dose!"

Dr. Nandy was baffled. Not least because, besides the Zoloft mentioned above, I'd taken over the years at various points the antidepressants Celexa, Paxil, Effexor, Wellbutrin, Anafranil, and Tofranil.

I finally tried the Prozac and Ritalin combo. But my place didn't get any cleaner and I went off them.

■   ■   ■

So, you ask, how was Sunnywood aiding me at all with the boxes piled up in my apartment? I often asked this myself. As did Cosima. No one at the Behavioral Health Clinic had expertise with hoarding, severe or lite. There were no community services for the problem, no support groups.

"I feel like what I'm doing in here is constructing a *poem*," I once exclaimed in Dr. Equis's office. "The poem of myself."

Exactly, I expected to hear—so quit wasting time! Instead my Lacanian nodded, in affirmation.

"So you are," she agreed.

Dr. Equis was an acute, startlingly attentive listener. She spotted themes flickering across categories: how my inner mess fitted into my outer clutter.

"You don't just hoard *things*," she declared one day, as I went on about accumulated miseries of all kinds with my parents. "You hoard *emotions* too."

Not letting go was an obvious feature of my clutterbug character. But her comment was subtler, it struck deep—so deep, I had a sudden vision of my whole approach to living. And how I tried to cope with loss.

With the most painful of losses.

I bowed my head, overcome.

■   ■   ■

There was a fragile box, lodged with obsessive care in the mildew-scented depths of one of my entryway closets. I unearthed it, my heart thudding, the morning after the Dr. Equis session above. It was cardboard, sunken-cheeked with age: 13 inches long, 11 inches wide, 6 inches deep. "*DENVER*" and "*FRAGILE*" had been handwritten (by me) on the top, straddling a cross-ply of packing tape, blistered and brownish, the color of aged fingernails. I had not brought myself to open this box since closing it more than twenty-five years before. It was light in my hands. I brought it over to my studio area and sat beside it on a cleared patch of floor. I rocked back and forth, gazing at it. It contained just a few delicate things, buffered in newspaper, that had belonged to my mother—or, more accurately, that were among my mother's effects when she died.

One of these was a small cut-glass hand bell. The bell my mother bought to ring for aid at home in the last stages of the illness that took her. That left me and my two brothers, in our mid-thirties, six years after my father's death, orphans finally.

■   ■   ■

My mother died in 1984, in the early spring, from lung cancer. She was seventy-six years old. Sudden flare-ups of memory of her final hours in Denver would still make me wince and twist away. They were lodged in me like a geological fault that I kept planked over. Or like a handful of her relics I kept hidden away in a closet in a cardboard box.

Question for the home curator: Where and how do you keep a tender thing that also reminds you of your mother's harrowing dying?

A friend of mine shared a fair definition of trauma: You witness a loved one's suffering you were never meant to witness. It overloads your emotional capacities. Things don't "resolve." Things lodge pent-up in your psyche, waiting to unleash their monster seismics into any new big shock that comes along. Such as happened in the late eighties, when a girlfriend unexpectedly dumped me. And then again three years ago, during Cosima's health scare, when the dates kept chiming and compounding. Cosima got her frightening emergency CAT scan on January 28—my mother's birthday. When, trembling, I called her surgeon's office a couple of months later to ask for the biopsy results, it was in April—on the day my mother died.

The mouse I'd more recently killed in my woeful kitchen had me flickering back to mice in another kitchen. The one at our red-clad family split-level in Denver, where I went to stay with my mother while she had chemo. The chemo turned my elderly widowed mom—the dottily regal, wise, laughing little person, so full of goony poetics and gumption, who'd changed her name from banal Ethel to the concocted euphony of Ethella, or Thella for short—into a wraith tottering about the curtained dimness of the living room, her long thin gray hair, usually drawn back tight in a smart bun, flapping lank around her shoulders as she moaned in distress. One evening, feeding her tablespoons of awful pink liquid diet she struggled to keep down, I spotted past her a mouse scurrying along a floorboard. We had an infestation of them: little verminous heralds of the collapse and ruin of everything.

I couldn't alarm my mother by calling in an exterminator. I set out traps at night and rushed upstairs from our downstairs bedrooms in the morning to dispose of the stiff puny corpses before she tottered across them. One night I even saw one flit across her bedside slippers as she sank down onto her pillow. Dread engulfed me; I floated on it as I lay in my father's bed in his old separate room, where he'd slumped to the floor six years before, with his last words a dazed non sequitur, "Thella, we're not in the Black Forest anymore." My brothers had put in their innings here. I didn't have a job and wasn't married, so I had little excuse not to be called on most for this duty. Other than my terror. I was torn away from my bohemian self-preoccupations in downtown New York, exiled back to the Denver sticks. Where our family and our home were tumbling down—sliding away underwater, as my story would later put it, the one I read aloud in Dr. Equis's office at the Behavioral Health Clinic.

Was it at this stage my mother acquired the cut-glass hand bell that sat inside the taped, sunken-cheeked box beside me now? It was an object so characteristic of her, highfalutin but tenderly eccentric, suggestive of grande dames but employed without grand airs. Did she keep it to ring among the pillboxes on the night table in her bedroom? Or was it by the couch in the living room dotted with her knickknacks and my old man's career memorabilia, where she'd sit for hours draped in a purple throw blanket she'd crocheted herself, fixed in broodings I'd try to buck her out of with a joke? She appreciated my quips, I really believe; they cheered her up. They were much of the little I could do for her, a guy almost helpless about life's practicalities, a guy who clutched his head, and groaned a lot, at a loss what to do.

I couldn't recall now: was the hand bell one of the few personal items that went along with my mother to the hospice where she consented to be taken out of the hospital? She was only semiconscious by then, her puny ruined lungs incapable without an oxygen mask. But what use would a hand bell have been to her? My brothers whispered their goodbyes through the paraphernalia of the hospital bed, and left me and my mother's sister, in from South Africa, to handle the rest. The rest meaning a peaceful dignified passing, after the ambulance transfer to the hospice. But that's not what happened.

Then again, I think I did remember, vaguely, the cut-glass hand bell on the barren night table by her hospice bed. More clearly, her liver-spotted hand, with its long up-curving groomed fingers, reaching out to adjust the angle of her little gold-rimmed square alarm clock, another totem from her cozy bedroom at home. I remember her hand trembling, visibly quivering. I remember the searing pathos, the violation, at the sight of that alarm clock, a domestic icon meant to soothe her, to cozify this stark alien room. It made the ordeal hideous, a hideous sham of solace.

There was no peace and little dignity to my mother's end. When the ambulance arrived to take her from her hospital bed, she started squirming and went from semi-comatose to wide-eyed nonstop panic. Of the sixteen hours that followed at the hospice, I remember rushing down a lot of night-lit corridors, pleading for nurses or attendants or whatever the hell you call them at a hospice, to come and do something. But morphine, I was told, would kill her. My aunt had gone home to sleep. I remember forcing myself to smile down at my mother from alongside, a quivering smile of helpless terrified false reassurance, as she writhed and gasped and bleated in sweat-soaked sheets. It was like keeping company with a person drowning in shallow water for hours and hours. "*I'm so sorry you have to go through this,*" she whispered up to me, teeth chattering. I had to go out to the hall so she wouldn't see me as I wept by the door.

Sometime after dawn my aunt reappeared. But she'd forgotten her pills at the house. I drove off frantically to get them. Perhaps some subtle understanding was operating between the two elderly sisters, that I needed to be away to release my mother from her struggles. When I got back, it was over. In that form, at least.

■　　　■　　　■

I sat beside the box now, my arms clasped tight around me. The little alarm clock must be in there too, along with the cut-glass hand bell. Also a little flat hard rubber fish, colored red, that had belonged to my father, which my mother had kept.

After her death we three orphaned brothers rented out the house for a couple of years. Finally we put it on the market. When the time came to dispose of the material contents—we gave our father's papers to the university—I couldn't face going out. My brothers went to Denver without me. I listed some requests. What each of us took from our old family split-level, and what we did with those takings, spoke of our stories. My twin, Tug (as he was called now), with a young family of his own and years of group therapy, shipped back, among other things, silverware and plates from the dining room, and the upright piano my mother had bought herself as an indulgence after my father died; she would play the couple of tunes she'd written in her younger musical days in London, which she claimed had been stolen by her bandleader. Tug installed the piano in his house outside Boston and began teaching himself scales. My younger brother, Palle, who'd always bought my mother sumptuous presents (I'd send a birthday card, hectically inscribed) and was long openly contemptuous of my father, kept exactly . . . nothing. Me, I asked for some of my father's books and a few small items of my mother's. Among the latter: the contents of this box marked "*DENVER FRAGILE.*"

I ran my hand slowly along the top of it. No, I still wasn't prepared to open it. Besides everything else, that felt like another violation. A desecration. I was ashamed to bring out what was in the box into the shambles of my place—my "place of disarray."

Maybe this was just another way of saying that for all of Dr. Equis's attentions, I hadn't yet learned how to grieve properly.

■　　■　　■

Every January around my mother's birthday, things would get very rocky and troubled for me. During the most recent of these stretches, when the memories were flooding back raw in my Lacanian's office, I'd suggested to Dr. Nandy that I likely had post-traumatic stress syndrome. I'd just never been diagnosed properly.

At this latest piece of do-it-yourself *DSM*, he took a deep breath. He produced his smartphone. He read off the diagnostic questions. He toted up the point value of my answers. Yes, he admitted, my score met the threshold. He didn't seem very enthusiastic, if I can put it that way.

He asked if I wanted a medication. I told him I'd become progressively leery about all psychopharmacology, particularly antidepressants in my case.

Dr. Nandy knew this already. I'd earlier brought up, among others, the withering critique of the effectiveness and safety of psychological drugs by Marcia Angell, the crusading former editor in chief of the *New England Journal of Medicine*.

"Marcia Angell is full of shit!" Dr. Nandy had retorted. Drugs, properly prescribed, helped.

Things were a little frayed in his office.

Anyway, I was satisfied with his diagnosis. I left it at that.

■   ■   ■

How many years had it been since my mother died, Dr. Equis asked me.

"That's a long time . . ." she said, when I told her.

"You think I hoard my pain and hurt too?" I asked her quietly.

"I think your pain and hurt and grievances were what you could carry with you, moving about so much as a child."

This image of myself as a child clinging on to injuries for his possessions made me throb with sudden tears yet again. I seemed always to be bursting into tears now in Dr. Equis's little windowless office. I was getting my Alice Miller quota of anguish and

then some. I started packing Ray-Bans for my exits through the
waiting room.

■   ■   ■

"You know, I think we're making progress in here, despite you
being a Lacanian," I announced, sincerely, two and a half years
after we'd commenced and four months or so into my Project. My
analyst had learned to roll with the punches. "Now please don't
make a cut on this," I added quickly—"cut" being the term for the
provocative Lacanian practice, one that had shocked and angered
me the first time Dr. Equis did it, of ending a session early and
abruptly if the analyst felt an important point had been touched
on—"because I have something to show you."

After stalling and resisting, I'd decided to bring in photos of
my apartment shambles. This may sound trivial, but it wasn't—for
either of us. I was allowing both sides of my mess, external and
internal, to meet up, at least for a glimpse.

"I think I need a cup of coffee first," murmured my Lacanian,
rising to fiddle with a French press at her tiny office sink, while I
brought out Cosima's iPad.

Grinning shyly yet proudly, as if about to disrobe, I took a
breath and began the slideshow of my pigsty.

"*Oh*," said Dr. Equis.

She leaned close, peering at my colorfully swamped counters
and piled floors. She seemed surprised.

"You look surprised."

"I was afraid it would be all hoarded trash," she said. "But it's
really more like clutter. Almost *organized*, in a way. A place where
somebody's in the midst of working."

I felt relief—and a pang of disappointment. I did not consider
myself a full-blown hoarder, someone suffering from an out-and-
out pathology. But I did want some shock value for my mess. I'd

come to take a certain secret pride in it, even. It was a dramatic and richly intricate problem spurring an existential far-reaching Project to try to fathom and resolve. Surely it deserved respect for being impressive and alarming—for putting my relationship with Cosima at risk?

"Dr. Equis, you're confusing everything," I protested. "You're not supposed to be saying this!"

She gave one of her shrugs. She sat back sipping her coffee, looking amused.

"No wonder you say you've got writer's block!" cried Dr. Nandy, squinting at Cosima's iPad when I took my pigsty and pony show into *his* office. "I'd be completely distracted in that environment!"

"Would you say it even looked like *hoarding*, then?"

"Yes, I'd call it hoarding."

"But mild," I countered.

"Yes—mild *hoarding*."

"O-kay," I nodded, perversely gratified. Dr. Nandy at last had come through!

At my next session in Dr. Equis's office, I detected a change in the environment.

"Wait a minute," I said, scanning the scarcity on top of her filing shelves. "Have you . . . *cleaned up* in here?"

Yes, she replied, she had.

7

Mastering Disaster

Then it happened again.

My doorbell rang.

My spasm of alarm flared close to panic at the answer to my cry, "Who is it?"

I opened the door a crack. Héctor the super loomed before me, cradling white boxes in his beefy arm.

"New CO detector," he said. "I gotta come in." Héctor is tall and muscle-bound, but his voice is thin and high. The squeak of doom.

"Not now," I sputtered. "I'm in the midst of—some cleaning! Next week!" The words sounded so wretchedly furtive I added recklessly, as if not hiding anything: "And you need to look at my faucets, they're in pretty rough shape." I forced a laugh. "Really old!"

"Okay," said Héctor. "Then I bring my boss maybe."

Immediately as I closed the door I was engulfed in horror. I clutched my head.

"What have I done?"

"What have I done?" I repeated desperately to Cosima that evening. "My faucets are leaking nonstop! Who knows what damage I've caused? *And he wants to bring in the Bubonic Weasel!*"

"Whoops," said Cosima. And she gulped in genuine empathy.

The Bubonic Weasel was the longtime managing agent of my building. He was such a tormenter of tenants we'd actually called the cops on him once for trespassing. Then I had to hire a lawyer several years later when he tried not to renew the lease. It cost me thousands of dollars in legal fees and months of seething anxiety. Every time the rent bill appeared under my door from him I wouldn't leave it out visible—or in contact with anything; I would immediately carry it into the bedroom and quarantine it deep from sight in my filing cabinet. To shield myself from the malevolent karma of this evil talisman, this anti-Hotel Meurice stationery eating away at my serenity and security.

And now I'd gone and exposed an opening for the Bubonic Weasel with the faucets!

My faucets were leaking. Really badly. For months. Because I didn't want the super inside. And owing to this flagrantly irresponsible housekeeping half my bathtub was streaked a grisly mineral blue-green from the shower head's drip drip drip. The shower tiles were mascara'd with mold. The pipe to the toilet dripped even more lavishly. And the kitchen tap didn't just leak, it half-gushed a continuous stream.

Ugly phrases—*property damage, failure to maintain*—singed my tenant brain. I'd intended to get to all this in the course of my Project. Eventually.

Now my system of procrastination had been thrown into upheaval by Héctor and my careless mouth.

"Oy, oy. But maybe he won't come," muttered Cosima, pulling the sheet to her chin, while I huddled beside her, tossing and turning under my weight of blankets, throws, and coverlets.

■   ■   ■

Next morning first thing I hurried off to Roosevelt Avenue, the neighborhood's main drag under the rumbling elevated 7 train, and from the second 99-cent store I entered I chose a set of plastic funnels—the most inexpensive set, a detail obsessionally important to me somehow. After additional anxious calibrations—*vibes* were involved—I chose the sunny blue funnels over the pink ones.

Cheap plastic funnels, we're talking about.

I also bought a rubber shower hose (white), and back in my bathroom I rigged up a Rube Goldberg contraption in the shower. The largest funnel I seated down in the drain, where it directly caught the lethal drips from the shower head above. Then right below the shower's leaky hot water handle I hung with string a smaller funnel fitted into the mouth of the hose, which I'd cut in two after removing the spray head. Beads of water ran by capillary action from the handle down the string into the smaller funnel, then down the hose into the drain alongside the big funnel. I did likewise with the leaky cold water handle, employing another small funnel and the second part of the hose.

It was a device worthy of a fourth-grade science project. Maybe with a hint of *Aliens*, the movie. It was demented, it was delightful; I stood back beaming. *Drip! Drip! Drip!* all harmlessly into blue funnels and then into the drain. I got my camera and documented my handiwork. To take a shower I would simply lift the funnels delicately to the side, and then return them to position.

But what about the blue-green stain? Distress gripped once more. I retreated into my dining area. And was confronted by the snowdrifts of plastic grocery bags which would greet Héctor —*and possibly the Bubonic Weasel*—on entry. With a sudden howl, I began snatching up bags—tearing through my immobility, grabbing the billowy flimsy excesses accumulated over years and years. Ferociously I stuffed them into larger bags—almost every one of them, save for a few too pretty or too useful (for size, durability), which I put aside. Then I took a photo. Then I shoved them down the trash chute in the hall.

I did the same with the load under the kitchen sink.

There were no pangs as when tossing my old pasta bowl. Just a rush of empowerment at finding the will at last to rid myself of their burden—of their portion of absurd, clingy fearfulness: "How will I cope with not having enough plastic bags should I need one?"

I threw out 131 plastic bags in all. I counted, for my Project.

■   ■   ■

Similar inspiration sent me darting over to my laptop to go googling.

Plastic grocery bags, I now learned, are the world's most popular consumer item, the second largest trash item after cigarette butts. They were born in the early seventies; the familiar ones with handles, the "T-shirt" bags as they're known in the trade, appeared a decade later. By the mid-nineties four out of five grocery bags were newfangled plastic, not old-school paper. They were thinner than a human hair—soap bubbles of high-density polyethylene thermoplastic. Americans collectively use some 100 billion of them per year, while the average American discards some 500 of them annually, after a per-bag use of about twelve minutes. (Not in my case! I corrected.) Their environmental impact is terrible. Not biodegrading for twenty years at least, they clog seas and waterways.

I picked up a specimen I'd kept, and really eyeballed it. It was the most common type in my stock—from Met Foods, the chain supermarket two blocks away. The body color was white, the logo thick-lettered in blue with a red design accent. "PLEASE REUSE OR RECYCLE AT PARTICIPATING STORE," declared large red letters at the bottom. No problem here. My place was a shrine to reuse. Bags shrouded every perishable in my sad fridge and freezer, they double-lined waste receptacles in my kitchen and bathroom, they hid clots of T-shirts and socks in the bedroom.

But what of this recycling invitation? Which wasn't actually "recycling" but "downcycling," since plastic bags aren't turned into new bags, they go into the making of plastic lumber. Was "participating store" just PR hot air?

I found myself—for the sake of my Project—out on the street, hustling over to Met Foods from my unfinished labors. There was a cubbyhole at the side of the building for bottle returns, where toiling tiny Central American ladies queued with their shopping carts stupendously towering with picked-over recyclables. I darted through a pause in the line and stooped to address a man behind a small cramped counter. "I'd like to recycle this," I announced self-consciously. I waved my specimen plastic bag. He stared back, at me and it, from under his sweat-darkened Yankees cap. Silence. "Recycle—" I repeated. "This bag!" Irritably he ignored me, waved forward the bottle lady behind me. "Inside," he muttered, confusingly.

I drifted away, red-faced. But excited. Had I just exposed Met Foods' phony bag recycling program? What meant "inside"? There wasn't any bag recycling facility inside!

Actually there was. A specially designed large barrel was pointed out to me, over by one of the further checkout registers. I never went through there so I'd never noticed it. And it was practically hidden away. I deposited my bags, on an awkward note of disappointment.

I hurried back to my place. Mounting the stairs peevishly, I bumped right into Héctor. Cradling more white boxes.

"Hey, know what?" I blurted. "Why not just give me the detector, I can set it up myself—save you time!"

"Okay," said Héctor. "Sure."

I tried not to look elated as I took it from him.

"And the water leaks?" Héctor remembered.

"In a couple of weeks, okay? They're not so bad *really*."

Héctor shrugged. "Okay."

Back behind my door, heady with self-congratulation at having finessed some breathing space, I climbed onto a chair with the new CO detector. Carefully I maneuvered it overhead onto the mounting screws of its predecessor in the ceiling arch by the bathroom.

And fumbled it.

The detector fell to the floor and exploded sensationally into many plastic pieces.

■   ■   ■

That very evening, Ron Alford entered my life.

He was waiting in the depths of an Indian restaurant, examining the menu. Bollywood music warbled overhead. He wore a battered baseball cap with the logo "Clutter Masters" and a saucy little gray D'Artagnan goatee that spiced his square owlish features. He suggested a slightly bohemian, perhaps philosophical, job site engineer. I figured him for his mid-sixties; turned out he was over seventy. Age didn't inhibit his bluster.

Earlier in the day, while reassembling the exploded detector —it was miraculously unbroken, and worked—I'd taken a break to indulge in some more fitful hoarding research (mostly). On YouTube I came across a man in a respirator mask clearing out hellaciously cluttered spaces. His name was Ron Alford. His outfit, trademarked as Disaster Masters, specialized in handling hoarders in crisis. Ron was the Disaster Master himself, who'd been profiled on MSNBC and featured on *The Life of Grime—New York*, a hoarding series the BBC tried to launch over here.

Instead of getting back to my needful bathroom and kitchen, I'd impetuously called the number on his main website; he seemed to have several. He answered.

"You and *400 other people*," he snorted when I explained I'd like an interview.

But we could meet that very evening, he suddenly cried, if I wanted to buy him dinner. I sputteringly suggested Jackson Diner, a popular spot on 74th Street, my neighborhood's Indian drag.

"So?" said Cosima, eyes bright, when I came reeling in at 10 p.m. "*So?*"

■　　■　　■

Where to start with My Dinner with Ron.

"Two words," the Disaster Master announced, "will get me to pay close attention to you [as a would-be client]: '*Yes, Ron.*' Two words will turn me off faster than anything else: '*But, Ron.*'"

Meaning if you asked for Ron's help—he never solicited, people came to him—it was his way or the highway. His way involved italics.

"I *know* you," he informed me personally, as a self-confessed clutterbug, at various points once the curry got flowing.

"Write this *down!*" he also variously exclaimed, to me as interviewer.

I could barely write fast enough to keep up with the spray of invective and propounding.

Clutterers Anonymous: "What a joke, they go to listen to those others' problems so they can rationalize to themselves, '*At least* I'm not like that poor son of a bitch over there!'"

Professional organizers: "The fucking *blind* leading the blind."

Books about organizing: "You're looking at a guy who's thrown in the garbage more *books* by Julie Morgenstern than any other human being *on the planet!"* (Julie Morgenstern, author of *Organizing from the Inside Out*: "Oprah's *butt girl*.")

Self-help books generally: "Not one of the fucking things *works*. Reading a book on tennis, you're gonna come out an Andre Agassi? *Ain't* gonna happen! You need a *coach*." Meaning Ron.

And as for shrinks:

"I would *never*," declared Ron, "allow a shrink to come with me on a cleanup—*ever*. They'd just waste my time, and get it wrong. Why? Because they don't take you into the *future*, they're too busy digging in the *past*."

But cognitive behavioral therapy, specifically, didn't seem to operate like that, I mumbled into the spray.

"There's this guy," Ron ploughed on, "Randy Frost, sitting out in the woods, at Vassar or *wherever* he teaches—"

"At Smith. I'm going to interview him—"

"Writing books, giving talks, getting funded by the *drug merchants*—"

"I don't believe he's so hugely about drugs—"

"Where's he get grants?" demanded Ron. "It's *all* about drugs. They say they're gonna make a drug gonna cure hoarding? *They're so full of shit it's unreal!*"

How many hoarding situations, he wanted to know, had any shrink personally ever handled? A *handful*—whereas he'd done three, four, five a week.

"But since all these *TV shows* and *amateurs* have shown up," he added sourly, "they've almost put me out of business."

It was the grumble of a pioneering veteran with thirty-plus years at it, who'd refused to go on Oprah despite, he claimed, five calls from her producers. Because he didn't want his clients "paraded on any *OH MY GOD! network*."

So what was his first cleanup job? I asked.

Not *cleanup*, he corrected. *Life transition*. His first such job was in the early eighties, for a college professor on Long Island who went away for the winter. Leaving his furnace to die, his pipes to freeze and burst, and water to flood everything.

"*Huge* misunderstanding!" Ron spooned up more of his chicken curry. "Real hoarders are *chipmunks*. So many people living with *stuff*, they're not hoarders, they're *dysfunctional!*"

Such were his clients. They numbered health care workers first of all, then teachers and government employees—almost all of them "brilliant, but completely *dysfunctional!*" So they were thousands of times more likely to have a flood or a fire than so-called "normal" folk. Why? Because they didn't take care of their house or apartment, only attending to what they wanted to.

"They don't take care," Ron summarized collegially, "of what *you and I* think they should."

I blushed and mis-swallowed my goat vindaloo, me and my untended premises.

No, proclaimed the Disaster Master: it wasn't any *hoarding*. It was the fear and inability to let things go—*that* was the key dynamic.

"I invented the word 'disposophobia' fifteen years ago 'cause I got tired of shrinks telling me *blah blah blah* and I looked at them one day and thought, You haven't a fucking *clue* what you're talking about!"

I had to say, "disposophobia" did have an incisive ring to it. And the notion resonated intimately with me.

"How about this?" I then asked him. "Emotional trauma as a trigger for the reluctance to let things go?"

Ron wasn't interested. "I tell people straight up: I don't care if you were raped by fifty Indians when you were twelve, because there's *nothing* I can do about that. Well, I can have empathy but *guess what?* If you continue to recycle that *Poor poor me*, you ain't *never* gonna have a future, pal!"

What people lacked, he announced, was a *plan*.

Meaning a practical plan to prevent disasters, and a practical plan to handle them if they happened. That was the name of his overall approach to his business or businesses (there seemed to be an interlocking welter of these; advising how to deal with insurance companies was his root activity, I gathered):

"The Plan."

■　　■　　■

With all his blather and bluster, I warmed to Ron. He was so colorful as to be visible from outer space. *A trash-talking transitioner of trash.* And he had his vast experience and keen insights. Obviously, it seemed to me, he had a chip on his shoulder as a self-described Florida high school dropout, who'd nevertheless earned a pilot's license—he'd had a stint in the Coast Guard, then some years selling insurance for Prudential—and found himself surrounded by clueless "experts" and "brilliant but dysfunctional" clients.

Finishing our beers, we got around to my situation.

"So when did your squeeze lay down the ultimatum?" he asked.

"Some months ago now," I admitted sheepishly. "Actually, a large number."

"So what's taken you so long?"

I explained about turning my decluttering into a Project. How I even restrained myself at times because of that. "I've turned it all into an art and research project!" I laughed, as if bemused by my silliness.

"*You're so full of shit,*" said Ron.

"Maybe," I murmured.

Then I cleared my throat. Would he take an informal glance at some photos of my clutter? I brought out Cosima's iPad.

He leaned over the plates and bowls, peering at the iPad gallery.

"This is your man cave . . ."

"Well, *writing studio*."

He grinned. "Love the vacuum cleaner with all that shit on the floor surrounding it. I may have a hundred pictures of vacuum cleaners like that!"

"But you think it's no big deal, as these things go, right? It's not that bad?"

"That's exactly why you go to those *fucking* meetings!" Ron erupted. "*Write that down*. You are an *At Leaster*. That's what you are, I've *got* you again! '*At least* I'm not that bad!'"

■ ■ ■

"So is Ron coming to your place?" Cosima wanted to know.

"Are you *fucking* kidding?" I said. "Ever hear of Red Adair?"

As Ron had carried on, I'd suddenly thought of that old dare-devil oil-field firefighter. I asked Ron if he'd ever heard of him. He said he'd never met Red Adair but he'd dedicated one of his books to him. (He'd written several, in fact, mainly about the insurance racket, all self-published.)

"*Do I want a guy in my little reliquarium who thinks of himself as Red Adair?*"

Furthermore, I'd stopped by my lair on the way over and already there was an email from Ron, thanking me for the meal and describing the interview as high old fun, followed by his advice that if I really wanted to do a worthy book I'd best have him over to my place and obediently submit to his orders (this with a parenthetical smile).

He then made a poetic critique of my marooned big vacuum— and characterized my piles of things as thought-triggers that reminded me of what I'd intended to do with my things, only more things got in the way.

It all made me gaze fondly over at Nadya's shipwrecked Kenmore PROGRESSIVE Direct Drive. And at my dusty piles. I *liked* how they triggered thoughts.

Next morning another email was waiting: Had I reviewed the various materials he'd sent with the previous email or was I simply back online panning for newer material? He was wise to me, he declared (another parenthetical smile).

I gave a sniff. In fact, I was doing exactly what Ron described. To my annoyance, he was spot on.

He continued that he'd located an old page on his server which I should check out. It constituted, he informed me, the outline for my book.

It was a Web page called "The Clutter Masters of America (Formerly Professional Organizers of America)," on his site *The-Plan.com*. The site seemed awfully . . . cluttered. I was to call when I was done to give my response.

I scanned the text with slapdash authorial scorn. I noted a couple of decent, familiar points that stuck out in a foam of blather about credentials and unmatched expertise. I also noticed a combative passage about typos: "On this Web page are several typographical errors. Most Disposophobics will find these errors faster than understanding the contents of our message. Some will get stuck on the minutia and forget why they came here in the first place."

A weird sentiment to be forwarded to a writer! Didn't Ron have Spellcheck? Or was this a gambit to entice a would-be client?

I took a deep breath and called him up. His reading recommendations, I said, were "very illuminating."

"But I'm not really ready yet, at this point," I went on— stammering a little despite myself—"to have you, or anyone else, come to my place right now."

"*Jesus Christ*, I wasn't angling to get *hired!*" Ron snorted.

I reiterated, though, that I'd like to come along on one of his jobs.

He said there might be one the day after next.

■   ■   ■

We rendezvoused at 9 a.m. in the lobby of an upscale apartment tower a few blocks away from the UN. I'd been right around the corner only a week before, at a friend's cocktail party for visiting Russian authors. Ron wore a smart black baseball cap with a "Disaster Masters" logo, and a similarly designed T-shirt. After he touched base with the super, we rode the elevator up to the twenty-seventh floor with two of his black-T-shirted crew. Seventy per cent of his customers were over fifty-five, Ron had told me. Today's client was a retired high school science teacher, a bachelor in his eighties. He was a repeat client from a decade earlier. Once again overwhelmed and under pressure from the building management.

We entered a large studio apartment. I didn't know what I would see. I'd scanned enough videos and photos to have a sci-fi scare vision of the possibilities. Stuff packed to the ceiling à la the Collyer mansion? Goat paths between towers of newspapers, fetid junk, and whatnot still in store wrapping?

I found myself in a short dim crowded entryway that prefaced a large main room—one that was covered in a jumbled flood of cardboard boxes and pale and translucent plastic bags of all kinds. The bags eerily caught the light from the wall of windows looking out at other high apartment blocks beyond. Areas of this indoor flood—on the two large, almost buried sofas—were at least waist high.

Three others from the crew were already at work, edging about in silhouette, methodically sorting and filling big dark trash bags. One of them was Ron's wife and partner, Melissa, a pert San

Antonio native and professional organizer several decades younger than Ron. Her teenage daughter was assisting. The third figure was a young guy from Ireland who worked in Disaster Masters' office.

Melissa lowered her respirator face mask to greet me. They were looking to save things of *real* value, she explained, principally money and important documents, jewelry, and sentimental memorabilia of, again, *real* value, such as family photos—all mixed in with everything else. They would clear out the non-valuables, the clutter: the myriad of old prescription bottles, the heaps of expired jars, cans, and boxes of food, the multitude of old magazines, newspapers, telephone books, and miscellaneous paper stuff.

Disaster Masters sold itself on knowing how to handle the whole process: the emotions and concerns of the client, the worries of the building super and management, and the final code-proper disposal of what got tossed. And would follow up, supposedly, to keep the client on the right track. (This part remained vague to me.)

The little question being begged, of course: *real* value in whose eyes?

The client himself sat off at the far end of the room on his clogged bed. He was tethered to an oxygen tank and leaned on a cane, even while seated. He was portly and bald, and made me think of the Caterpillar from Alice in Wonderland reimagined by William Burroughs—perched in agitated silence in his pale blue old sweater and dark 1950s-style sunglasses as the work went on around him, with occasional consultations from Ron and Melissa. No one else spoke to him. I was not introduced. I had to bite my tongue now and then, such as when Ron breezily inquired why he had all his fingertips covered with Band-Aids.

"'Cause I bite my fingernails," he squawked. "'Cause I'm *anxious!*"

Of course you're anxious, I thought. Strangers, effectively, are rummaging through your private world, judging the "value" of your things, heaving them away. I'd be freaked out myself.

Ron was aware of the client's anxiety too, from a more practical angle. "Lives at the top of the building," he said to me, gesturing at stacks of unopened Poland Springs bottles all about. "He gets the water pressure problems, so he worries about going thirsty." Similarly the kitchen cabinets were packed solid with toilet paper, plastic wrap, crackers, tins of sardines. Because the client didn't go out much anymore. There was a lightweight wheelchair parked by the bed.

Everyone, the client included, wore a respirator face mask, a serious item with a pert plastic snout in the center. But no melodramatic pseudo-hazmat suits or the like. I pulled my face mask on and started lending a hand. My heart, though, was really in using my camera. Ron—who was snapping away throughout; he documented all his jobs—had a strict ground rule: no photos whatsoever of the client. Client privacy was paramount. As they hauled sacks of trash down the elevator, the crew's cover story was "renovation."

Despite Ron's okay and obeying his rules, I felt weirdly furtive and feverish, hurrying with my camera to catch at fleeting riches of outsider-art moments when the client wasn't in the frame: old scribbled to-do lists on index cards idiosyncratically (obsessively) constructed into fan shapes held by an arc of paper clips; the crowd of rubber bands collected ritualistically on his cane handle (I slipped over while he was in the bathroom); more ancient to-do lists scribbled on slim yellowing paper bags, like penal colony poems from an archive.

These all were someone's intimacies that I snapped away at (having snapped away at my own). If anyone had tried that in my place, I'd have punched him. But maybe I was just approaching the opportunity like a real photographer—ruthlessly.

Along the side of the main room away from the bed ran vast

jam-packed bookshelves. The wall and the ceiling by the book-shelves' window end were peeling and decrepit. Shades of the der-elict ceiling in my own bathroom. Along the top and piled on the floor in front were stacks of girlie magazines, the sort I knew well from my own past. Copies of *Mayfair* mostly—so innocent now, so prim, obsessively so perhaps, in their brown paper wrappers. The nostalgia of brown paper wrappers! The hardest-core porn you could ever imagine was now instantaneously available on your home computer screen, in brain-scalding onslaughts.

The crammed bookshelves kept enticing me. Especially the old paperback detective novels. My God, the Maigrets! *Maigret and the Killers! Maigret and the Strangled Stripper!* I doubted they were in print in English any longer, and if they were, it was with-out the savor of these cheap editions from the sixties or seventies. To come across them by sheer serendipity like this—not selling for $20–30 now in a bookstore or on a sidewalk, wrapped in plastic—gave an extra sizzle to their allure. I ached to have them.

But I doubted the client would ever accede to parting with them. I'd heard him and Ron differing about the books on these shelves—about books in general. The client and I were broth-ers against Ron. "I haven't read a book in fifteen years!" he'd boasted at the Jackson Diner. Collecting books of "value" (that word again—meaning monetary value) was one thing. But the old paperbacks and such on the shelves here were simply dis-posophobia, he argued. Though he wasn't going to twist any-one's arm.

"But when you gonna have *time* to *read* all the ones you own you haven't read?" he debated the client, as he'd debated me two nights before. "And why hang onto ones you've *already* read?"

I could imagine how Ron would disparage my chewed-up Mickey Spillane volumes. Or my copy of *No Orchids for Miss Blandish*, a brutal noir tale from the thirties which I'd idly picked up for a dollar on an Istanbul side street and devoured and kept on my shelf—smelling the multiple fragrance of its hardboiled lingo, of its English author's hothouse dream of America, of the sleepy passageway where I bought it—every time I saw the spine.

Or my father's books under Cosima's piano.

Or, hell, maybe even the piano itself.

I spent lunch at a nearby Greek diner with Melissa and her daughter, who was along on a job for the first time, while Ron headed elsewhere with a yen for Mexican food. (He was, I'd learned, a great fan of the Food Network.) Disaster Masters' website described Melissa as the compassionate talent of the outfit, and she had an appealingly empathetic, warm—and modest— way about her. We talked about her excitement on first meeting Ron at a conference in 2005, where bigshots of the organizing world had gathered, people like him and Barbara Hemphill. Who's Barbara Hemphill? I thought. This was an entire professional universe I knew nothing about. Melissa and Ron lived in the tony enclave of New Milford, Connecticut; they rented out cottages on their property.

The talk turned to psychologists. Melissa declared they were a little hurt and angry that Randy Frost had never talked to Ron, given his long experience with hoarders and his insights. She also announced that she would stand her ground against *any* psychologist about the condition responsible for hoarding: it was depression.

"And then one day, it lifts," she said, "and people want to clean up their places. And they reach out."

On the walk back after lunch, Ron suddenly flung up an arm to point at a line of trees ahead. Could I climb them all at the same time, he demanded. It was a trope I'd already heard at Jackson Diner. He contended (*knew*, rather) that the source of anxiety and depression, which resulted in clutter and hoarding and so many other ills, was conflicting thoughts. *Trying to do more than one thing at a time.*

"And people who think they can multitask are the *worst!*" he repeated anew. "They're full of shit! *Can't be done!*"

Then he took another swipe at owning books.

"If you want any book," he declared, "you can always go to the library."

I shook my head in disbelief. I used libraries all the time; I'd go chasing down books at branches all over Queens and Manhattan. It was another way of exploring the city. Growing up as a faculty brat I'd loved to roam university library shelves, browsing for a serendipitous discovery (an early version of Internet surfing?). Books weren't just "other worlds" between covers; they were my various *selves* between covers. I wanted to possess them, have them by me to be revisited, to be popped into, to be relished anew. Or admired as aesthetic objects. (A good book didn't read right with a bad cover.) What's more, books intimately retained my physical experience of them—dog-eared pages, bent pages (though I'm not personally big on marking, myself). My unread books constituted more worlds and selves ready at hand to be explored and maybe cherished—when after being ignored, or resisted for whatever reason, be it by chance or sudden purpose the mood magically struck. And I'd open up the pages.

I guess Ron had never felt that way. He was no friend of Walter Benjamin.

Back up at the client's, the clear-out restarted with more than half still to go. The afternoon grew tedious and claustrophobic. There were so many documents, so many prescriptions to be gone through—grueling labor requiring concentration because checks and bank books might be mixed in the jumbles. For me the shambles had lost its grotty novelty and turned mundane and dreary, even though the two couches were coming into clearer view. It all felt like some enormous practical-nursing task. A great cache of old batteries was uncovered that would have to be carefully disposed of. Then Ron discovered the list of follow-up tips he'd left for the client ten years before. While the client was in the toilet again I got in a photo of the lineup of five alarm clocks on the bureau near his bed. A poignant shrine to anxiety. But the furtiveness was getting to me.

Last act of the day, the crew tackled the shopping bags of books clumped obtrusively at the foot of the bookshelves. The client protested. But the word was: he had to winnow. The books couldn't "live on the floor." Melissa sat in front of him, and went through each bag, holding up every book and insisting, gently but unswervingly, that he decide: Keep? Toss? The client shifted around in his wheelchair, anxious at the decisions. I shifted around anxiously too. In one of the bags I'd spotted a cheap old paperback of *Thrilling Cities*, Ian Fleming's travel book. My eyes widened. I hovered with bated breath, biting my tongue as Melissa held it up for the client's verdict. When he said glumly "Okay, toss," I managed to restrain myself from yelping in glee.

"I'll handle that," I said. And stashed it in my shoulder bag while no one was looking.

We knocked off at 3 p.m. Out by the building service entrance, a small but substantial dumpster was full of our discards. There was still a whole further day's work to do. Ron didn't reveal what he was charging for the job. I gathered it wasn't cheap. Money wasn't an issue for the client. Ron never billed by the hour but for the full procedure, based on an initial assessment that cost at least $250. His philosophy jibed with one attributed to Red Adair:

"If you think it's expensive to hire a professional to do the job, wait until you hire an amateur."

I said my goodbyes at Ron's van, which deliberately was unmarked by a logo. Again, for the sake of the client's privacy. I wouldn't be joining in the next day, though I'd be keeping in touch. Ron was in a mellow mood. He teased his stepdaughter, who teased him back harder. He wore his baseball cap backward.

I waved to the van as it drove off. Then I turned and hurried over to the dumpster. Checking to see if anyone was watching, I peered in, scanning for any desirable books from the client's discards I might have somehow overlooked. I wanted to be sure.

I had the vivid mental image of myself ending my day of hoarder decluttering by dumpster-diving into the squishy rubble of bags and boxes—diving literally, feet kicking above me. But I saw nothing, hesitated to reach in, then with a glance around, strode away.

Back behind my own door, I gazed about at the rumpled dusty coziness and thought: "Well, *at least . . .*"

I thought this without irony, mind you.

I took out my trophy *Thrilling Cities* and cleaned up the cover and browning page edges with a paper towel dipped in spray cleaner. Some of the pages were close to brittle as I briefly leafed through, and there was an aged smudge at the bottom of the cover. But still, a worthy little specimen. And memento.

But where to put it?

Because I suddenly was afraid *Thrilling Cities* might have mold. And now it also brought back the depressing vision of where it had been, all that piled translucent grubbiness.

So I just left it lying on my entryway bookshelf—at the doorstep of my place, as it were. Where it would stay, as part of my decor.

8

Dodge Days, or Letting Go of L.A.

I'd brought back the respirator mask from the Ron job as well. I wore it now as I resumed preparing for Héctor, and the awful possibility of the Bubonic Weasel.

There was a heap of ancient *Gourmet* magazines crammed in beside my dining table. I assaulted it. It was like spading into an archeological site of my past with Cosima—and from before then, when my ex-competitor was the man on the scene. To relieve the agitation, I sought my usual online distractions. Where I came across a documentary: *Packrat*, by filmmaker Kris Britt Montag. It was a portrait of her hoarder father. There was a long interview with Randy Frost, and with Ron, too. Ron, in fact, was listed as an executive producer of the film. The Disaster Master talked from his office. I paused the video on my laptop. His office sure looked . . . *cluttered*. Did Ron have a problem himself? I'd asked at Jackson Diner. No, he'd retorted: he had a *time issue* 'cause his head was such a fount of ideas!

I resumed the video.

"As you can see from my office behind me," the Disaster Master told the interviewer, "I have a bit of a disposophobia problem myself."

My jaw dropped under my respirator mask.

■   ■   ■

My glee lasted till the following night.

"You're having me and my mom over for dinner."

I blinked at Cosima. "What? *When?* Are you crazy?"

"We cook for you and feed you all the time. So you can do it for us now! And now you've thrown out the plastic bags, throw out your boxes!"

"But they'll be *useful*," I protested wildly, ambushed, reeling. "Do you know how hard it is to find good boxes, from the liquor store and supermarket?"

"I'll buy you new ones as a present when you need them! *How many months has it been?*"

Oh. So that was it. Somehow the months had stretched on . . . and on. Had piled up. Accumulated. What with my interviewing and researching. And distractions. And procrastinations.

Not to mention our travels. Since Cosima rang at my door I'd gone with her to Madrid, Marrakesh, and St. Petersburg besides Moscow. Also quickies to London, Paris, Rome, and Naples. And Istanbul, twice. And Vienna, where, amid our schnitzel tastings and coffeehouse trawls, I'd interviewed the director of the Sigmund Freud House about the father of psychoanalysis's vast collection of statuary objects (which were in London now, having accompanied him when he escaped there in '38). Had they cluttered his office? I wanted to know. "No! Freud was not messy," rebuked the director. All these trips supplied fresh cheap souvenirs that clogged my apartment and thousands of new travel pix that clogged my laptop.

I'd made *some* headway, true. But there was so much yet to do . . .

"Can't you see I'm trying?" I bleated wanly. "Why are you browbeating *now*, when I accomplished heaving my bags?"

"Because you still have no urgency!" she exclaimed. "So you've discovered Ron is a clutterbug, la-di-da! How's *that* helping you clean? And how long d'you think my patience is going to last? Tell me!" Her eyes flashed that way of hers. "Tell me—*how long?*"

"Gee, I don't know, Martha-from-*Who's-Afraid-of-Virginia-Woolf*," I replied bitterly. Caught once again in the jaws of reality. (Dr. Equis once commented that Cosima and I sometimes sounded like Edward Albee's Martha and George—"But in a loving and playful way," I'd corrected.) "As long as it takes, I hope. It's a *Project*."

"*Cleaning up* is your project! That's your problem," she said, much more bitterly. "You think I'll just put up with this forever. That you can go on borrowing money from people forever!"

Now *that* again. An unfair, if true, blow regarding recent aid from an old friend. Since I had nothing to say to make it look any better, I sat in heavy-breathing silence.

Sickened by the familiarity of it all.

"You need to cook dinner for us," Cosima repeated. "To challenge yourself. You used to make that lovely pasta with zucchini when we met, remember?"

"That was before you turned into Medea," I muttered.

"Ariadne," she corrected. "The wonderful heroine who leads you out of your stinking labyrinth. Yes, Ariadne! 'Cause I'm sick of being called this idiot Cosima!"

"*Sorry*," I retorted vengefully. "For the time being I think I'll stick with Medea."

"*Whatever*," she said. "Anything's better than Cosima!"

◼   ◼   ◼

Back in my place I surveyed my surroundings in despair, mixed with choking panic. The threat of the Bubonic Weasel was bad enough. Now I was supposed to whip up a dinner for my James

Beard Award-winning Medea, and Nadya, another fabulous cook?
Here? Since my last decluttering effort and epic farewell to the
ancient cracked bowl, my kitchen had come to remind me of an
alcoholic who'd managed to comb his hair, shave somewhat, and
clean off most of his jacket; but you didn't want to peer too close
and smell his breath.

And even if I did manage to cook, what about my bathroom,
should a guest wish to wash up before dining? And where were
we to savor this hypothetical feast? My dining area decor still featured checkered plastic tablecloths deputized to drape over various marooned boxes and bags—many still holding Medea's left
behinds. There were my own boxes and shopping bags, too, mostly
brimming with cassette tapes accumulated over three decades.

My precious tapes! Their absurdly fragile outdated technology
still embodied the *savor* of my musical soul. I'd gotten passionately
into world music and Latin music, living in L.A. in the late eighties
and early nineties. Cassettes were cheap dosages of these sounds—
ephemeral, not acoustically "serious." And for that reason I felt a
special pleasure in hanging on to them. Pain though they were.

Just to *do something*, I fitfully began organizing the tapes.
More than half were bare cartridges separated from their cases.
In my hand was a compilation of Colombian cumbias. A sweet
Colombian girl had made it for me from her mother's record collection. I'd played some of it when I guest DJ'ed on KCRW, the
great world music NPR station out in L.A., where my friend Tom
was then music director. Where was the tape's handwritten case?
I dug around . . . and found myself examining an empty case for
lovesick country balladeer George Jones. That was another great
tape. Where was it? The minutes drifted on by.

At the rate I was going, it would take hours to straighten out
just this lode of cassettes.

Ron said people couldn't declutter solo, they needed a coach.
But I didn't want Ron coaching me here, blithely insisting on "keep

or throw." But I needed to get Héctor and Medea and Nadya and the Bubonic Weasel, the whole lot of them, off my back!

I needed to *challenge* myself, to discard something *big, somewhere* in the apartment!

Like a guy storming into a bar to start a brawl, I entered my bedroom. There stood my archaic Cardio Glide exercise machine festooned with T-shirts and jeans. I squirmed. I wasn't ready to see it off. Where would I hang clothes other than in my wretched closets? In fury I stalked around to one of those closets, wrenched it open—and seized hold of a red cardigan wedged under the piles on the high shelf. I tore it out. My heart beat fast.

The cardigan had a red paisley-on-paisley motif and a zipper instead of buttons. It resembled something a sixties' English Mod would wear; I called it my Paul McCartney cardigan. I'd had it for over two decades. I still wore it now and then, but only here at my place because Cosima—make that Medea—hated it. She hated it because she knew I always wore it with an accompanying pang. It had been a Christmas present from my then girlfriend in L.A., who dumped me two weeks after giving it. Thereby launching me, a rickety bloke with unresolved grief from his mother's death, into a blackest void of depression. My personal corner of the abyss William Styron described in *Darkness Visible* and Andrew Solomon in *The Noonday Demon*.

And yet I'd hung on to this demonic red (psychologically *blood red*) cardigan all the time since. Because, silly to say, I liked its cozy Paul McCartney style. Because it reminded me too, somehow, despite everything, of my enchanted vision of Los Angeles when I first arrived there, before disaster hit.

I held the cardigan in my hands, not sure what to do. I bunged it down on the saddle of the Cardio Glide. The Cardio Glide occupied half my bedroom—a skeletal moose in black metal, its sweeping handlebar like a pompous set of abstract art antlers draped in unwashed laundry. No, I never exercised on it; it was absurdly awkward. So why did I keep it?

Because I'd helped Medea lug it here a year after our secret romance began, when New York again seemed a dewy hopeful world for me . . . like L.A. had been, despite all the heartbreak.

L.A., *my* L.A. of the late eighties and early nineties. The thoughts of it carried me out to the counter against the green wall in my studio area. There, beside the brown and gold shopping bag from Hotel Sacher in Vienna (newly acquired), lay a big two-foot-square color photo print, still rolled up even though Tom, my musical friend from L.A., had sent it almost a year before. I edged the Sacher bag away, spread the print open.

■   ■   ■

That's me—me and my secondhand '67 Dodge Dart muscle car. I'm posed jutting out over the grill like a human hood ornament. It's a striking image, one of the signatures of the photographer Michael Grecco, who shot it mock-monumental style, from below. The magazine version of it ran as a double-page spread in a 1991 issue of *Buzz*, a Los Angeles glossy of the day. I'm wearing brown hepcat Ray-Bans and a bottle-green suit jacket and pearl-gray shirt I had tailored in Mexico. As pictured I weigh twenty-some pounds less than I did when the clothes were fitted. A breakdown burns off those extra kilos . . .

She was a painter, much younger than me, eccentric and pretty, with a brogue from her childhood in Ireland. The very moment my art world pal Mike introduces us on my third night in L.A., I'm smitten. I'm on tour with a new book, doing "performance art" readings. (The same Mike will later introduce me in New York to she who would be known as Medea.) I fall head over heels for the Irish girl and L.A., and move in with her right away while still keeping my sublet in New York. After a year of enchantment, she comes down to visit me for Christmas in Mexico, where I'm on movie location with a small role as the physicist Edward Teller (an awful man whom my physicist old man despised) in a Hollywood production, *Fat Man and Little Boy*. A "surefire blockbuster" about the A-bomb at Los Alamos, *Fat Man and Little Boy* will bomb to bits on release. So will our relationship. I grow annoyed with her down in Mexico, where she gives me the Paul McCartney cardigan. She's so artily scornful about Hollywood, and I'm in weird shape from stress, the pressure of being an arty type myself, a "literary performance artist"—meaning an arm-flailing amateur—sharing scenes and a hotel with Paul Newman and John Cusack. And the undertow, I'll come to know, of the trauma of my mother's death. My Christmas visitor gets food poisoning; I shout and rage at her. I shock the both of us.

So I should know I'm on shaky ground when I get back to L.A. She's obsessed 24/7 with an art show she's mounting. I sulk at being ignored, I who've been on camera with Paul Newman. I blow up again. And suddenly, just like that, she announces it's not going to work. To my horrified uncomprehending disbelief, she dumps me. It's over. Those are her words, in her narrow kitchen where the sweetly ditzy folkloric mask is hanging which I bought her for Christmas:

"I just realized: it's not going to work. It's over."

■   ▣   ▪

A breakdown. That's what I, the guy in the Ray-Bans and bottle-green jacket in the photo, am shakily recovering from, propped up by medication. After my expulsion, I'd gone reeling back to dreary midwinter New York, not knowing what else to do. There in the gray, I sank—a stone coffin—into a zone of desolation I never imagined existed. At its worst, before the meds kicked in—

this was pre-Prozac days, I was given a then-new "tricyclic" drug called Anafranil, which, honestly, saved my sanity, although first it made me a tad berserk with anxiety—I felt as if some critical protective layer of my very existence had been shorn off. Such raw terror, anguish of abandonment, catastrophic loneliness, aching longing engulfed me that I gasped in awe at their epic force even as I struggled. Perhaps I was unconsciously reenacting my mother's death scene, playing both parts, her and me. All I could do, all day, much of any night, was pace back and forth and writhe and gasp. And talk. I talked nonstop, a filibuster of reality, a bug-eyed logorrhea about the girl in L.A.

"Boy," quipped my friend Mike. "Am I glad I'm not you!" Other friends, they just ran away.

■　　■　　■

And then there I am, back in L.A. again, rumbling the sunshine in my Dodge Dart.

The nomadic lifestyle begun in my childhood goes into hyperdrive. In my three L.A. years P.D. (Post-Dumping), I move twenty-five times, from short-term sublets to housesits to friends' spare rooms (some of them repeats)—mainly from beachside Santa Monica and Venice to Hollywood's seedier lowlands and hummingbird hillsides. It's a precarious, crazy life, which suits me and my broken heart and state of mind to a T. Los Angeles is full of people like me—itinerant and obsessed, if not with hearts and heads quite so cracked.

I haul around only a suitcase and a box or two. The rest, mainly boxes of cassette tapes and my review clips and gig posters and flyers, I stash in Tom's garage in Venice. Back in New York, I still have my storage space heaped with things from my parents—and from my various relationships gone bad.

What anchors my world those driven, Dodge Dart days are my

"literary comedy" readings at clubs and cabarets, my stabs at movie pitching, and a new book of stories I finally start on, *The Sadness of Sex*. (Which will end up very sadly when adapted for screen by a man who'd just filmed Michael Jackson.) With the scornfulness of a true artist/bohemian I ignore my bank's overdraft warnings while writing my lovelorn opus. And the bank responds eventually by not only closing my account but fixing such a stain on my credit rating that it takes over a year and a half and my begging in person, despite having long paid off the overdraft, to get an account at any other bank.

And I can't let go of my ailing secondhand Dodge Dart.

Its transmission falters, its brakes grow permanently faulty—a miracle I never broadside anyone—and a bad gasket becomes so moth-eaten I chug through the fanciest blocks of Wilshire Boulevard billowing smoke like a movable incinerator. Once I look up in the rearview mirror and recognize Bobby Short, the swank cabaret singer, sitting in a natty classic Mercedes coupe right behind me in the rolling black cloud of my spew. Still I cling on to the car as its ox-blood paint job turns mangier and blotchier, and the driver's door won't open anymore.

Because I bought the Dodge Dart with my L.A. true love who dumped me.

Talk about *really* not letting go.

I don't mean stalking her. I mean lovesick pining and pleading and useless abject apologizing, an inability to accept "We're over" that reaches atomic proportions. For a year after we break up I exist like some Monty Python knight who can't admit he's been defeated, rendered limbless, hacked to a stump. Because she'll still call me every month if I keep silent, and then even agree to meet, enough to tease a madman's hope, a madman who's in group therapy now, beating his guilty breast. But she won't resume as I want.

So there I am, practically radioactive, incandescent with my sadness of sex, churning the freeways in my decrepit beloved Dodge Dart.

■　　■　　■

Mercifully in '91 she moves back to Ireland.

The car continues to be my link to her—and to my first, halcyon vision of L.A. as a place where the days are ever balmy and blue-skied (in fact, L.A. was having a historic drought when I arrived) and after the years of straining for attention in downtown New York, I'm getting some of my share on radio, in the papers, even on screen (besides the movie in Mexico).

The other, equally important reason: I can't face the hassle of buying another car. The practical challenge overwhelms me. So I keep shelling out money for smoke-spewing, brake-pumping temporary patches.

The Dodge Dart finally exits my life in 1993, while I'm visiting New York for a couple of weeks, book finished, mulling a move back. The city of Hollywood tows the shambolic carcass from where I've left it gathering dust on a winding pretty lane under an orange tree.

Just a few months prior to this, the first academic paper on the condition to be known eventually as hoarding disorder is published by Randy Frost and a Smith College student collaborator—so launching this field of psychological study. Among other things, hoarding behavior is described as the sufferer's attempt "to avoid emotional reactions which accompany parting with cherished possessions."

A man who cannot let go: that would be me.

■　　■　　■

I returned the photo print now to the counter's mush under the green wall, thinking, as I always did, that I should get it properly framed. But when? The print rolled itself up once more. An artifact of an extravagantly itinerant time of my life.

Surrounded now by artifacts of my extravagantly itinerant current life with Medea.

From the jumble by my writing table I pulled clear all the Japanese Muji notebooks I'd used for taking notes on our travels. I toted up the trips: twenty-seven over the nine years leading up to that fateful buzzing of my doorbell. The fifty-six destinations those trips involved were scribbled in disorderly block letters swarming the notebook covers, as if inky spiders had snowshoed across them.

And already it was another late afternoon. With my decluttering yet again stopped in its tracks, courtesy of my wandering mind straying off down its byways. A mental style from hoarder and clutterbug central casting, from any distracted case history by Randy Frost and company.

And my self-conscious Project was at it again too—always eager for researching more odd angles, counting up further "colorful" details, dredging through reminiscences, photo-documenting, calculating stagings. Reluctant to plain *do* something.

But I needed to *do something!* I needed to scream! I screamed!

I turned on my heel, grabbing up my "general use" pink scissors (not my "private" yellow ones reserved for positive objects), and stormed back into the bedroom. I seized the red Paul McCartney cardigan off the Cardio Glide saddle. We cling to things out of love but also out of hate—I recalled Dr. Equis's words. Not just out of hate, I thought; out of their ties to twenty-year-old pain and hurt.

Grimly, savagely, I sliced into the cardigan where a sleeve joined the body. My pink scissors made a squelching crunch though cotton-acrylic blend. *Squelch crunch*. I jerked clear the sleeve by the last red threads. I went for the other sleeve. *Squelch crunch*. I was butchering a cardigan. I hacked up through one side of the sleeveless body, then other. I was the Sweeney Todd of paisley. I grabbed up the floppy blood-red remains and bundled them into two plastic grocery bags and crammed them down the chute in the hall.

I came back inside, breathing heavily. A touch wildly. What did I feel? A rush of liberation! Amazing what throwing out something felt like. And yes, sadness, a pang of that, too. Because I'd liked my Paul McCartney cardigan.

To drown out any regrets I went at the Cardio Glide. With a loud curse I stripped off its laundry. Then I had an inspiration, God help me. And He did. I found a perfect song on YouTube as the soundtrack for the occasion: a Roy Rogers tune in praise of Trigger.

Cackling and chorusing along, I dragged the antlered Cardio Glide out through the dining area. Then another inspiration hit. I rushed back to my laptop.

Might Roy Rogers have been any kind of hoarder or clutterbug himself?

By God, he might have!

A "lifelong pack rat," a travel site on my laptop described him. Before closing in 2009, the Roy Rogers–Dale Evans Museum was "packed to the rafters with the stuff he [Roy] could never throw away." Another website declared that Roy "collected nearly every detail from his life . . . held on to everything he could. In today's world, he might have ended up an episode of a hoarding television show" (!). Instead, of course, he created a museum.

But he was another man who didn't want to let go.

Tickled pink, I returned to the Cardio Glide and photo-documented it poised to depart through my front door. Then I dragged it on its final trail along the hall, into the elevator, and down to the basement trash room, where I photographed it alongside discarded chairs and busted lamps—waiting like a doomed animal in a kids' tale to be carted off to the glue factory. Chuckling away, I took some abstract shots of the gray and green walls of the fluorescent-lit space.

All this chuckling and snapshooting was another means, I realized, of distancing myself from any pains of sentimentality. Happily no one came along and saw me.

■   ■   ■

"I hear you're having us to dinner this weekend!"

I ran into Nadya in the lobby. Had I thrown out my boxes yet? she wanted to know.

The mother-and-daughter drumbeat.

Just to end it, once and for all, I stalked upstairs and grabbed a dozen of my precious, carefully selected empty boxes, and piled them up high in my entryway, like a display of big game I'd bagged. Photographed them. Then furiously hacked at them with my box cutter, almost dangerously, tearing apart with bare hands whatever pieces were still joined, so my fingers ached. Stamped flat the lot. Photographed the "after" shot, so puny-looking and deflated. Got rid of it all.

Fury: it really helped things along.

"Use the power of discomfort," counseled *Master the Clutter*, an e-book Ron had co-authored. "Get mad at the clutter."

On the other hand, there was the perspective of Bruce Chatwin, the great travel writer: "The man who sits . . . in a shuttered room is likely to be mad, tortured by hallucinations and introspection."

And given to psychodramas involving sweaters and cardboard boxes.

Whatever, the floor of my studio area suddenly possessed airy space. I could do my calisthenics here now, if I wanted.

Of course, there was still the little matter of my blue-funneled bathroom and its looming inspection, my kitchen facing the threat of proper cooking being attempted, my dining area under the shadow of two self-invited guests eager for repayment of their hospitality.

And figuring out how to disguise the rest.

9

Home Comforting

Cheryl Mendelson has a Ph.D. in philosophy, and a doctorate in law as well. She is also a novelist.

She is also the best-selling author of *Home Comforts: The Art and Science of Housekeeping*. Described as *The Joy of Cooking* for domestic upkeep, this was the 884-page tome I'd weighed on my bathroom scale way back when my Project started. I'd planned to study and consult it as I went along. Then I'd ignored it.

I found *Home Comforts* now under a pile of books on the floor in my bedroom. Hefted up its several pounds; blew the dust off the cover. Sneezed. Started batting through for tips.

The table of contents listed a section on "Cleanliness," which contained, among others, chapters on "The Chemistry of Household Cleaning" (too detailed for a hectic search for quick leads) and another on "Resilient Floors" (ditto).

Lugging the book out toward my kitchen, I scanned the "Food" section. In the chapter "Cold Comforts" I read:

> The refrigerator . . . has taken the place of the hearth . . . The
> image of a woman's face lit by the fire as she stirs a cheerfully

*bubbling pot has been replaced by the image of someone's face lit
by the refrigerator light as he or she peers in . . .*

I stopped, and started to laugh. A sickly, barking sort of laugh.

Oh, dear Ms. Mendelson! I wanted to cry, *I admire your book
and look forward to its practical wisdoms. God knows I need some!
For now I won't even mention my kitchen floor, unwashed in months.
Or my kitchen walls flecked with vintage grease. Or the blackish fuzz
around the bottom of the stove.*

No, I'll just ask you to consider the un-hearth *that is my
refrigerator.*

*When I open my fridge door, dear Ms. Mendelson, I first descry
the brown gunk where the side walls meet the fridge floor. Sundry discolorations spatter nearby. I've cleaned the fridge exactly once
in all the years I've been here. In the door shelves still stand grubby
(very grubby) jars of stuff from ten years ago. On the bottom interior shelves, bizarrely, like rich folk wedged into steerage, lie bottles
of Veuve Clicquot, vintage 1996, and 2004 Collio Friulano from
prestigious Italian producer Venica, and various other fine wines
stored here for want of space at my girlfriend's (she's a food critic).
Dish towels, once gaily colored and unsodden, swaddle the wines
against the moisture leaking from the freezer. On the upper shelves
lodge my various fruits and lunch veggies, bundled (natch) in cloudy
old plastic grocery bags.*

*But the freezer section, Ms. Mendelson—oh, the freezer section!
Defrosted by me yet again exactly once. Marooned there amid the
ancient ice huddle a few beribboned, rock-hard little haute pound
cakes (after-dinner gifts from star chef David Bouley's Danube restaurant, long closed) and a plastic container of something reddish and
menacing from a trip (when?) to Morocco.*

Some hearth, *this, at which to conjure the comfort of food! Dear
God, help me, Ms. Mendelson!!*

I slouched into the bathroom, where my anti-drip Rube Goldberg hoses and funnels still dangled above the tub.

Home Comforts didn't seem to mention blue-green tub stains specifically. Chapter 41, "Bathrooms," under the section for "Porcelain Enamel Tubs," addressed "hard water" stains and recommended a solution of white vinegar and water. But was my tub porcelain enamel? Or was it fiberglass or acrylic, in which case Ms. M recommended a paste of baking soda? Either way, both cleaners seemed much too feeble.

But "vinegar" set my brain clicking. Hadn't I read that the father of Jacques Lacan, my shrink's grand mentor, was the sales agent for an illustrious French *vinaigre* producer, Dessaux Fils?

"I must use white vinegar somewhere," I bubbled later to Medea, "for that rich Lacanian resonance! Ms. M says it's a good all-purpose cleaner."

"Who's Ms. M?"

"And *guess* whose favorite vinegar Dessaux was, the red kind?" I added, delighted. "*Julia Child's.* Cool serendipity?"

Medea looked at me almost pityingly. "You're not aware that if you're ever clueless enough to mix vinegar and bleach, you'll make *chlorine gas*?"

"I will?" I sounded clueless.

"Anyway, for cleaning, Wipes are the thing!"

She disappeared into her kitchen and hurried back out with some colored flat packets. They contained solution-soaked Kleenex-y towelettes, which she'd recently become noisily fond of. She mimed adoring kisses at them.

"Here!" She thrust a green packet labeled "Scrubbing Bubbles" at me. "Use this for your tub."

"Are you joking?" I gave a snort, seizing back some dignity. "My stain requires *serious stuff*."

Consulting Ms. M. more attentively next morning, I realized she suggested a product called Lime-A-Way for severe tub trouble.

Lime-A-Way sounded no more cataclysmically harsh than the "lime and rust jell" I'd already been using. I smeared some more of the jell on the stain. I thought I detected further effect. If I squinted.

But what of all the hoary moldy grouting between the bathtub wall tiles? On Ms. M's advice I sprayed with diluted bleach (no cute addition of vinegar). Then, standing half-naked in the tub with the hoses maneuvered aside, sweating in the used respirator mask I'd kept from my Disaster Masters day, I scoured with a toothbrush. Not just any toothbrush, of course. I spent minutes curating the right un-brandmarked one, digging though my dusty batches of airline toilet kits from our travels in a bedroom closet.

Toothbrush, bleach, and elbow grease: they got the job done.

"Good call, Ms. M!" I saluted. "You're a comfort, truly."

But now once again I faced shopping—for the equipment to tackle the bathroom and kitchen floors. Shopping meant likely ensnaring myself in yet more grueling calibrations of aesthetics, emotional effect, utility—not to mention price.

Still, I set off enthusiastically. I saw the bright side: the opportunity of introducing totems of cheer—little domestic gods—into my place.

■   ■   ■

"Look at this sweetly orange, cheap plastic bucket," I announced to Ms. M on my return from tramping Northern Boulevard, the big traffic artery from Manhattan along which 99-cent Korean emporiums hawk their housekeeping wares beside Colombian empanada joints and Peruvian *pollo asado* places. "And these rubber gloves whose purple will contrast with the bucket artfully. And this brush."

I waggled the petit wooden-handled item I'd acquired simply for its fierce red bristles.

"You see, Ms. M," I confided, "even as I pursue the practical, color is important for the things around me. And don't Frost and

Steketee note how people who clutter and hoard are very sensitive to the aesthetics of objects?"

Ms. M and I were becoming quite the pals.

But I had an exasperating session with her now, trying to determine, for the sake of the appropriate "cleaning product," what type of tile covered my bathroom floor. The Internet was no help either. So I just settled for the bottle of all-purpose Señor Limpio that merrily caught my eye in the aisle at Met Foods on 37th Avenue.

Then yet another inspiration struck. Away I hurried to Patel Brothers, the bustling Indian supermarket among the sari and gold shops on 74th Street. Out I emerged with a bottle of Dettol.

The Dettol of my childhood!

Except it no longer came in a glass vessel such as the one that broke on my dusty way home from Scottsville Government School in that memory-snapshot from long-ago Pietermaritzburg. This bottle was plastic; its round-shouldered shape seemed more banally streamlined than I recalled. And the pale green label proclaimed "First Aid Antiseptic." The turbaned clerk assured me it cleaned floors "better than any American stuff."

Proust may have had his madeleine, but I had my Dettol—the world's *biggest selling* antiseptic! (So claimed its manufacturer.) There, behind my door, I unscrewed the cap and for the first time in the arching span of the decades I dipped my nose for *a temps-perdu* whiff. The smell summoned to mind . . . hospital floors. Generically. That was it.

But no matter. Because I'd made a sensational discovery.

"Wasn't available, Ms. M, when you wrote *Home Comforts*," I murmured. "The *magic* of Mr. Clean Magic Eraser!"

Having seen a breathless reference online somewhere, I'd picked up a package experimentally at Met Foods. In my kitchen I wetted slightly the white sort-of-foam-rubber sponge—it was almost weightless—and swiped, ever so softly, at a grimy light switch plate. Presto! *The grime vanished!* I tried it on a patch of wall, on a floor tile, on light switch plates and the grubby door areas near the handles. It was practically hallucinatory.

Magic Eraser's special material apparently was a plastic foam called Basotect, made from melanin resin. Basotect's main other use was for soundproofing. Its "open-cell" structure—lots of air with tiny fibers—enabled it to be super-abrasive yet super-flexible. Essentially it operated like a pencil eraser or super-fine sandpaper. Or to my mind, a wizard's wand!

"Listen to you!" hooted Medea as she served us her basmati and lentil pilaf at dinner. "But I still prefer Wipes."

I flapped a dismissive hand. "I'm giving a Magic Eraser as a present to your mom," I announced. "Though I note that the company which makes Basotect—BASF in Germany, the biggest chemical company in the world—was once part of the IG Farben chemical consortium. Which was so monstrously complicit during World War II."

"You took time to learn this?" Pause. "You mean you aren't single-mindedly focused on the tragic consequences of the Bubonic Weasel busting into your place and seeing your mess?"

"Focused, focused," I lied. I pressed my temples. "And thanks for bringing up the Bubonic Weasel to haunt our evening!"

"And you aren't preparing to have me and my mother for dinner?"

"Who said I wasn't!"

"Oh. Thank you," said Medea's mom, looking bemused by the almost weightless Magic Eraser package next day. She was tidying up after an Italian Renaissance-themed dinner party. "And there are your housewarming presents," she smiled, pointing to a T. J. Maxx bag. "So when are we coming to dinner?"

"Soon, soon!" I bleated.

It was a comfort to be back in my place with Ms. M. "*You* I can confide in," I told her warm and astute author's photo. "Without being harassed!" Again I floated on dusty air with the Magic Eraser as smudgy spots disappeared under fairy-tale swipes. Though the excitement did wear down kind of quickly—just like the expensive eraser itself. "Best used sparingly, eh?" I muttered to my Ms. M.

But in indefatigable high spirits I now went bumper-vacuuming with Nadya's elephantine upright. Then, with my new blue-shafted sponge mop and Señor Limpio, I attacked my miserable bathroom and kitchen floors. A nostalgic splash of Dettol turned the contents of my yellow bucket milky. I got in the nod to Lacan, too, and scrubbed with vinegar under the kitchen counter.

As the soundtrack for my "cleaning production" I settled on some 1960s' musica Cubana classics. When all was done I broke into a sweaty cha-cha-cha, hugging *Home Comforts* to my chest. The horrors of my fridge and kitchen cupboards still awaited, hidden from sight. But my God, after years and years my woebegone kitchen—to an intruder's glance, at least—was once more a place of passable comfort and cheer.

These words rang a little echo. Cha-cha-cha-ing to the dining table, I flipped through *Home Comforts* to where Ms. M had quoted from a W. H. Auden poem. It celebrated his new kitchen at home in Austria as

> *again the centre of a dwelling*
> *not, as lately was, an abhorrent dungeon*

And then I hooted and shook my head.

"Oh dear Ms. M!" I chided tenderly. "Don't you realize you've quoted a poet who was *notorious for the messiness of his housekeeping?*"

Whereupon I was compelled toward my laptop, past where my boxes had once sat heaped, to extend what I knew of Auden's calamitous domesticity. Yes: when he gave up his notorious apartment of many years on St. Mark's Place in the East Village, the Salvation Army refused the poet's sofa because of its horrendous condition. His place had never been other than an "absolute mess," according to one commentator. To my amusement, Auden's literary executor, I saw, was one Edward Mendelson—who was, further, a professor at the Collyers' old alma mater, Columbia.

Then I gasped.

"Auden's literary executor is *Cheryl Mendelson's husband!*" I sputtered to Medea. "I just emailed him. How amazing for my Project: a simultaneousness interview with both Mendelsons! Of course I didn't mention my intimate little dialogues with his wife."

"*What intimate little dialogues?*" said Medea. "*What's going on?*"

Prof. Mendelson wrote back to say that alas his wife was no longer interested in being interviewed about *Home Comforts*. But he was always happy to discuss Auden. I asked how messy and cluttered was the East Village apartment, exactly? Could I send along some pictures of my own mess? How might it compare with that of one of the great poets of the twentieth century?

He passed on the idea.

"Because no one's living space is comparable to anyone else's," he wrote, "and I can't imagine that it would make sense to say that one image was more or less cluttered than Auden's flat."

But he rated the poet's living style for me:

"The desk and tables were covered with disordered books and papers [BY *ditto!*] except for the dining-room table, which was pristine and had a fruit bowl in the middle. [BY *semi-ditto?*] The ashtrays were overflowing. [BY *ugh, non-ditto.*] The bookshelves were cluttered and disordered. [BY *big ditto!*] The books themselves were stained with cigarette-ash. [BY *ugh, non-ditto!*] The kitchen counters were cluttered. [BY *non-ditto, proudly, fingers crossed.*] But the chairs and sofas were perfectly orderly and comfortable, though shabby. [BY *semi-ditto?*] The shelf with the expensive Tandberg turntable was pristine. [BY *non-ditto?*] Auden was highly selective about what he wanted to keep clean and neat and what he didn't care about. [BY *non-ditto . . .*] Very fastidious people (like Vera Stravinsky) were clearly appalled. [BY *ditto, per Medea.*] To less fastidious people . . . his flat and house were cozy and comfortable. [BY *um . . . semi-ditto?*]"

So much for Auden and me.

At this point I recalled another East Village Englishman who was even more notorious for his housekeeping. Quentin Crisp, of *Naked Civil Servant* fame, made a point of never lifting a dust rag or anything prefiguring a Magic Eraser. (He lived alone, whereas Auden had a partner, Chester Kallman.)

"After the third year," Mr. Crisp once assured the tidying world, "the dust doesn't get any worse."

■   ■   ■

But how did a clean, well-kept house become the desired model?

I thought of Amsterdam, where Medea and I had spent part of recent summers, where along cobblestone canalsides we'd peer through uncurtained windows into spotless designed-to-death living rooms. An anti-Questin Crisp of a town. Fabled Dutch cleanliness had astonished visitors all the way back in the seventeenth-century Golden Age of Rembrandt and Vermeer, and even earlier. These hyper-scrubbed interiors and exteriors, what's more, were not only at the abodes of the wealthy, as was the case in Renaissance Italy, but among all classes.

Art historian Simon Schama argues persuasively for the influence of puritan Calvinism. Starting in the sixteenth century, cleaning house metaphorically scourged the dirty demands of the flesh, the impure lures of the material world. Housekeeping enacted a morality tale. Schama's assessment jibes with anthropologist Mary

Douglas's pronouncement that dirt was ultimately "matter out of place." That notions of dirty versus clean are cultural creations.

But maybe, in fact, Holland owed all to the sound of mooing. Two Dutch historians, Bas van Bavel and Oscar Gelderblom, recently argued that many Dutch households of the sixteenth and seventeenth centuries kept a cow for milk and cheese—which required strictest hygiene. The big influx of country dairy-farm girls to urban areas as housemaids more deeply established these hyper-clean habits.

Perhaps that's what I needed to galvanize me in Queens: take up a little cheesemaking.

On the other hand, the Dutch Golden Agers believed, like everyone else in Europe at the time, that hot baths were dangerous. So their houses were spic and span but the occupants stank.

■   ■   ■

Further such research for my wide-ranging Project sent me off to Chelsea in Manhattan.

I was ushered into the pleasant, book- and art-crowded apartment of Dominique Nabokov. Dark-haired, slim, with old-school offhand chic, this well-known French-born photographer had shot two series of *au naturel* Polaroids of the un-fancied-up, unpeopled living rooms of cultural figures: *New York Living Rooms* and *Paris Living Rooms*. Her photo of Quentin Crisp's studio apartment showed a glum, thickly blanketed bed with clothes slumped across it, a long pole of some kind angled against it, and books piled upon a movable radiator at its foot.

"Did the place feel squalid?" I began.

"What is 'squalid'?" asked Nabokov in rich French tones.

"Very unpleasantly messy."

"No," she informed me. "*I* wouldn't like to live like that, but he was so at ease in that surrounding. I had a feeling I was with an intellectual," she went on. "Very often intellectuals—maybe not American—don't care about their surroundings."

"Was the dust visible?" I pressed.

"Certainly! I didn't look at it but I'm sure. But living in New York! If I don't dust every day, after two days I have dust everywhere!"

Auden, it turned out, was a close friend of her late husband, the composer Nicholas Nabokov (cousin of Vladimir). She'd visited the St. Marks' apartment though never photographed it. She laughed.

"He was a man, so not domestic, he didn't know what to do! But I have a theory," she declared, "that Americans have lost contact with nature. They are so obsessed with washing everything clean. But we're animals after all, so I sort of admire people who can live like that, not that I'd like to live that way."

Her admiration even extended to Taylor Mead, the impish old Andy Warhol superstar whose entry in *New York Living Rooms*, a tiny Lower East Side space, was the one most suggestive of a hoarder's habitat—claustrophobic, crammed, everything mixed on top of everything.

"And the smell was unbearable!" Nabokov exclaimed. "*He had eighteen cats!*"

But even so. "You see, I admire people who are oblivious, like children," she said.

I flashed to Ron the Disaster Master. I wondered what he'd respond.

Would the photographer agree to look at some of my early photos?

She peered at my iPad.

"It's messy, no?" I suggested. "It looks a little cleaner now. But Taylor Mead's comparatively was much more intense?"

"Yes! Because of the stink—those cats! In a one-room apartment! But your place . . ." She sought for *le mot juste*. "In French
we say, *desordinée*."

Disorderly.

■   ■   ■

On the subway returning to Queens, I thought of Andy Warhol
himself. His famously insatiable collecting of art and objects, high
and low, certainly suggested hoarding. At his death, his brownstone on the Upper East Side was so packed only two rooms were
habitable. But Warhol was a serious and knowledgeable collector.
And someone who'd been to his brownstone told me that all was
well kept within. No shades of Mead or Crisp.

There were, though, Warhol's "Time Capsules"—cardboard
boxes into which he placed bits and pieces from his daily life, until
eventually he just swept into them whatever was on his desk at the
Factory—business cards, books, drawings, matchbooks, magazines,
invoices, receipts, what-have-you. A hoarder's potpourri. By the
time he died he'd amassed 612 identical such boxes, kept in storage.

But things weren't what they seemed, Matt Wrbican told me.
Wrbican is the chief archivist at the Warhol Museum in Pitts-
burgh. "It was a Midas touch idea," he explained. "Turning trash
into treasure." Warhol, that nose-puller, planned to display his
essentially identical, unopened Time Capsules (only differences,
labeling) at his blue-chip gallery, Leo Castelli, in New York.
They'd be for sale, all the same price.

"So you wouldn't know what you were getting," said Wrbican.
He'd been overseeing the opening and cataloguing of the boxes,
now held by the Warhol Museum. "Some Time Capsules are full
of nothing but newspaper clippings. But there's another with over
two hundred artworks by Warhol."

Homer and Langley would've been baffled.

"And tell me," I said to Wrbican. "In your photo on the museum website, I couldn't help notice that your office looks a little cluttered. Do you have an issue there?"

Yes, Wrbican acknowledged. He did.

■   ■   ■

Back behind my door, I walked over to ponder the foot of the wall just outside my bedroom. The dust had been gathering on the floor there into a feathery gray rubble over the past couple of weeks. I'd left it alone to admire as the golden afternoon light slanted across it . . . a little pensive showpiece of decay.

I mused on Dominique Nabokov's defense of disorder as the way of intellectuals and *artistes*. It was touching and reassuring to me. And confusing to my Project! Sure I was honored to be in the company (as it were) of Auden. I thought again of Proust, how apparently the dust lay about his cork-lined room "like feather boas."

But then I wouldn't want to live like Quentin Crisp or Taylor Mead.

I wouldn't want to live like *I* was living!

I felt an immediate impulse to vacuum this scrap of dust, as a gesture of change—then resisted. I was too weirdly attached to this patch of household dirt.

I squirmed and twisted, gripped by the familiar agitated bind. I rushed out to the dining area, to find any junk mail to throw away instead. And as if on cue, spotted the new rent bill.

The Bubonic Weasel's avatar, thrusting under my door.

Suddenly I felt overwhelmed. My most intimate sense of security was menaced by this lousy little object—this prim off-white envelope with "Excelsior Management" in the see-through window. Even as my Project was turning life in my apartment into an immense rickety contraption swarming with protocols, calculations, decisions on how precisely to proceed, contradictory urgencies. I felt as if I was trying to maneuver a weird fragile bulk through my narrow days—another ever-more-awkward Rube Goldberg rig, a monstrous variant of the things in my tub and sink. And while I struggled with my overwrought burden, I was under threat from rental authorities hungry for any excuse to go after me. Not to mention the pressure from wannabe dinner guests!

I snatched up the envelope and rushed it into the bedroom and plunged it into the filing cabinet. Then I wrestled the upright vacuum over and sucked the showpiece dust into oblivion.

And then I stepped around the bucket and mop in my brightened kitchen and wrenched open the narrow standing metal cabinet, the one which Nadya had given a sneak-tidying years ago. I was unable to resist hurriedly photographing the shelves; but now I didn't linger as I normally would have to mull each ancient item. I just crammed several shelves of stuff unmulled into plastic grocery bags. The plastic was flimsy. I cursed having thrown out my boxes.

Grim fury, that was the ticket. It seemed the necessary state to galvanize me and my distracted mind into decluttering action. A focused empowerment. And in turn it seemed to require the pressure of immanent threat or unbearable crisis to force it into being. Or as Samuel Johnson put it, when a man knows (or fears) he's soon to be hanged, "it concentrates his mind wonderfully."

But where now to dump these uncleansed bottles, cans, and whatnot? Weren't you supposed to clean disposables before recycling them? Was I supposed to spend an hour emptying everything into the toilet?

■　　■　　■

That night a skulking figure en route to his girlfriend's apartment hurried under cover of darkness to a public trash basket on
a Queens avenue where he illicitly unloaded his bulging grocery
bags of uncleansed recyclables. He tensed in expectation of accus-
ing shouts from the nearby stores. But no shouts came.

But he was in a mood to deal with them if they did.

■   ■   ■

Next day, I shocked myself and went straight at the fridge.
Cold-bloodedly I consulted *Home Comforts*, without a wisecrack.
I no longer had private words for Ms. M. (Frankly, since I was in
touch with her husband, I was embarrassed at where things had
gotten to between us.)

After unplugging the fridge as advised, I pried from the
freezer the David Bouley mini-pound cakes in their stiffened gift
ribbons and, as advised, thrust in a pan of boiling water and closed
the door. Not fussing with any food styling, I photographed the
pound cakes, then likewise the bottles and jars time-capsuled in
the lower fridge.

I crammed everything into plastic grocery bags.

But then I couldn't resist the tug of two tiny antique jars of
fruit preserves in their paper mini-bonnets. Didn't preserves keep
forever? I set them aside.

Then in fifteen frantic minutes I:

—hauled out the fridge's disrespected wines, cleaned the
moldy labels, stood 'em on the floor in the dining area; snapped
their photos.

—wriggled loose all the racks and shelves, purple-glove-scrubbed
them all fervently in the sink after unrigging the blue funnel
there.

—jerked loose the ice slabs in the freezer, sponged down the
compartment with mild detergent rinse.

—dragged over the Jobian upright and sucked at the nether-worlds of dark fuzz by the fridge sides.

And my emptied refrigerator now blazed at me. I snapped its quick portrait: a still patchily discolored zone, but strangely serene.

The cute fruit preserves tasted vile.

Evening came. Again I humped my overloaded illicit bags to a public trash basket and hurried on into the night. Triumphant.

"But Jesus, it'd have been nice to have those boxes you promised!" I added to Medea, after recounting my heroics over a bottle of our current favorite Nebbiolo. "Look at my hands still from huffing those bags!"

"Our poor suffering *artiste*," she said.

But then she cushioned her jibe by surprising me with a present: a set of new happy-red frying pans.

I was touched, despite the unspoken implication. "But first things first," I cautioned.

■   ■   ■

Those first things had kept waking me in clenching dread at 4 a.m. I mean the inspection by Héctor. Followed by a bust-in from the Bubonic Weasel himself.

■   ■   ■

Except Héctor was no more. He'd been replaced.

"Call me Tod, short for Todor," the new super greeted me in his windowless basement office. He was heavyset, Bulgarian—and genial, it appeared, especially after my hasty attempt to immediately get on his good side by mentioning Hristo Stoichkov, the great Bulgarian wiz of the soccer field, on whom Medea still harbored a crush from the 1994 World Cup.

With my heart thumping, I brought up my leaky faucets.

■   ■   ■

"You got a lot of books!" said Tod as I hurried us past my tidied but still piled-up dining table.

We stood in the bathroom and beheld the great blue-green stain, the dripping drips. (My Rube Goldberg thing I'd stashed away under the sink.)

"This stain got bad a month or so ago," I commenced lying airily, "must be the hard water or maybe it's—"

Big Tod ignored me and clambered into the tub. "Lotsa people in the building got this," he muttered, squinting up and down. "Old pipes."

"So you're not going to need," I asked gingerly, "the managing agent? To come in?"

"Why, you want me to? Okay, I can—"

"*No no no!*" I assured him.

The story went the same for the faucet in my brightened kitchen. No mention was made of the unpretty sight of my stove area; the doors of the ancient derelict cupboards, at whose interiors I'd taken a gander and shrunk from in dismay, remained unopened. (As did the shut-tight bedroom door.) Though Tod did notice the paint peeling off the kitchen walls, to which I'd been oblivious, and offered to have his painters come by.

"Thanks but I'm not quite ready just now!" I replied. "But soon!"

Half an hour later, the existential threat was over. Leaks and faucets fixed; bathtub regrouted (stain left as is); $30 tip dispensed. *Bubonic Weasel kept at bay.*

I called Medea euphorically.

"From Bulgaria? Maybe he knows Stoichkov!"

"Huh? What, personally? Why would he know the major national sports hero?"

"It's a small country."

That night we opened a bottle of good Spanish cava in cele-
bration. After we'd toasted, I asked how her mother would react
to what I now contemplated. Because the day had spawned a wild
urgent ambition in me.

Medea snorted. "Why would she care *what* you did with that
piece of junk?"

So next day, in the basement office of Medea's super, Oswaldo,
I unloaded Nadya's longtime burden of a gift, the oppressive Kenmore PROGRESSIVE Direct Drive upright vacuum. I'd debated
destroying it but it was too big, and after all it did still work. But
I didn't want it existing in my building. Oswaldo was grateful, if
wide-eyed.

Then I went back to my place and hauled out from a front hall
closet the old gray Eureka canister vacuum, busted for years since
I slammed it in a fit of pique while borrowing it from Medea. I'd
kept it all this time because perhaps it could be fixed.

Perhaps.

Now I photographed it ritually by my front door. Then I did
my thing and hacked its cord into pieces, and snapped off its front
lid, and bashed off two of its wheels. After leaving the carcass
in the corridor trash closet, I made a trip to a Queens mall and
triumphantly carried back a new Eureka Mighty Mite—a bright
yellow pet bug of a vacuum that made my heart sing.

"So much depends on a yellow Mighty Mite," I quipped to
myself, revising William Carlos Williams's poem about the importance of a red wheelbarrow.

I knocked on Nadya's door to share news of my purchase and
apologize for passing along her gift.

"That awful thing?" she said. "I can't believe you still kept it.
But aren't you having us for dinner?" She smiled. "I've still got
your housewarming presents."

"Soon, soon," I promised, smiling back my tight beleaguered
smile after turning to regard the big shopping bag she indicated.

I emailed Medea's and my friend Melissa Clark, the food col-
umnist, asking for some recipe suggestions. I'd long meant to do
so. But hadn't. Waiting for her reply, I went distractedly trawling
through her recipes online.

And promptly got swept off into the awful mess at the
National Arts Club.

10

The Real Stuff

I t had a luridness worthy of the Collyers.

Juicily, the *Times* detailed the scandal enveloping Aldon James, longtime president and resident of the National Arts Club (NAC) in Manhattan's tony Gramercy Park. He'd been ousted and drummed off the club rolls, accused, with his twin brother, John, of misusing club funds for years, to "compulsively hoard" sensational amounts of stuff in the NAC's spaces and residential apartments.

Surreptitious online photos and YouTube videos showed offices and hallways clogged with paintings, statuary, antiques, clothes, boxes, knickknacks, and all manner of rubbish. At a certain point, dozens of dead and stunned baby zebra finches had been found by the gated exclusive park in the square. (The embattled Aldon, a bird fancier, denied having anything to do with it.)

As with the Collyers, the James twins appeared to be independently wealthy. But unlike Homer and Langley, both Jameses were equally hoarders and, in the case of Aldon at least, feverishly sociable. I'd met Aldon once, actually, in passing, when I'd given a literary reading staged at the NAC. I recalled an eccentric figure in pink-tinted spectacles and a bow tie and dandified suit, scooting through the Tiffany-ceilinged premises with a little dog at his heels.

That was the scene of the current histrionic outrage and dueling litigation: an architectural landmark, the club's Gothic Revival headquarters. Messy poet Auden had been a club member!

"You should go talk to these James weirdos," urged Meddy (as I'd taken to calling Medea now, to her peculiar annoyance).

"Easy for you to say," I snorted. "Apparently they're not very friendly. John James has a conviction for tax evasion—he spent time at a psychiatric hospital as part of his sentence."

"Cool!" Meddy grinned.

So, giving in, I steeled myself with memories of my obit phone calls for a suburban Philly newspaper right after college, and rang the Jameses' intimidatingly high-powered lawyer. I left two messages.

Nothing.

I wrote Aldon a flowery letter, care of the attorney.

Nothing.

For want of *somebody* to interview, I tried the NAC's attorney. He called right back. Roland Riopelle was bluff but amiable, a fan of conversation. He was an ex-U.S. attorney for criminal matters, with an M.A. in English lit. From Columbia—where else?

After the requisite badmouthing of his opponents ("sad little men"), he sighed.

"Barry, it's all about not being able to let go," he philosophized. *"They just can't let go."*

"I know the feeling," I philosophized back. I wondered, might he have any problem with clutter himself?

He chuckled. "I do."

He then clarified that the James Group (as the twins and their friend Steven Leitner were called in court proceedings) still occupied certain NAC apartments, but some had been already reclaimed. The hoard from those was being held at the club pending the outcome of litigation. The Jameses claimed it was valuable. Riopelle called it junk.

"Could I take a look?" I exclaimed.

Riopelle had no objection.

"Good luck with your clutter project, Barry," he said when we hung up.

"I'm coming too!" cried Meddy.

■   ■   ■

We were shown the NAC's now-decluttered offices by the club's new, dark-mustached general manager. He hailed from Lazio, near Rome, so Meddy babbled to him in Italian as he then led us up to the "Giffuni apartment," occupied till a few years before by one Flora Giffuni, grande dame founder of the Pastel Society of America. The James Group at their peak reportedly utilized twenty of the club's various spaces, included four apartments they officially leased.

"*Wow!*" cried Meddy at the Giffuni threshold. And went bolting across.

Under a cliché artist-studio skylight the contested portion of the Jameses' notorious hoard loomed. It resembled a crammed yet semi-orderly antiques flea market. Or an estate sale with everything piled on tables, shelves, the floor. But not entirely dusty. And no boxes, no bogs of plastic bags à la the Ron the Disaster Master job.

"This isn't how it looked before," the GM assured me, as Meddy disappeared from view. Apparently the hoard had been house-cleaned.

I was eager to press for James scuttlebutt, but the ambience of ongoing litigation hung in the air. I wandered through the bric-a-brac snapping my arty-doc photos: a high jumble of chairs, lamps, and lampshades; shelves hodgepodged with pretty ceramics; a dog-sized carved lion nuzzling a brass spittoon by more lamp-shades. I'm not much of one for yard sales and antiquing; I get bored pretty quickly. The excesses of the Giffuni apartment didn't stir a sense of personal empathy—all the more for having been cleaned up to this extent. I poked around looking for more suggestive signs of the Jameses' hoarderly chaos, such as the pile of chairs and lamps, and things more intimate or revealing. In the kitchen a big black and white photo, much askew in its frame, leaned against the stove on the floor: Aldon and John posing with Princess Di and Pavarotti. I snapped a picture of this picture, this strivers' trophy souvenir, poignant for where and how I was seeing it. For how I was appropriating it for my own, unauthorized souvenir. I felt furtive, like a sneak with a camera.

■   ■   ■

I found Meddy in the main room, hectically pawing through a vast table glossy with ranks of bowls and plates. "Ooh, what gorgeous vintage *Limoges!*" she cooed. "And precious *Wedgwood!*" Ferociously she examined trademarks of various saucers and serving pieces. That's how she shops, in a snatching, almost savage way, compared to my careful loitering and pondering. The James lode had her agog.

She turned and rushed off to a rack of clothes.

"My God, this is sixties Chanel!" She shook a jacket's label in my direction. "Look!! And *original* Pucci silks, for God's sake—in perfect condition! D'you have any *idea* how hard these are to find?"

"Just remember *you can't take any of it with you!*" I warned loudly, sharing a wink with the GM.

Meddy stayed oblivious. Enraptured.

Downstairs I cleared my throat at the front desk and asked how I might possibly leave a message for Aldon.

"How 'bout his cell phone number?"

"Really? Great," I gulped.

■   ■   ■

"Hello? Mr. James?"

"Yes." His tone was polite, not hostile.

I introduced myself, mentioned my letter and messages, fumbled out that I'd like to interview him "about, um, objects and art and their resonances."

He asked abruptly which publications I'd written for. I dropped the most impressive names.

"I'm in a meeting right now," he said. He'd told me he'd call back and took my number.

For the first minutes afterward I actually felt thrilled that I'd snared him.

■   ■   ■

Lying in our domestic bed, I brooded over Aldon's continued silence. Gloomily and idly I was flipping through my copy of *Stuff*.

All at once I screamed. I writhed up in the bedclothes.

"What's wrong?" yelled Meddy. *"Is it a bedbug?"*

"The James twins!" I sputtered. "They're one of the case histories. Under a pseudonym, of course—*but it's them!*"

Chapter 10 of *Stuff*, "A Tree with Too Many Branches," featured a pair of twins named Alvin and Jerry. Like Aldon and John James, they were bow tie-wearing eccentric sons of wealth. They'd dropped out of college. So, I knew, had Aldon.

Stuff's twins lived at "a hotel" and made use of many rooms there.

Frost had visited them over several years since the one called

Alvin first telephoned him to announce that he and his twin were "modern-day Collyer brothers."

Each of these twins occupied a capacious penthouse apartment at the "hotel," in which the vast two-story main room of both held a pathwayless sea floor of disparately valuable paintings, sculptures, lamps, antique furniture, jewelry, knickknacks—all draped with scattered clothes—the lot at some places six feet high. The penthouses were uninhabitable. The twins resided in other smaller "hotel" apartments—barely habitable for the hoarding there too. Sometimes they slept on the floor, the beds being overloaded.

Thanks to *Stuff* I was apparently peering right into the Jameses' hoarded sanctums. Into their minds and stories.

A gothic miasma pervaded all, a perverse whiff of the Collyers and their domineering mother in the Harlem brownstone.

Alvin and Jerry, reported Frost, were carrying on family tradition. Their distant and critical father had collected books and magazines, though in a strict, orderly way. It was the twins' reclusive mother, a passionate shopper and hoarder, who was key. By her last years some 5,000 paper bags had accumulated in the family's "mansion." Most of its many rooms were crammed with bric-a-brac and artworks. Loaded in the basement: "Kleenex boxes, paper towels, and one hundred dried-out deodorant tubes from the 1960s." What's more, the twins' mother was overprotective and controlling, keeping her "genius-level" sons at home much of the time, away from other kids. She kept them out of most of the other rooms of the mansion, too, having arranged those just to her liking. She arranged the twins' rooms as well. She even decided how they dressed daily.

Helen Worden hadn't been able to probe Langley and Homer beyond their Harlem threshold. But Randy Frost got guided tours from Alvin and Jerry. They didn't see their monstrous jumbles as mess. What they saw were layers and complexities: art objects of exquisite beauty and value mixed with trinkets and

mementos accorded equal footing because of their evocative richness, their aid to memory, their stories.

"There is a physicality to my memory," said Alvin. "I have to
have the physical connection."

"Everything here has a story," said Jerry. "And I remember
them all. If I get rid of any of it, the story would be lost."

As if their hoards were their Proustian external hard drives.

The twins went by daily to savor their dusty tumults. In this
they behaved like collectors, not simply hoarders.

Despite their high intelligence, Frost noted, they easily lost focus
and had trouble with organizing and decision-making. And their
speech rambled on and on, flooded with unprioritized detail, with
Collyer-like formalities. Their minds spun so rapidly, thoughts
and reactions branching off in so many directions at once, they
despaired to keep up.

"Hoarding," wrote Frost, "is a kind of giftedness, a special talent for seeing beauty, utility, and meaning in things." Many hoarders regard themselves as artists—which might be, Frost speculated
almost rapturously, because "hoarders are more intelligent or creative than the rest of us, their worlds filled with an appreciation of
the physical world that most of us lack."

But this gift came with a "curse"—a wild overload of information matched to "an inability to organize." And a further inability,
again, I would hasten to add, to perform the task crucial for any
genuine artist: cutting, editing. Letting go.

■   ■   ■

I was caught now in a feverish dilemma. Surely I'd stumbled on a
scoop, a Helen Worden opportunity. No one in the press had yet
twigged to the *Stuff* case history. I could probably do my own juicy
little item for the *Times*. I'd written for the paper over the years
(about my movie misery with *The Sadness of Sex*, for example).

But then I'd have to call Randy Frost for comment right away.

But I also needed to talk to him for my greater Project purposes.

And I wasn't ready yet.

And I'd be treading on awfully delicate turf about Alvin and Jerry and the James twins—blowing the confidentiality of a psychologist's professionally disguised interviewees. Which wasn't the deftest way to ingratiate yourself with someone you're hoping to entice into a special interview in their office.

But proper reporting required me to ask Frost for comment, if I was going to write about who the twins in *Stuff* really were.

I writhed. I found Frost's Smith College number and, feeling slightly out of control, dialed.

"I can't comment on whether anyone may or may not have been a patient or an interviewee," he replied flatly. Frostily.

Silence.

I stammered that I—I understood. But on another matter, more importantly, could I possibly interview him, sometime, for my Project—in his office (did I sound like a stalker?), which was near where my father's was when he taught at Smith?

"Oh, your father taught here?" said Frost, thawing a little.

He told me to email him.

■   ■   ■

"It's been fun talking about all this," says Randy Frost. "But I'm not sure you've got what you needed."

I'm a little surprised, even taken aback by his pronouncement. We're deep into freewheeling conversation in his light-filled, bland, sparse office at Smith. The past lies close around me. My father's first book-crowded office sat diagonally across the wide lawn outside in the brisk autumn sun. The postmodern psych department building where I now perch, Bass Hall, was grass in my faculty-brat days. I recall a muddy college fair right about on this very spot . . . and my father in his trench coat, jovial but dictatorial, ordering me and my twin, Tug, to leave early with him to keep him company in the family Buick while he drove home. My father, big on forced companionship.

"What makes you say that?" I inquire of Frost.

"Because I've done a lot of *asking* questions and not *answering* them."

Ah.

Here I am at long last interviewing the pioneering grandmaster of hoarding studies, coauthor of several books and over one hundred scientific articles on the subject. And instead of acting as inquiring sufferer seeking deeper knowledge, I've gone sprawling on about *my* sundry opinions, experiences, and impressions.

I've brandished lookalike Langley and me on Meddy's iPad. "That's fantastic," Frost's managed to insert, with a little hoot. "*I like that!*"

And displayed the iPad's gallery of my mess, documented at its most disorderly. "Probably relatively mild," he's offered, peering cautiously. My chirp: "That's what I thought too! It's improved much since these photos."

Whereupon I've launched into a windy discourse on the subtleties of my slush—how when I acquire, say, postcards of the glamourpuss Macarena Virgin in Seville, I keep them in their purchase packet as a sort of curated ensemble.

Frost (edgewise): "Staying pristine?"

Not so much *pristine*, I roll on, as retaining the acquisition experience. A kind of *positive* contamination (I have the negative type too). As if trapping a happy mote in the dust of time. "Or it's like Dickens's Miss Havisham—*but with a bow!*"

Frost (seemingly tickled): "*Miss Havisham with a Bow*—there's a title!" Then (wedging a few more words in): "Interesting about 'contamination.' In *Stuff* we talk about a very anxious ten-year-old kid with a fascinating hoarding behavior. He had a birthday party, everything great. One of his presents was a pair of pants—which he refused to wear, because they were associated with this special happy day. If he wore them on an *ordinary* day, it would ruin the specialness of—"

"Randy, I completely understand!"

Am I really interrupting him, in high spirits?

Frost (laughing): "You understand the—"

Barry (re-interrupting): *"Are you kidding? That's me!"*

Am I merrily comparing myself to a very anxious ten-year-old?

"Fascinating . . ." murmurs my interviewee.

■   ■   ■

Randy Frost, the Harold and Elsa Siipola Israel Professor of Psychology at Smith, possesses an empathetic calm, warm with a mildly prim parsonish air, perhaps from his roots in small-town Kansas. He's been at Smith since the late seventies. He's a tall man, sixtyish, large-limbed and balding, with a wide gray mustache and wire-rim glasses. Today he's jacketless in a long-sleeved taupe shirt, crisply pressed, with a pen in the pocket. But his collar, poignantly, is a little frayed. I like him immediately.

Taking myself in hand now, I ask what drew him to hoarding. Something personal?

Frost shakes his head. He'd long been interested in what might underlie OCD—something more fundamental that caused intrusive anxiety-making obsessions and the compulsion to repeat actions to allay those anxieties. He thought perfectionism, the focus of his early research, might be it.

And then he laughs at the whole business.

"All these categories are made up!" he exclaims. "We give them names, assume that makes them real. But they're hypothetical *constructs*. What struck me was perhaps there's a more basic construct that might underlie OCD."

In the early nineties a seminar student of his named Rachel Gross wondered at the lack of research on hoarding, which was then categorized, along with perfectionism, as a feature of obsessive-compulsive personality disorder (OCPD)—the "anal-retentive" condition distinct from OCD, despite the similar terminology. Hanging on to useless items was considered one of OCPD's various symptoms—though if the hoarding was "extreme," there was thinking it should be ascribed to OCD.

A confusing, dimly examined situation.

And why Gross's interest in hoarding?

"Because growing up in New York," Frost replies, "she was regaled with stories about the Collyer brothers."

Ah. *Them.*

Gross and Frost placed an ad in local newspapers for "pack rats and chronic savers" to interview.

"We expected ten to fifteen responses. We received over 120."

Out of these interviews grew their seminal 1993 paper, "The Hoarding of Possessions."

So what exactly causes it? I know that contrary to popular images of Dust Bowl parsimony, hard times and economic deprivation aren't essential. You can be rich and hoard: see the Collyers (see the James twins).

I have my own pet notions of an "underlying" condition, which I'm eager to try on Frost.

Recently I'd spoken to another prominent psychologist, Dr. Fugen Neziroglu, coauthor of *Overcoming Compulsive Hoarding*. She floated a hypothesis that gave me an ad-hominem jolt: the common thread among hoarders she treated, she'd come to believe, was moving a lot as children.

"Perhaps," Frost responds now. "Though more the *loss* of things because of moving, than the moving itself."

How about depression? Almost 50 percent of pack rats suffer from this disorder—a hallmark of which is indecisiveness, which acutely afflicts hoarders. And me.

True, says Frost. But the major evidence shows that people will hoard regardless of their mood.

"So then what about as a response to trauma?"

I'm steering things back to my terrible health scare with Meddy, which stirred up the anguish of my mother's death. In the wake of which my clutter went out of control.

Frost nods. Hoarders do report significantly more trauma in their histories.

"But those who appear to hoard because of that," he refines, "do so at a later age than those who began *before* their traumas. What's more," he goes on, "though hoarders generally claim more traumas, they report comparatively far less PTSD [post-traumatic stress disorder]. So perhaps the hoarding operates as a buffer."

In other words, my old refrain: clutter as comforting environment!

Indeed, Frost cites the case history of "Bernadette" in *Stuff*. Sexually abused when young, she was raped by an intruder as an adult. Her hoarding commenced after that. Over time her family house (she'd married later to a minister) became a chaotic bunker stuffed with her out-of-control shopping, which served both as a calamitous self-soothing and a protective bulk. Her therapist painstakingly helped her declutter—and it was during this process that PTSD symptoms about her rape first surfaced. She was able to resolve these through therapy.

■   ■   ■

We break for a lunch. Over gourmet sandwiches at a little gastro-spot near campus, I'm eager to discuss hoarding's entry in the new edition of the *Diagnostic and Statistical Manual of Mental Disorders*, the *DSM-5*, due out a few months hence.

The periodically revised bible of what constitutes psychological illness, the *DSM* is the most influential mass of pages in American mental health. Published by the American Psychiatric Association, it comprises checklists of behavioral symptoms that ostensibly remove fallible human judgment and conflicting psychological orientations from the process of diagnosis. The *DSM* doesn't interpret causes, it only describes manifestations. But practitioners of all stripes bend to it: its codes are required by insurance companies.

For decades the *DSM* has been thick with controversy, not just for freezing out the old-school psychodynamic "art" of the therapy encounter, but for its explosion of listed disorders—from 182 in 1968 to over 300 in the year 2000 edition. Drugs for these new conditions (many of them pathologizing what seem merely difficult behaviors; the category of bipolar disorder for children has been a notable disaster), have mainlined billions of dollars to the pharmacology industry. Psychopharmacology has become a booming, not to say exploding field.

To its credit, the upcoming *DSM-5* will make hoarding—to be called "hoarding disorder," not anymore "compulsive hoarding"—its own discrete entry. No longer will it be parked, as it is currently and ambiguously, under both OCD and OCPD.

What's more, the inability to discard will now be the lead symptom, ahead of excess accumulation.

I think of disposophobia—Ron the Disaster Master's term for an unwillingness to let go, which he insisted was hoarding's true underlying condition.

Ron with his harsh words about Frost and his ilk.

"Yeah, I know who he is," says Frost, sipping at his jumbo artisanal lemonade. "Draconian" is how he characterizes Ron's "I'm-in-charge!" approach. The trouble with it, says Frost, and with the self-help books Ron disdains (though he's coauthored one himself), is that they don't get at a fundamental relationship between hoarder and objects.

"So what," I ask, munching my Vietnamese bahn mi baguette, "does?"

The answer so far, "not with complete success," is a tailored version of CBT (cognitive behavioral therapy) that Frost and his colleagues have developed.

CBT is the dominant form of talk therapy these days, the "gold standard," as its proponents tirelessly call it. Combining exercises and even written homework to change a person's current ideas (cognitive) with gradual exposures to what's feared or avoided (behavioral), it focuses narrowly on symptoms. The woolly mysteries of the unconscious don't figure. CBT is short-term, much studied ("evidence-based," goes the endless touting), often used in tandem with drugs, and beloved of insurance companies.

"What we do," explains Frost, "is get people to think hypothetically. What would happen if you, Barry, threw out that postcard wrapping? You make a prediction: 'If I throw this out I won't be able to stand it.' You keep track of how you feel. You find you don't feel so horrible, you were able to bear it."

"*If*," I counter, thinking of my Seville Virgins ensemble.

"And the only way to discover that is to treat it as an *experiment*. If I say, 'You've got to throw all this out'—that's wholesale cleaning. But if I say, 'Here's just one object, I know it's gonna be tough, but do you think, just as an experiment, you can see what it's like?' That's different."

I chew on my porky baguette and his words. I've managed to throw a good number of things away during my Project. Because I'm not a full-fledged hoarder, after all.

As for difficulty discarding as the new lead symptom in the

DSM-5, Frost, who was an advisor to the revision process, says caution was emphasized. Current research shows 90 percent of hoarders acquire excessively; the 10 percent who claim not to will probably prove to indeed do so. Hoarding still means taking in too much, as much as not letting go.

■   ■   ■

Finally, the elephant in the room.

A recent experiment (led by Frost's sometime collaborator, psychologist David Tolin) has churned up much media froth by showing that brain scans of hoarders display comparatively excessive agitation in the decision-making prefrontal cortex when faced with a throwing-away task. Hoarders' brains respond differently from those of non-hoarders, is the implication.

"Sure, brain scans are glitzy," I muse, "but their import, I dunno . . ."

Frost is dubious too, I'm happy to hear, and unlike me, articulate. The brain is *plastic*, he notes—responsive and reactive. So if someone has a psychological problem, there'll naturally be differences in how their brain functions.

"But is this brain function *causal?*" he asks. "Or is it a *correlation?*"

That is the chicken-or-egg question on which psychology today is turning.

Or *has* turned. I mis-swallow my lemonade at the "big deal" Frost decides to share with me.

The National Institute of Mental Health, the source of government money for research, is no longer interested in the *DSM*.

"Tom Insel [NIMH's director] has personally told me," Frost confides grimly, "that proposals based on *DSM* symptom descriptions will not get funded. He wants to move toward neurostructural or neurofunctional markers of disease—to come up with a construct that links to brain functions and mechanisms. Not that he isn't interested in hoarding; he is. Just not in 'hoarding disorder.' What will get sponsored? Neural imaging."

"Taking the 'mental' out of mental health," I sputter, astounded. "The *DSM* is reductive enough—now they want to quantify everything?"

For Frost quantification isn't the rub. It's the lack of interest in the phenomenology—the lived experience of the condition.

"There's a lot of research in hoarding now, but most of the researchers don't understand it. Because they haven't paid attention to its phenomenology. But in my opinion the phenomenology is where you have to start."

His emphasis here makes him sound almost like an old-school psychodynamic shrink. But one who, ten minutes before, stated that he didn't believe in the unconscious. That he didn't always give special weight to hoarders' childhoods. That he rejected "repression" as a mechanism; he cited "avoidance" instead.

"So it will be hard," Frost repeats, "to get funding for things that aren't brain scans or some kind of biological marker."

"What are you going to do?"

He wipes his lips once more, slowly. "Well, we won't do the research. Because we won't have the money."

■   ■   ■

The massive *DSM-5*, pilloried for its glut of recategorizations of disorders (goodbye Asperger syndrome) finally rolls out in May 2013, weighing in at 3.2 pounds and 991 pages. Thomas Insel, the top U.S. mental health official, greets it with the stunning pronouncement that he doesn't consider it a sound "scientific" resource for understanding psychological problems. He then backtracks diplomatically, saying it's the best we have for the time being. As for the time to come, the NIMH is putting major funding into the Human Connectome Project—to establish an extensive database mapping the functions of a healthy brain, for diagnostic purposes.

■   ■   ■

I walk back with Frost onto campus to collect my overnight bag from his office.

"The mental health field hasn't progressed much in the last ten to fifteen years," he ruminates. "Maybe a whole reconceptualizing is needed. But to require everything be solely brain-based, that's a little hard to take."

So how *would* he characterize hoarding as he currently understands it?

"I think there's some kind of developmental stall. People get stuck where everything in their orbit becomes a part of them. We have all these little clues—trauma, depression, *emotionally* deprived family background. Even body mass. But no one thing characterizes everyone. There's something *there*—but what exactly? Ultimately the cause may be more physiological, a combination of things. But I think the information-processing deficits we find in hoarders—rather than the attachment to objects—are probably what's *genetically* transmitted."

Genetic vulnerability paired with a certain environment. That's his best guess, overall.

"*But,*" he then adds: "What the hell is the environment? Is it something about how people relate to each other, how parents relate to children? Maybe there's other stuff we don't know. We have such a limited picture right now."

As we say goodbye, he surprises me with a quiet, unexpected gust of feeling.

"You know, I envy the experience you're going through with your project. Hoarders are such special people. Doing *Stuff* was the best thing I ever did."

■   ■   ■

Before heading for the bus onward to Boston to visit my twin brother, I make a hurried slog just off campus in another direction. There's a Victorian house, standing by itself amid an expanse of turf near a modernist college building where I took cello lessons from a coed as a convulsively shy twelve-year-old. This gray and white Victorian structure held my father's second, major office—the Persian-carpeted demonic mill where my brothers and I labored at packing his books. I walk in. I don't recognize the place, its staircase and hallway now wallpapered in clubby dark green stripes. I have no idea where his old office was. There's no one about. I sneak a furtive photo of a hall bulletin board and, taped to a closed professorial door, a Red Chinese postcard.

Impulsively, softly, I knock. No answer. Furtively, I try the handle. Then I scuttle away.

■   ■   ■

My genetic clone lives in a three-story house in a suburb of Boston. It's been a year—or three?—since I've been up. Tug is the well-socialized one of us. Successfully married for years, with twins of his own now out of college and a good living he earns from his own TV production company. In the nineties he received two Tony nominations for a Broadway musical drama he wrote about South Africa. I think of Tug's life as having gotten set right by his marriage and years upon years of group therapy.

Variations on a theme: We both wear goatees, Tug's a bushy half-beard, mine slender and mainly mustache; the fringe of hair on my head is close cropped, Tug shaves his entire pate. Neither of us, though, sports a Jamesian bow tie. We have no punch-ups like were said to break out between Aldon and John—despite which they were inseparable. But Tug has always wanted to embrace our twinness, to be in touch. I haven't. So while relations between us have improved, there's still ever a wary tension, a chronic edginess. The projected reality show that brought him and his crew into my cluttered place several years ago was titled *My Brother Is Driving Me Crazy*.

■   ■   ■

For me, being a twin meant having a second self loose in the world, beyond my control: a sci-fi doppelganger whom I was powerless to stop bumptiously breaking into song at fancy restaurants or bursting into irritatingly deafening guffaws in small theaters. It meant never having a birthday that was just mine alone. It meant having my quirky individualities jarringly duplicated, even my thing for colorful socks. More grotesquely, it meant contested ownership of my most intimate personal histories, such as the time in Meddy's living room when to my outraged disbelief Tug claimed that my father's intervention with me as an infant—that grisly "toilet training" episode—really happened to *him*. We actually argued about it. We argued about who was who in our grade school pictures from South Africa.

My sense of wanting possessions just for myself, not for sharing, surely sprang from all this.

I didn't resist, though, our mutual animosity toward our father. Palle, our younger brother, shared it too. Palle kept his distance from us as well, the painful result, no doubt, of growing up as the third wheel behind a noisy pair of curiosities.

"So what did you think of my place," I ask Tug now, "that time you came for shooting the video?"

It's soon after my arrival at his three-story home. We stand with pre-dinner low-alcohol beers in his backyard amid a scatter of suburban autumn leaves.

Tug's face assembles into one of his serious, sympathetic, "group therapy" looks, as I call them. "It made me sad," he informs me, "to think you were living like that, and that you were ashamed about it too. I wondered if your state of mind was as cluttered as your apartment."

His ascribing "shame" to me instantly sets me seething. But I bite my tongue and ask if he has clutter problems himself. I know he does but I want to hear him answer in his own terms. Yes, indeed, Tug replies. He and Beth (his wife) both have clutter issues since forever. It was only when he looked into attention deficit disorder—he's been diagnosed with it—that he felt at last an insight into why he was that way.

"Sentimental value and 'it's still perfectly good' keep me hanging on to things," he tells me. "And I don't have the patience to sort." Now he uses a computer calendar to stay on schedule and makes "lists and lists."

Going in for dinner, I bring up the drawing of Bertrand Russell.

Signed by the philosopher himself to my father in the 1950s, the framed portrait hung by the stairs in our house in Denver. Since my mother's death it's hung by the stairs in Tug's house. By rights it should have been mine to keep, as the philosopher's namesake. But I couldn't bear its presence. So I left it where it was. Then over the years I've started to feel that obviously the portrait belonged with me—acknowledging of course my twin's good shepherding of it over the decades of my lack of interest. But I've just known how he'd resist—typically! astoundingly!—if I ever asked for it back.

Which he now does, hemming and hawing. I bite my tongue again, bitterly, but not pressing, not wanting to disturb our evening.

The next night, I return to his house late from dinner in Boston with friends of Meddy's and mine. And on my bed, there's the Bertrand Russell portrait.

I find Tug and hug him.

11

The Notorious Bungalow

What differentiates a collector from a hoarder? Both passionately accumulate objects; both are intensely attached to them. Indeed, consumer sociologist Russell Belk notes that collectors see their collections as extensions of themselves, and suffer as acutely as any declutter-resistant hoarder if these are lost or destroyed. Objects serve as a means of comfort, even as repairers of damaged selves. Collecting, however, is considered respectable behavior, while hoarding resides in the shadows of pathology. The collector is an empowered soul, showing selectivity, a focused ordering sense, and a decisiveness in acquiring. Even if, as Belk again notes, collectors will call themselves (smilingly) victims of a madness, an addiction. But they're proud of their objects, proud to display them to others. And they engage with their acquisitions—handling them, admiring them, researching their histories. They will let go of something to acquire another that better serves the theme, and needs, of their collection.

Hoarders amass, without sharp selectivity. They have no compunction about owning multiples of the same thing, as opposed to unique items to complete a set. They don't take public pride in what they have, are generally burdened and shamed. Not only don't they display their objects to others, they don't engage with their acquisitions themselves in much more than a perfunctory way. They don't take care of their things, but can't part with them, however miserable the state these are in. Their accumulations take over their disorderly living spaces, which become unfit to be properly used, or even inaccessible. Hoarders are powerless before their possessions; there's an inertness to them—both hoarder and hoard.

Of course, there can be overlaps between collecting and hoarding. Gray areas. The line of separation isn't always bright.

■   ■   ■

The reflections above came to mind as I sat talking to Nicho (short for Nicholas) Lowry. A friend of a friend, whom I'd known slightly some years before, Nicho is president of his family's Manhattan auction house. He's also a veteran on-screen appraiser for PBS's *Antiques Roadshow*, conspicuous in his riotous three-piece plaid outfits. Initially I'd contacted him hoping that as a member of the National Arts Club he might have an angle on Aldon James. Yes, he told me when we met for lunch, he'd run across Aldon many times at flea markets—was amusedly wary of him. But he'd never seen the twins' infamous hoards.

But as for hoarding, as such, said Nicho, "You're talking to the right guy!"

A "self-diagnosed class two hoarder" was what Nicho called himself. The scale was his own, from one up to five. "Clutteritis," he dubbed his condition.

Nicho was a huge fan of the *Hoarders* series on TV. "When I started watching with my then girlfriend," he told me, "she said, 'This show is all about you!' I said, 'I'm not a hoarder!' She said, 'You're a hoarder—*how many ballpoint pens do you have?*'"

About four hundred, it turned out.

"She said, why didn't I get rid of some of them, then? I said, *Okay, I will!*"

It took Nicho about six weeks, going through all the pens—from airlines, from hotels—each with a little story to tell, a memory to reignite and tug. Eventually he had to cram pens by the handful into bags and run them down to the trash room in the middle of the night so he wouldn't change his mind. He now had less than fifty.

I said I found the hoarding shows too awful to watch. I'd seen a brief excerpt or two; they struck me as exploitative freak fests. "One of the leading brain researchers of hoarding," I noted, "Sanjaya Saxena, told me he feels the same way. He used to go on them as an expert but he refuses now. They won't yield air time to how proper treatment works."

Nicho shrugged. For him *Hoarders* struck a chord. He said he could relate to the mom crying "when her kids tried to get her to toss her 30,000 unread magazines."

To be accurate, Nicho qualified, he had hoarding *tendencies*. He wasn't crippled by them. Indeed, he assured me, "People come to my house all the time." His personal style was, simply, maximalist.

And unlike me, Nicho was a serious art collector, building with his auctioneer father the finest collection of Czech posters outside museums. In my mind he began to loom as a distinctive bridge figure: collector and sub-hoarder; connoisseur on *Antiques Roadshow* and fan of hoarding TV.

We arranged to watch a show together at his place. As we parted he told me people's reaction to his apartment was a litmus test. "I consider my surroundings a manifestation of my internal world," he declared. "This is what my head is like, this is what my place is like." He didn't regard his "clutteritis" as negative—a problem that needed curing. He thought what made people hoarders (of his scale) made them more interesting.

"The Happy Hoarder," I told him. "That's you!"

■   ■   ■

Nicho lived in an art deco building around the corner from the National Arts Club. His place was maximalist, all right.

The small crowded main room was part English men's club (handsome old leather sofa, a coat rack piled with hats, some dry-cleaned shirts and a cricket-style striped jacket draped on a café chair), part curiosity shop (a huge sculpted eyeball staring from its high spindly pedestal), part art dealer-collector's lair (a speed-swept Czech art deco poster of a motorbiker on the wall, a por-trait of Lenin propped on the floor).

"This house is pervaded with an ADD outlook," said Nicho. "It's meant to hold my attention."

Nicho's place was more object-crowded, for sure, than mine. But conspicuously, it was clean—a maid came every two weeks. It also seemed object-*happy*. Nicho engaged with his things. He'd actively acquired them and they gave him pleasure. "Sur-rounded by the objects he possesses," wrote cultural theorist Jean Baudrillard, "the collector is preeminently the sultan of a . . . seraglio."

After I peeked into his petite kitchen (fridge door tree-barked with stickers, magnets, and notes), and admired his display of restaurant and bar matchbooks in the artwork-crowded hall, we settled on his leather seating with popcorn and a bottle of Alsatian Sylvaner to watch a hoarding TV show.

In the picturesque tony village of Westcott outside London, a three-bedroom bungalow and garden were engulfed by hoarding so extreme the mass was visible on Google Earth. To enter and exit his home, the owner had to wriggle body-length right under the ceiling on top of his piles. It took him forty minutes to get from room to room.

Obsessive Compulsive Hoarder, the show was called—a TV

documentary I'd come across and brought along about "Britain's Most Extreme Hoarder," a man named Richard Wallace.

"Awesome!" cried Nicho. *"Terrifying!"*

Richard Wallace lived—"existed," as he put it—in a couple of burrows within the debris of old newspapers and grocery packaging. We watched him cook his daily arduous supper of two boiled eggs on a gas stove he lit by scraping a match amid towering flammable walls of stuff. He slept in a chair.

"Definitely more intense than the American shows," offered Nicho. "I don't think *Hoarders* ever had such a fortress of a house."

A kindly local landscape gardener, delightfully named Andy Honey, broke through the village's standoffish hostility to the hoarder and his monstrous clutter in their picturesque midst. Andy helped Richard start on the long road to decluttering. He got others to pitch in on the junk-buried front yard.

Thirty tons of rubbish were hauled off.

A lot more remained, though. Richard wept quietly on camera now, registering his situation.

"On an American show," said Nicho, "they'd have him *freaking out*."

"My message to anybody thinking of collecting things," said Richard Wallace: *"Don't."*

Under the big staring eyeball sculpture, Nicho and I exchanged a look.

■   ■   ■

Only child and village loner, Richard Wallace had become a hoarding celebrity thanks to the documentary which aired on Britain's Channel 4 right before Christmas 2011. Over four million viewers had tuned in. There'd been a sequel doc since, and Australian and German TV had come to film. Major London papers had run profiles.

Richard had lived all his life in his family's bungalow and adjoining semidetached four-bedroom house (into which Andy Honey and his family had moved after decluttering it). His father, Maurice, was a bus driver and traffic warden; his mother, Freda, worked at the grocery store right nearby owned by her father, Frederick Balchin. Richard had inherited not only the two houses he crammed with his stuff, but five similarly crammed garages. Overall property value, an estimated one million pounds. For a time Richard held a job as a TV repairman. During the last years of his mother's life he was subsidized by the government as her full-time carer in the bungalow. Since her passing he delivered newspapers in the village, rising at 6 a.m. daily. He'd never married, never had a girlfriend, had no real friends.

As a child Richard collected Dinky toy cars (he still had some of them). But his proper collecting began as a teen with *Practical Electronics* magazine (he still had the copies). Following the death in 1976 of his father—a man who liked to throw things out—he began seriously archiving papers and magazines, keeping them "tucked away" in piles in various rooms. But a year's worth of papers would stack to the ceiling; it didn't take long to accumulate a roomful. His mother kept things more or less in control. Once she died in 2005, at age ninety-one, his hoarding became "ungoverned."

And then in 2010 a young documentary filmmaker, Christian Trumble—Richard's *benevolent* Helen Worden—sought him out after seeing him patronized in a TV interview following his legal victory over the local county council's attempt to make him clean up his property. And then Andy Honey entered the picture.

■   ■   ■

The commuter train pulled into Dorking, a picturesque market town in Surrey adjacent to picturesque Westcott village. It was four months later. Meddy had wangled us a three-week apartment exchange in London.

Andy Honey rumbled up in his old work van, his shorts spattered with grass from a neighborly chore. He was no longer, though, a gardener. He'd become a hoarding advisor.

We turned off in Westcott by a pub, the Prince of Wales, and then we walked over to where a figure was standing in a cluttered yard by a brilliantly white plastic tent. The tent was the size for a small wedding.

"Mr. Wallace, I presume?" I announced genially, trying not to beam at my good fortune.

He looked like he did on TV—a mothier, gentler, more bald cousin of the old hambone horror film star John Carradine. His face was nobly craggy-nosed and a bit skull-like. He wore an old green zippered cardigan over a grayish checkered shirt, and black pants. He was about my age. Not as gaunt as on TV; he'd been eating more than two eggs a day.

Andy left us to get on, and Richard led the way into the noto-rious brick bungalow.

The astounding ceiling-high masses in the documentary I'd seen, figments of a claustrophobic subterranean bad dream, were reduced now. Meaning we could edge along a goat path through the clutter and shambles. Stacks of newspapers loomed just at shoulder height, topped with magazines, bottles, cartons, gro-cery packaging. We reached the kitchen where Richard used to so precariously scratch a match for his stove. He stood by, smiling demurely but hospitably as I tried not to gape.

"*Wow*," I gulped.

I'd never been anywhere like it. I was, at last, in hoarding Val-halla: ghastly, derelict, oppressive, aesthetically astounding, most piles and surfaces grayed with dust. But with a weird mundane coziness—because someone was *living* in all this. Had been for years. I recalled how Richard had reminded a TV interviewer: "An Englishman's home is his castle."

And the *smell*. At first I panicked, thinking I couldn't bear it. It didn't "reek"; it was high-pitched and punky, intimately piercing. Like the whole place was one long-moldering ancient intimate flesh.

I followed Richard as he went edging along a short narrow hallway into his main living area. It was formerly his parents' bedroom.

Another saucer-eyed *"Wow."*

Amid once cozily-papered walls, their pale leafy pattern streaked here, blotched there, a giant high mudslide of consumerist stuff appeared to have churned to a precarious, hodgepodge halt. The indoor hillside was made up—*in part*—of:

Old manuals and books (*CLASSIC CARS*, blared a spine; Richard was an avid car buff), old newspapers and magazines, VHS cartridges; high up, a jutting big cardboard carton for Miele (the vacuum cleaner maker; did he own one?); further down, uncovered smaller cartons, saggy and crammed, bearing tilted advertising logos—"Dell," "Free Range Eggs," "Vine-Ripened Insecticide Free" something; a couple of clunky pillows and alarm clocks; a Kellogg's Corn Flakes box, Weetabix box, Lyons French Sponge Sandwich box; bulky manila folders, clumps of sheets of paper; garish packaging for various Nestlé candies and cakes . . .

Buried underneath all this somewhere were the old beds, Richard informed me. A slovenly office chair was pressed against the mudslide; a wooden board, inserted into the mass, served as a desktop. The chair was piled now with condiment jars, soft-drink bottles, and a sack of something. The chair would be cleared for sleeping.

"And what's *this*?"

My gaze had fallen on another section of the hillside, where perched a crumb-scattered brass tray. On this gleamed Richard's white double eggcup, a poignant icon from the TV show I'd watched; one branch held the remnants of a brown eggshell. Alongside this eggy ensemble lay a dove-gray banana-like thing, frail and mysterious, almost surreal.

I pointed wonderingly.

Richard sniffed. "An old piece of bread," he informed me.

"Ah . . ." I said. For want of what else to say. (*How long could it have been there?*)

Now I noticed, by the tray, as if on display on the lid of a box for baked goods, some spindly swervy wads of dark hair, like oversized trout-fishing flies.

"You keep locks of your hair?" I piped lightly—hoping I wasn't leering or intruding on some awkward privacy.

"No, no," said Richard—slightly awkwardly—"it's a sample for comparison—of hair color."

(He dyed his hair?) I nodded. Feeling I'd intruded.

But then wasn't that what I was after? My own mini-version of the hoarder reality shows' prying voyeurism? My own fascination with the lurid spectacle that was extreme hoarding? Because in a way, a hoarded space was as gothic and gruesomely fascinating as a horror movie set—one constructed by an outsider artist, a troubled soul. I felt this, in truth, while reading about the Collyers and their hermit mansion, and then invoking their strange ghosts up in Harlem; while poking my furtive camera around on the Disaster Masters job; while wandering the Jameses' antique-shop glut and chasing after beleaguered Aldon. I admit I found something spooky and Poe-like, even mad, about extreme hoarders. How then wasn't I like Helen Worden and her ilk, and hoarder TV? Contaminated by a contemporary popular culture that gorged on voyeurism.

But then, as a callow reporter after college, I'd often felt like a voyeur, a creep and intruder, whenever I had to interview people in trouble or in crisis. Ringing up a house for an obituary. In other words, doing my job.

So who was I, really? A species of Helen Worden or a Collyer—a Collyer lite? How did people feel when they entered *my* place? Did I want to experience the "phenomenology" of extreme hoarding as an inquiring observer or to intimately compare myself against a true big-timer, to sound out our solidarities, find fellowship and insight? Or did I expect revulsion to distance me—or scare me into cleaning? Every time I hauled out my iPad gallery, I had a tangled agenda. I both wanted acknowledgement (yes, a hoarding problem!) and reassuring denial (not full-blown hoarding). And here with Richard, was I using the role of writer-interviewer really as a nervous shield, to keep the sufferer similarities at less-painful arm's length?

My ponderings were interrupted by Richard asking if I wanted to see more.

■　　■　　■

We resumed the house tour. Edging back along the way we'd come, I glanced at a dim room inaccessible for boxes heaped toward the ceiling.

Was it hard, I asked, deciding what to keep or throw?

Yes, if such decisions were thrust upon him. "But if I'm geared up to deal with something *collectively*," he declared, "then the decision comes quite easily. For example, I tend to hold on to packaging quite a lot."

I almost burst out hooting despite myself. "*So I've noticed!*" I replied good-naturedly.

"With a view to having one or two samples," Richard continued, unfazed, "because packaging changes. Manufacturers keep the price but reduce quantity, you're not supposed to notice it, but I do, because I compare. Not a lot of people do that." He was just being an exceptionally wily, thorough consumer, apparently. His aim was to have a couple of samples of everything and put them into a scrapbook or scan them into a computer (though he didn't own one as yet). "Having done *that*," he concluded, "then I don't mind discarding en masse. Rather than disposing of them slowly."

So in a sense what he was doing was *archiving*, I offered. I paused to steer my shoulder bag around a jutting heap of papers and snap another photo.

"Yes, but only the sorts of things of interest to me."

"Do you find decision-making hard generally?" (I was interviewing clutteredly.)

It depended on the context, he said. "Right from a child or teenager, if I'd go into a shop and get confronted with a choice of two or three things, I'd usually end up with one of each."

"Do you *collect* things as such?"

To which Richard Wallace replied, "I principally regard myself as a collector rather than a hoarder."

He followed this astounding pronouncement, which I found quietly delusional—but which I knew was how many hoarders saw themselves—by noting that "various studies" had determined that once one's collection interfered with "domestic arrangements," then "of course" it became hoarding. The "of course" was a touch of pure seeming rationality.

"And that's what happened to me," he admitted. "I literally ran out of space."

His voice suddenly rose at the existential absurdity. "You know you've got something," he cried, "but you can't *find* it because of the sheer scale of the stuff that gets in the way! So that's the same as not having it! Because of the sheer volume of the stuff! So it comes to the same thing!"

"Water, water," I quipped sympathetically, "nary a drop to

drink." In my own lesser way, I knew the feeling. There was the gift certificate from Nadya and Meddy I'd lost in the papery slush of my counters. The loss still stung.

"Absolutely right," said Richard. "The answer of course is to approach the problem logically and allocate a certain space for certain things."

That was his solution, then. Space, organization, and "shelving" . . .

So much for Randy Frost and changing one's fundamental relationship to objects.

We edged around a claustrophobic corner, and then stopped because I wanted him to take my picture. I'd taken lots of him.

Then we entered his dingy bathroom.

The tub was cleared from the heaps I'd seen on TV, but it was filthy. The bathroom overall, though apparently in some use, was woebegone and derelict—wall tiles missing, wallpaper (where merry forest creatures cavorted) hanging in peels. The wooden lower panel of the bathroom door was warped and curling off. By the gross, grubby sink, another display of his locks sat beside two neat piles of rubber bands on a tall white carton for corn flakes. I thought of Ron the Disaster Master's old client and his rubber bands. The display here touched me: a small obsessive-aesthetic moment in the chaos. On the way out the cuffs of my jeans caught on the warped lower door panel and tore half of it right off.

"That's all right, all right," Richard murmured, waving away my embarrassed "Oh my God!"'s.

■   ■   ■

Outside, the white tent stood glossily in what was, I now gathered, Richard's backyard. The tent housed "temporarily" a bulky load of Richard's beleaguered newspapers: the tabloid *Daily Mail* (he'd

subscribed for thirty-four years) and more respectable *Telegraph*.
All awaited "sorting out" with an eye to scanning—along with,
naturally, heaps of packaging.

I pointed out that newspapers these days had searchable
websites.

"That's quite true," Richard conceded calmly. "Lots of people
have been pointing that out to me."

He hadn't yet accessed the websites himself, though.

At my request he dug around in the jumbles and brought out
some of the photos he liked to take with his old-fashioned film
camera. He held up those now bygone bearers of memories—
unartful snapshots. The grocery store refuse around us made a
fit background to his mother as pictured, shown by the shelves
of Balchin's Stores, the grocery shop Richard's grandfather once
owned. It was still there a hundred yards away on the main road,
under different management.

Whereupon the obvious penny dropped. Richard's packaging hoard was a tumultuous echo of the grocery store where he'd
helped out as a child.

We walked across the road to meet Andy at the Prince of
Wales pub.

■   ■   ■

THREE MEN IN A PUB
(TO SAY NOTHING OF THE PINK UMBRELLA)
A Brief Sketch

The dim Prince of Wales we have to ourselves. Wimbledon is being
blurrily projected on a wall. Above the bar hangs a busted pink
umbrella Richard and Andy haggled over on television. A dozen
potentially useful—i.e., broken—umbrellas remain in the bungalow.

Richard orders an orange soda (he doesn't drink alcohol, coffee, or tea). Andy calls for a pint (that jumbo English pint) of lager. I settle on a half-pint of real ale.

Andy is burly and cheerfully benevolent, a more keen-eyed, playful version of Winnie-the-Pooh. He's "good with people," you can tell. He's become a celeb himself, toasted by online forums for his kindness and fellow-concern for Richard. There's just been a play based on their friendship; they've gone up to Scarborough, the Yorkshire seaside resort, for a performance and appearance. Andy, who's forty, ran his own shipping business before the landscape gardening. He's given that up to be a full-time hoarding consultant. He's being paid to continue working with Richard, but is now also engaged with other clients as well.

"Andy's got his drawbacks," Richard commented to me on the phone before I came. "He's got a different train of thought to me, a bit more ruthless with stuff. We start off with an ordinary civilized discussion, then it gets a little more heated. But we get by. He helps with a faster pace."

TV celebrity culture has proved good to the both of them, thanks in no small part to the sympathetic director, Trumble. Richard is the opposite of the secretive Collyers and James twins. He welcomes cameras in through his derelict door—seems almost proud of his hoarding. It's made him a public figure and he basks in the attention. He's less private than I am! And there's a touching philosophical dignity and candor to him. He suggests an eccentric, that venerable English type, rather than someone disturbed. But that he can tolerate such a radical shambles—make his home in it: that's pretty unsettling.

But then look at what I was able to tolerate in my way.

The subject of boxes comes up.

Andy: "There's a shop across the road has boxes every day, we can get hold of them in a jiffy. And I say to Richard, if we get rid of his empty boxes—"

Richard: "But you need boxes to put the things I want to keep *in*."

Andy: "Why don't we get rid of the boxes, Richard, and create that initial bit of space—"

Richard: "And two weeks later you'll want more boxes!"

Barry (gust of solidarity): "I know how precious good boxes are from the liquor store!"

Richard: "Wine boxes are strong."

Barry (giddily talking shop): "Yes, strong! My girlfriend Meddy challenged me to throw mine out, said she'd buy me nice new ones to replace them. So I threw them out—and she still hasn't got me the other boxes!"

Andy (switching to Barry): "But have you *needed* a box since?"

Barry (suddenly on the spot, resisting being easily handled): "Yes, a couple of times! Okay, maybe not as badly as I thought . . ."

Andy: "So when you *needed* the box that you threw out, what did you do?"

Barry (scoring on him): "Cursing I put the stuff in bags—but I had a whole thing I couldn't throw out because I hadn't a box for it!" (Unable to recall exactly what.)

Conversation now wanders briefly to time travel, a pet interest of Richard's (he thinks Einstein got it wrong), then on to regular travel—of which Richard has done almost none. He's been on a plane exactly once.

Exactly being the word.

"Not a jet, a turbo-prop Viscount, with four engines, in 1965, from Gatwick."

"Richard's got a fair memory," grins Andy.

And all at once I think of Borges' short story, "Funes, the Memorious." A young gaucho, Funes, is blinded in an accident, after which he can recall everything he's ever seen or experienced—in hypermagnified detail. It's a wonder but a monstrous burden. Funes is engulfed by his excess of remembrance.

"My memory," he complains, *"is like a garbage heap."* (My italics.)

The line leaped out when I read the story again recently. Isn't Richard with his memory, both mental and material (the archival heaps overwhelming his properties)—isn't Richard a real-life cousin of poor memorious Funes?

Except the material has overtaxed Richard's memory capacity: *he can't find things.*

He's half-Funes.

And then what about me, with my mementos of travel, my postcards, calendars, receipts from Tokyo eyeglass shops, old train tickets, foreign newspapers—all slushed about?

In my way I was part-Funes too.

Finally it's time for my iPad show-and-tell.

"Low to moderate," Andy rates my clutter gallery.

Richard shrugs. "Looks normal."

To my great satisfaction they both squawk at the photos of Langley and me.

■   ■   ■

Waiting for my train back to London, Andy and I sat chatting in his van. I'd return in a week to accompany Richard to a new support group that Andy had helped launch. He'd grown to realize, he told me, that he—Andy, the former gardener—had a gift for aiding hoarders. The TV documentaries opened a new life to him. There were TV-series possibilities to explore; he now had an agent; the small decluttering company he'd joined had ambitions to expand on a national scale.

He'd come to Richard's aid initially out of sympathy for the underdog (the director, Trumble, did likewise). His empathy and sensitivity, he confided, were inspired by watching his mother's struggle with depression.

I told him I sympathized myself with the pain of depression. And that he and Trumble were striking a blow against the freak shows of reality TV.

And now I learned that somewhere deep in Richard's chaotic hoarded jumbles, there was—supposedly—a set of crucial financial documents. But where? That was one of the urgencies to all the decluttering and sorting underway. But it was slow going with Richard. "A five-year project," Andy put it. Despite so many tons of stuff having already been removed.

"A very *Dickensian* situation," I murmured.

■   ■   ■

Meddy was waiting for me for late dinner at the Newman Street Tavern, a young chef's intensely locavore gastro pub in Fitzrovia. Over bowls of cockles, she grinned at my pub lunch photos. Then waved away with a yelp my shots from inside the bungalow. During the Cornish lamb (with a red from Mount Etna) she announced we "had a problem."

She didn't like being Medea. "Or Meddy—I *hate* Meddy."

I sighed magnanimously. "Jesus, all right. But I'm not calling you Roxelana or whatever."

"Why not?"

"*Because.*" Then it occurred to me. In London I'd found a secondhand copy of the *Fawlty Towers* scripts.

"Sybil—from *Fawlty Towers!* That's you perfectly: Sybil!"

"And you're Basil!" she cried. "*Basil*, what are you doing? 'Just trying to kiss you, my sweet.' Well, *don't!*" She laughed, delighted.

"I already have a name, thank you," I told her.

To my amazement, poking around online next morning, I learned that Prunella Scales, the actress who immortalized Sybil Fawlty, had lived in Westcott as a child. She was now eighty. I immediately scrounged up her agent's contact and wrote asking to pass along a note:

Did Ms. Scales possibly recall Balchin's Stores, Richard Wallace's grandfather's grocery?

Promptly I received a forwarded reply:

Dear Barry Yourgrau:
I do indeed remember Balchin the butcher in the village of
Westcott, where my parents lived before the war of 1939–45.
But after the war they moved . . . and we lived on rabbits shot
by my father and brother, and ducks or hens which we kept
for their eggs.

Best wishes,
Prunella Scales

"You heard from Sybil Fawlty?" Her namesake's eyes were wide as saucers.

"Yes—can you believe the coincidence?"

"Oh, can I be Prunella instead?" she burst out. "*Oh please, please!*"

"Jesus, okay."

"*Yes!*" cried my Prunella. "*Basil*, what are you doing? 'Just trying to kiss you, my sweet.' *Well, don't!*" And she laughed in glee.

12

Freud's "Dirty" Couch

Like Richard Wallace (sort of), the father of psychoanalysis began intensively collecting around the time of his father's death in 1896.

So emotionally precious did his 2,300 items of antique statuary and objects become to him that when the ailing eighty-two-year-old Freud escaped Nazified Vienna to London in 1938, he brought the whole lot with him, along with his analytic couch and many of his books. The antiquities were faithfully reinstalled in Freud's handsome new red-brick residence at 20 Maresfield Gardens in comfortable Hampstead—in the same month, as it happened, that Helen Worden's first article threw its glare on the Collyer brothers of Harlem. In 1986, following the death of Freud's psychoanalyst daughter Anna, the house became the Freud Museum, London.

Art historian Janine Burke called Freud's passionate collecting his "personal form of therapy." He liked the hunt, the wheeling and dealing. He traded for pieces. And if he'd had to leave it all behind in Vienna, he intended to start anew in London. Curiously, he wrote almost nothing about collecting as such. The artist Louise Bourgeois, who spent years in psychoanalysis in New York—and whose living room was among those Dominique Nabokov photographed—wasn't overimpressed with the results, despite the museum quality of some pieces.

"How could Freud have an eye for aesthetic quality," she wrote, "when the aesthetic of some of these objects is so low?"

Be that as it may, I sniffed the gaudy roses by Freud's Hampstead front door now, and went in to meet a young research psychologist named Ashley Nordsletten.

Nordsletten, a Minnesota expat with an Oxford M.A, long blond hair, and much good humor, had coauthored a recent prominent study on collecting versus hoarding disorder, to test the projected new *DSM-5* criteria. Her coauthor and Ph.D. supervisor at the Institute of Psychiatry at King's College London, was David Mataix-Cols, who'd headed the team that formulated the hoarding entry for the *DSM-5*.

Nordsletten had interviewed hundreds of London hoarders and collectors in their homes. But she'd never been to Freud's house. I'd asked her to join me.

We entered Freud's study.

"Yes," said Nordsletten—expertly scanning the Persian carpets; the ranks of books; the statuary in cases, on shelves, on tables; the prints and photos; the legendary couch; the crowded desk with its strange chair like a skinny, leathery maternal extraterrestrial: a whole "private museum," as one commentator put it—"my immediate impression is of a collector, not a hoarder. All the major spaces are usable. Everything being confined and meaningfully placed where it is."

And *no dust*, I murmured. *No smell*. And despite the plethora of things, no sense of Nicho Lowry's clutteritis. Orderliness prevailed.

At my request, Nordsletten gauged Freud on Frost–Steketee's Clutter Image Rating Scale—1 being the lowest, 9 the Richard Wallace-style highest. She gave Freud a 2, because of the amount of his stuff. From 4 upward was when things became "problematic," she explained. Most furniture in a room would by then be out of commission from things piled on top, much of the floor impassable. The collectors she interviewed usually fell well below that threshold. I told her I counted myself, at my worst, between 3 and 4. For some (Freudian?) reason I'd neglected to bring the iPad. But I'd much improved, I assured her.

We leaned close over Freud's desk. Massed figurines—he collected Egyptian, Greek, Roman, and Chinese works, but nothing from Africa—occupied so much of the surface, there was barely room for his writing pad.

"I find this *claustrophobic*," I declared, in the hushed tone both of us were using even though we were alone.

"My personal preference," Nordsletten half-whispered, "would be not to have the desk so crowded. But you see, he's left himself space to work, he's been able to stop himself from putting *everything* on the desk. I've read how, when he acquired something new, he first brought it to the dinner table, to appreciate it. That's a collector." She paused, considering. "I would like to ask Freud," she declared, "*why* the sculptures are on the desk facing him. Interesting to hear his perception of that. Seems so intentional."

I said that Freud moved the objects around each time he was working on a new project—like a miniature Greek chorus to his thinking. He called them his "old grubby gods." And they all gazed at him despite his being someone who famously didn't like being looked at.

Nordsletten nodded, assessing on. "I imagine if you took him away from this space, he could probably tell you *exactly* what's on his desk and why it's there. A hoarder would not be so aware that way."

I thought of Ron the Disaster Master's challenge to me over Indian food, to list from memory twenty things from my clutter that I'd rescue in a fire. I hadn't tried; I'd regarded it as one of his

"I gotcha!" gambits. But certainly, I now ruminated quickly, I'd take my box of old spiral-bound notebooks and story manuscripts, my beleaguered laptop, my mother's cut-glass hand bell (if I could find it), a certain yellow Cutty Sark whisky box, a small painting done for me by the Scottish artist Steven Campbell, my old family photos, Polaroids of Prunella I took in our early days . . . how many was that? Could Freud have provided such a list? Would it simply be the antiquities on his desk?

Their petite size was a surprise. "Freud's toys," Louise Bourgeois called them. Almost no object rose over a foot and a half. From my reading I'd had the impression of things being much bulkier. Which would fit with my pet theory of massed objects as physical *company*, as a nurturing consoling bulk: an environment playing mother's bosom. Call it a "transitional" environment, to bend Winnicott's "transitional object" to my use.

A few feet over from the desk, we inspected the sumptuous original analytic couch. Technically it was a chaise longue, stuffed with horsehair. It made a slumping lumpy mass, voluptuously covered by a rich Persian rug and dark velvety pillows. A thing from the *Arabian Nights*, though a little faded right where decades of hips had sunk. The rug had been a present to Freud (I later learned) in 1883 from his brother-in-law and distant cousin, Moritz—whom Freud in a letter to a colleague described as suffering from "pseudologica fantastica," i.e. compulsive lying.

So that's where so many troubled souls had reclined to pour out their appalling intimacies, their wrenching, preposterous dreams: *on a gift from a pathological liar.*

"I kind of want to lie down on it," murmured Nordsletten. "Though maybe it looks dirty."

"*Dirty?*"

I leered softly.

"I mean, it looks worn, 'dirty' isn't fair."

"Interesting you came out with such a term!"

"I suppose the connotation is it looks old and worn, therefore you think 'dirty.'"

(In fact, the couch was about to undergo a major restoration project.)

"I guess these days in America," I said, "you'd put a sheet of paper over it, like a doctor's examining table. Though being allergic to wool, without the paper I might be squirming around, itching."

We moved over to the other side of the study.

"I do find the whole room *suffocating*," I exclaimed, "despite its orderliness, maybe *because* of its heavy, museum-like orderliness. With all these rugs everywhere draped on the shelves, all these books, those glass cases, all this *stuff*." I tried to imagine the awful labor of packing it all up. It was chilling.

Nordsletten chuckled. "I think my research has raised my threshold of discomfort. I walk into a room and so long as I can see the floor, then it's okay."

The chill I felt was intensified by ghosts of my old man's offices—those albeit lesser versions of where we were. On cue, right there among Freud's books I spotted the name "Arnold Zweig" on a spine. Zweig was a German author (no relation to Stefan Zweig) who long corresponded with Freud and even proposed writing his biography (he was declined). Zweig was also a friend and collaborator of my father's. During World War II they together edited a lefty political magazine in Palestine.

To not think anymore about family, I went out into the sunshine of Freud's back garden with Nordsletten. She now informed me that an estimated 30 percent of adults in the U.K. were collectors of some kind, whereas only 2 percent met the strict diagnostic requirements for hoarding disorder. The figure was much lower than I'd always heard, I protested. Because it applied to the full-blown pathology, she explained. Clutter could be problematic well below that level. I grunted. I was a case in point.

Like Frost and his colleagues, Nordsletten pegged hoarding to a mix of genetic vulnerability and environment. And noted that hoarders, surprisingly, were often perfectionists. I recalled something Christian Trumble, the TV director, had said to me: "Richard's a perfectionist, you know."

And like Frost, Nordsletten admired the intelligence of hoarders, their creativity, their seeing the use in things. *Their* things, that is, not other people's. Hoarders' attachment to possessions somehow didn't extend beyond their own.

"Why?" Nordsletten wondered. A mystery . . .

I told her of my intense feelings I called the *My-ness* of my possessions great and small.

Then I took a breath and confessed, there by the roses in Freud's back garden, that I cut up cardigans and tore apart vacuums so no one else could have them.

"That's not something I've come across," Nordsletten responded thoughtfully. "Most individuals I've had the pleasure of interviewing have been quite focused on the preservation and continued use of their objects."

And then she offered a confession herself: she had a bona fide hoarder in her family. He was an older long-divorced relative who lived alone in a small house navigable only by goat paths. The back rooms were completely inaccessible. He had numerous TVs, only half of them working, and a number of cars, again only half of them functioning. This relative's career was in a protective-service occupation. Meaning, he would know full well the hazards of his living conditions.

"But I've never interviewed my relative for research," Nordsletten noted wryly.

When he died, the family would face the shock of dealing

with what he'd left behind. It's a shock common to families with hoarder relatives.

■   ■   ■

Ravaged by cancer, Sigmund Freud ended his life (via a fatal dose of morphine, administered by his personal physician) in September 1939. His sickbed had been moved to his study among his antiquities, his books, his rugs, looking out at his back garden. His last reading matter was *The Magic Skin* by Balzac—with its famous description of a glutted, tumultuous, dazzling antique shop, where "a thin coating of inevitable dust covered all."

■   ■   ■

There were more roses, a lot of more, where I met up with Prunella to stroll in Regent's Park. I worried that she'd spent the day hobnobbing with some handsome young hotshot chef. But instead she informed me that she'd gone to an exhibition on the history of dirt at the Wellcome Collection, the medical history museum. And found it "profoundly fascinating."

"The idea that dirtiness is culturally conditioned," she announced as we started ambling. "That 'dirt is matter out of place,' which is a quote from the anthropologist Mary Douglas."

"Yes, I read that somewhere," I noted drily. "But not in *Home Comforts*."

Prunella had adored the show's section on housecleaning in Delft in Holland in the seventeenth century, "How housecleaning was linked to morality."

Actually there was new thinking, I informed her, that it arose from dairy-farming hygiene.

There was another section, she said, the Nazis' Hygiene Museum, where dirt was intertwined with "racial impurity." "But that's the big question," she declared. "Is our universal revulsion at dirt and filth a Darwinian hygienic protection against microbes? Or is it indeed culturally conditioned?"

"And why not both? So now you're interested in all these issues? Are you trying to move in on my Project?"

"*Our* Project," Prunella corrected grandly. "Not only am I an adorable character in your book. But by now I can write a better book than you on hoarding and mess."

I wasn't going to argue with her; she was probably right. Instead I watched the Adorable One as she stopped at a bush to pull close a mammoth golden rose, and press her nose into it.

■   ■   ■

The Wellcome Collection, it turned out, is based on the prodigious collecting of millionaire pharmacist and philanthropist Henry Wellcome. At his death in 1932 he had acquired some 1.5 million books and objects—about five times the holdings of the Louvre. No more than 10 percent of these could be exhibited in his lifetime by his overwhelmed curators; most sat in crates. While focused on the history of medicine, the collection includes diverse other things as well—weapons, fabrics, torture instruments, samples of hair from George Washington and Napoleon.

"As a result," notes the Wellcome website, "the collection has sometimes been criticized for lacking purpose or coherence."

■   ■   ■

There were no roses in the notorious bungalow's front yard, which I hadn't entered before. No Model T Fords.

But there were *lots of cars*.

I was back in Westcott with Richard—contemplating together the hulks of once-handsome machines crowded in stupendous decrepitude amid the purple-flowered weeds. They were some of the approximately eighteen (exact number uncertain), mainly Jaguars and Daimlers, that he kept here and in various garages. Black and white photos showed a very dapper young Richard Wallace, way back in the day, posing with a couple of sleek motors. He'd started collecting cars (secondhand) as a teen. His taste ran vehemently British.

None of Richard's cars were drivable. They were for "dismantling and restoring," he explained. When? I wondered silently, as he launched into a typically rambling, detailed answer of exactly how he'd handle restoration procedures. I thought of a psychologist's phrase to me, that hoarders give "twenty-dollar answers to twenty-cent questions."

"What's your favorite, then?" I asked when he was done.

An S-type Jag saloon car from 1966, much like the Mark 2 Jag that Inspector Morse drove on the TV series. It was stored in a garage nearby.

"Oh, can we look?" I inquired eagerly.

"Can't, I'm afraid," said Richard. "Car's blocking the door."

We headed away past a blue-tarped lean-to that bulged with battered newspapers, to go on around the bungalow and reenter it from the white-tent, backyard side. After another chat within, we'd take the bus to meet Andy at the support group meeting in nearby Leatherhead.

That *smell* again . . .

En route through the grungy little hallway to the main living area, an ensemble of dust-grayed boxes of lightbulbs on a sill caught my eye. An intuition made me stop and point.

"Broken?"

Yes, broken, said Richard. But there was a certain machine, "apparently," with which you could cut off the glass part and install new filaments.

I blinked at him.

"But Richard," I protested gently, "wouldn't that be *incredibly labor-intensive?*"

"It's just a silly thing," he allowed, with a slight, hapless laugh (he often used "silly" about his behavior). "But I do find it difficult," he sniffed, "to habitually throw things away *even though* they are essentially no good . . ." His voice trailed off.

He had boxes of broken television valves as well.

Broken cars, umbrellas, lightbulbs, valves. Richard kept them because they might be restorable or used for parts—as reasons go, a perfectly normal one. He saw them all as part of one man's principled if quixotic stand against our throwaway society. He meant to be practical. Except, of course, to everyone else his bulbs' practical value was a poignant zilch.

Really, Richard's busted objects functioned as embodiments of his *intentions*. They operated in the realm of symbols—not just never used, but effectively beyond use.

Was he always like this about broken things? I asked.

"To a certain extent," he said. "And then it developed out of all proportion. Which results in what you see." Ruefully he smiled.

We shuffled on; the indoor hillside loomed again. And now I tried out my pet insight about hoarded stuff as a self-mothering nest or security blanket, a "transitional" environment.

"I don't think that applies to me particularly," said Richard.

"*No?*"

I felt disappointed (even annoyed); his bungalow seemed so obviously that way.

But then Randy Frost had pointed out that many hoarders just wanted to have all their data accessible and at hand.

"I'm more like that," said Richard.

He wasn't sentimental either. Sentimentality drove so much of my hanging on, material and emotional, that I assumed it affected everyone who couldn't let go. But my assumption was a presumption.

A little lesson, I thought.

Gazing around at all the heaped masses, I wondered what it would be like to *live* in here. How to avoid a Collyer-style calamity?

"Anything ever fall on you?" I asked.

Yes. Piles of papers!

"They come over slowly, like that." He began miming. "You don't hear it because it's quiet. The whole pile comes over like *that*, and you get hit and then it sort of *slliiides* all over you. But you're able to resist it! Though it happens when you least expect it. You think it's stable and it isn't. You have to be careful. If you have anything on the top, it will come down. The trick obviously is to put heavy stuff at the bottom and get lighter. It's all about *weight*."

Did he ever think of keeping a diary of his experiences? I asked. Like the chronicle I was making.

"Yes, I ought to do that. Though it's just one more thing *to* do. Which can get in the way of what I'm trying to achieve!"

I gave a yelp.

"Exactly!" I cried. I beamed in fellowship. "I've found that doing my Project *gets in the way* of my decluttering!"

"Indeed," he declared, "I've found if you start trying to record every aspect of things, you need a complete day to write up the previous day. Of course that doesn't happen in real life. And in the end you give up and that's what happens."

I beamed again. Because here was Borges being echoed once more, in this dust-ridden jumble-clogged English village bungalow.

In a famous short fragment called "Of the Exactitude of Science," the Argentinian fictionist (a devotee of archives and catalogs) cited a prodigious map:

> . . . and so the College of Cartographers evolved a Map of the Empire that was of the same Scale as the Empire and that coincided with it point for point.

To be practical, though, maps need to shrink the scale of what they represent—not match up in size one to one. Richard wanted his diary to match up one to one with his days' experiences. A College of Cartographers' diary.

It was a beautiful expression of his disinclination to select, to cull. To let go of things.

I handed him my notebook and asked him to write his name and address. Which neatly expressed my own inclination for mementos.

"Richard B. Wallace," he began in careful block print. "(Former?) . . . Hoarder."

Then I videoed him reciting a little verse he'd composed about his stacks of *Daily Mails* and *Telegraphs*. "When I'm Keeping Papers," it was titled.

■   ■   ■

At the support group meeting in Leatherhead, there were more than twenty of us, spread round a vast table that took up most of a room resembling a glassed-in sun porch. Sophie Holmes, a local clinical psychologist, led things. Andy hurried in last minute.

Sophie had been on the second documentary about Richard and had given him a course of CBT therapy. He called her "very perceptive" about suggesting common-sense approaches.

A quiet aura of wise celebrity hung about Richard now and in the hobnobbing that followed.

"I don't think meetings can offer me much help any longer," he'd commented beforehand, as a veteran of sessions in London the year before. "But I can possibly help others, to as-it-were sort themselves out or advise the best way forward."

Leatherhead only met monthly (hardly adequate, I thought). This was its third time. After Sophie gave an orienting talk about hoarding, we split into smaller groups for what was essentially

Clutterers Anonymous-style confessionals, with one difference: we could comment on one another.

This provided the opportunity for the highlight of my evening.

I joined Richard in a smaller group. Where I realized, all at once, that I felt at home, there among those strangers. I was touched by the fellowship of our condition, whatever its exact form. I felt secure and collegial enough to confess, when my turn came, how I cut cardigans into pieces, how I tore apart old vacuums, so no one else could have them when I threw them out.

Richard's reaction was different than Ashley Nordsletten's.

"*That sounds stark raving potty,*" he exclaimed.

My jaw dropped. Not just at the violation of the principles of empathy, but at the notion of who was calling whom a nutcase.

"Richard just called me stark raving bonkers!" I sputtered.

"No I didn't," Richard shot back. "I said it sounded stark raving *potty.*"

13

The Red Fish

Back in New York, my own dust lay in wait. A familiar side effect of my traveling life.

I'd been gone four whole months this time—Istanbul, Amsterdam, London, a stretch in Copenhagen. What did I expect?

It was relentless, this New York dust, as the photographer Dominique Nabokov decried it.

I groaned at the labor ahead of me. That was the trouble with housework: it never truly *ended*.

But the dust spun a bit of poetry too. It added a painterly "memento mori" chiaroscuro, for example, to the semi-curated memento-jumble in the crèche of built-in display shelves in my dining area. I *liked* how it looked there. So did my camera.

After so long away, my lair struck me anew as the *semi*-curated hodgepodge of a *semi*-collector—one with a disinclination for the orderly responsibilities of collecting proper.

And now, post-London, my whole main room brought to mind Freud's decoratively laden couch. I eyed my postcard of it from Hampstead, sitting regally propped amid the mishmash on the striped piano top. It looked at home.

There was even a newly discovered Poe twist. The horror-

meister turned out to have penned an essay on interior decoration, "The Philosophy of Furniture." Therein he specified his
ideal pleasant room's color scheme: "the tints of crimson and gold
appear everywhere in profusion, and determine the *character* of
the room."

Red and gold were the very colors of the stripes on Prunella's
piano.

I'd come a long way, I reflected, since my Project began.

Number of visible cardboard boxes, empty or full: a mere seven
(plus a couple tagalong small ones)—down from the initial 45.

Number of visible shopping bags with handles: a measly six.

Number of supermarket plastic bags: a lone small waste-
basketful in the kitchen—no more tumbleweed colonies.

Gone: the behemoth Kenmore upright vacuum, the moose-
like exercise machine, the busted canister vacuum, the famous
red cardigan; all of someone's former boyfriend's old jackets and
tennis gear, stacks of unopened art magazines bulked on the floor,
a pair of woebegone hiking boots from the movie shoot in Mexico
twenty-five long years before; an even hoarier, deeply pitted cast
iron saucepan of the same vintage as the cracked pasta bowl I'd
forced myself to throw out in launching my Project.

And much more besides.

Arrived: a chirpy yellow Mighty Mite vacuum; a set of new
replacement Venetian blinds radiant in the bedroom; a dining
table habitually cleared of but a few books and folders; a wall of
bathtub tiles unmoldy because I wiped them down after shower-
ing in my nondrip tub; a fridge that I opened without brandishing
a crucifix and a head of garlic.

Of all the big items I threw out, I discovered I only missed, at
times, one: the red cardigan. I plain liked its plush hipster paisley,
and how it stirred, despite all, a certain happy vision of my time
in L.A. "Souvenirs," wrote Susan Pearce, the expert on collecting,
"are lost youth, lost friends, lost past happiness; they are the tears

of things." So then what on top of that is it to lose a special souvenir itself?

Also, the cardigan had still been wearable. But my regret was
petite and sweetly sad; not a grief but a romantic nostalgia for the
world I'd left when I gained Prunella.

Surveying my lair now, I felt a real change in its spirit, as if
some emotional feng shui of the place had shifted. Was that how
progress happened? Piecemeal. Organically. Not with brassy pro-
grammatic Project fanfares, but more like an *anti*-dust. Creep-
ing in, like a version of the poet's fog, on little clean feet? Was it
from the sheer cumulative effect of my Project experiences: the
insights from shrinks, the messy cultural histories, the empathy
I'd felt with Richard Wallace and friends (despite the "stark raving
potty")? Had my place improved by osmosis, with occasional outbursts of furious action spurred by the onset of visitors?

Suddenly I flashed back to the willowy figure of Corinne May
Botz. A marvelous art photographer of spooky narratives, Botz
was doing her own project, in conjunction with a group called
the Institute for Challenging Disorganization, about objects people couldn't let go of. Before leaving on my long latest travels, I'd
acted on a courageous impulse. I invited Botz to shoot my improv-
ing messcape. So I, a clutterbug who couldn't previously bear the
thought of intruders, had watched with a mixture of intoxica-
tion and anxiety as an elaborate black tripod camera went staring close-up at my dusty mementos. At the end, Botz announced
it was part of her project to receive an object in exchange for a
photograph—her photo being the sentimental aid to letting go.
(A strategy I was very familiar with myself!) She'd focused on my
cache of little sponge shoe polishers from far-flung hotels. To my
embarrassment I couldn't part with any one of them.

But Botz's visit had given me courage. Inspired, I'd invited in
others: a Ph.D. student psychologist who shared the case history
of a hoarder he was counseling; a pair of ladies from a hoarding

support group I'd very briefly attended in Manhattan (the group leader thought I talked too much), who nibbled on Nadya's cookies and weren't so sure about all my patterns and colors. I'd even tried to coax a visit, when he was in town, from Lee Shuer, an engaging young Massachusetts ex-hoarder who'd collaborated with Randy Frost on a training guide for the approach the Manhattan group was using. "I'm not Mr. Dispose-o," Shuer informed me genially, "I'm Mr. Save-o!" He'd winnowed his glut of bobbleheads and musical instruments down to the ones he chose to retain, and now proudly displayed those to visitors. We bonded sentimentally over being sentimental. Alas, he was too busy to come to my place.

No, I was no longer any Collyer-style recluse.

Granted, the shale fields on my long countertops and the Steinway hadn't been touched over the entire course of my Project. They'd even grown—though by less over time.

Granted, there was still the visual overload of checks and patterns all around—but that was my personal style. And admittedly, a few clumps of "fancy" shopping bags were wedged out of sight—there since forever, just in case needed.

Granted, a dinner for girlfriend and her mother still lurked in the cards.

And granted, my head was now a bewildered clutter of conflicting psychologists' views. Dr. Equis held to the unconscious, Dr. Nandy the Sunnywood psychiatrist was a believer in drugs, cognitive behavioral therapy involved much questionnaire self-rating and homework exercise—a quantifying approach I found deeply reductive, akin to marketing surveys. And what culture had CBT ever inspired, what literature and art? Randy Frost, so sympathetic to hoarders' interior worlds, shrugged off the unconscious. He and Ashley Nordsletten and others I'd spoken to plumped for the importance of genetic vulnerability of some kind (paired with a certain environment).

But in London just now, Darian Leader informed me that the notion of genetic vulnerability was scientifically "laughable."

Leader—the influential psychoanalyst who wrote the graphic guide to Lacan that Prunella gave me—further denounced as a dangerous "joke" any singular focus on symptom removal, a flaw he found at the short narrow heart of CBT. Hoarders, he even insisted, should be allowed to hoard, somehow, until they understood their reasons for doing so. His words stayed with me.

Then what were *my* reasons? The lingering trauma of my mother's death, amplified by a breakup—and reawakened by Prunella's health scare? My piling career disappointments, my anxious finances? My itinerant childhood? The possessiveness of being a twin who resented having to share an identity—an identity intimately expressed in objects, in things?

Or was the reason buried there in the underworld below the piano . . . the boxes of my father's books. I was a man clogged with father issues, and these boxes embodied him; they radiated his overbearing presence, and my conflictedness.

I'd taken the books from his home library in our Denver living room after my mother died. And kept them locked in my Manhattan storage space for years, and then hid them away under Poe's happy stripes, where Freud's postcard now sat. Like dark matter lodged in my unconscious (I believed in the unconscious).

Freud, that passionate collector of ancient statuary, compared psychoanalysis to the archeology of the mind. I'd cleared much of the oppressive physicality of my mess. This left me with the psychic space to realize more than ever that my Project demanded the emotional archeology Freud talked about. "You hoard not only things, but feelings," said Dr. Equis.

There was an old, old paternal beast lurking in the boxes in the shadows under the Steinway. I must confront it. Now was the time.

I swallowed hard.

■   ■   ■

He collected books mainly. A photograph of him in his Smith office shows him smiling proudly, posing "at ease" and proprietary by his burgeoning shelves.

When, after many years in Palestine, my father and mother fled the just-born state of Israel essentially overnight in 1948—reasons still shadowy—my father left behind some fifty-one crates in the safekeeping of the Hebrew University in Jerusalem. The crates contained almost 8,000 volumes (among them rarities like a fourteenth-century Koran), plus an illustrious correspondence with Einstein and Schrödinger, Thomas Mann and Hermann Hesse—not to mention a fine Bokhara rug and my mother's violin.

But alas all disappeared into the turbulent void of history, despite my father's pleading, remonstrating letters to Jerusalem through the decades.

Previously there was the extensive collection of books he left behind when he fled Berlin in 1933, as the swastika ascended.

In Denver he built up an enormous scholarly library—some 10,000 volumes—which he sold to a Japanese university in his last years. My share of the funds from the sale supported me for a good while as the main portion of my inheritance from my parents.

The Wolfgang Yourgrau Papers at the University of Denver now hold the books he authored and edited, articles he wrote, plus his further correspondence with Einstein and Schrödinger, with Bertrand Russell and Karl Popper, and others. After his death in 1979, loads of these materials had just sat bulked on the ping pong table in our garage, accruing mold and dust beneath a creaky tarpaulin. We his survivors were at a loss what to do with this burden. Then after Mom died, my brothers and I unloaded everything for his archives there at the university.

And I took away some of his personal library that stood in our living room.

My father acquired a lot of books in his life. They were scattered, many lost, across the world. They put my stashed clutter of boxes to shame.

■   ■   ■

It's almost a month since my return.

Wearing a dust mask and latex gloves, I finally drag away the Mexican blanket and shake it furtively out my window, releasing an unneighborly cloudburst of motes and bits by my downstairs neighbor's sill. Then I lift clear the piano top's striped fabric with Poe's favorite colors.

The boxes sit there exposed, mostly brownish. They resemble old, cheap, worn, much-traveled luggage. The fatigue of time lies sour on them. Sullen bones.

I begin wrestling them out, poking the vacuum head into the dimness and dust. Awkward going all round, as some are wedged in behind the piano's struts and the pedal mount. I am looking for an ominous set of initials. Eventually I waggle back on my knees and tot up the boxes, finally all out.

Thirteen.

None marked "W.Y."

I clap my head. Obviously I've misremembered where I put the sulfurous things. Richard Wallace's plaint mocks my ears: "*I can't find anything!*" I twist on my haunches and stare drearily at the folkloric pink and green fabric hanging down from the slush-loaded wall counter leading to the piano.

The counter is just a long board balanced on boxes of stuff (mainly books). The whole thing could come crashing down.

Up with *this* fabric, then; more awkward reaching in. And deep underneath I spot and delicately grapple out a Cutty Sark Scotch whisky box. It has a fine faded yellow color, with the great clipper in sail on its sides. No initials; but wrapping tape crisscrosses it in a palimpsest of layers. Layers that go back almost thirty years.

As I slit the plied tape with my box cutter (of cheery red plastic), I think of a traveling typewriter salesman Bruce Chatwin mentioned in an essay called "The Morality of Things." This salesman, whose circuit was faraway Africa, maintained a room back in England where he kept a strongbox. The strongbox held a few objects dear to him. Whenever he returned from his travels, he opened the strongbox to handle and admire the contents. He would add something new each time, and remove something old. The objects were his roots, his household gods.

My Cutty Sark box operates that way for me. I like to open it up and handle what's inside every few years. Hence the layers of tape. Though I haven't replenished it for a long time, and I never retire anything. I lift out now the beautiful lacquered bento box which my mother brought back for me from Tokyo in 1981. Then a steel drinking flask given me by my old mate, the Scottish painter Steven Campbell, who died tragically a few years ago; and paperbacks— by Max Beerbohm, by Maxim Gorky—that were precious reading from my 1980s. I photograph them all and return them.

A thought pings suddenly. The little red rubber fish my father liked to carry in his pocket, which I kept from Denver and which lies buried here somewhere in a box—it would be a whimsical thing to add to my Cutty Sark group.

Were it not once *his* . . .

And then I spy a first set of them under the counter—his initials, "W.Y."

■   ■   ■

BACKGROUND TO AN ARCHEOLOGY: ANCIENT HISTORY

My father, Wolfgang Heinrich Joachim Yourgrau, was born in Berlin in 1908. He was the only child of a Belgian Catholic father, Joseph, and a German-Jewish mother, Selma (née Federmann).

His parents divorced a year after his birth. Joseph went back to Brussels and my father was raised in Berlin by Selma and her dashing, well-to-do brothers.

Joseph's last name was actually Yourgray. The French-Belgian terminal "y" was Germanized to "u" during World War I by Selma, out of caution there in Berlin.

After the war, young Wolfgang visited his father periodically in Brussels, where Joseph Yourgray was a research chemist.

These were the givens, hallowed yet sketchy, as I knew them growing up—as my old man would tell tales of his earlier days, enthroned of an evening in his rocking chair in our living room in Denver, jumbo tumbler of pink gin and ice in hand. I say "sketchy" because my father brusquely dismissed detailed queries about his terrible, complicated times before South Africa as too painful. Off limits. And I never met Joseph or Selma or any of my paternal relatives, most of whom perished in World War II. So I settled for my old man's swashbuckling Weimar yarns of brawling with Brownshirts and taking a piss with four elderly Nobel Prize–winners in the WC of the physics department at the University of Berlin. Or his later Palestine tales of heroically publishing a political magazine whose printing press was blown up by right-wing Zionists.

I was raised and remained "post-religious," never identifying as a Jew. But I wore, and continued to wear, a feather of pride at my background blend of three-quarters Jewish (my mother's parents were Lithuanian Jews) with a quarter streak of Belgian Catholic. It was another "exotic" stripe in my flag on our special Yourgrau ark: us five who sailed under a name no one else in the world flew. As for the Yourgray part, who knew the exact story, lost in the tumult of time? Not me. I had enough of family growing up. I shied from probing my origins. The received narrative more than satisfied.

It compensated for all the paternal domineering.

■   ■   ■

The first crack in the narrative opened a few years after my father died in 1979. He was born in the city of Katowice, in what was then the German province of Silesia, so I discovered after the festschrift of academic essays in his honor came out. Katowice would become part of southern Poland in 1921. My father only arrived in grand imperial Berlin at age six; the train brought him, not the stork.

A small thing. But still. Misleading.

■   ■   ■

BACKGROUND TO AN ARCHEOLOGY: RECENT HISTORY

Then, as my Project went along, I'd gritted my teeth and connected with Tug about his longtime researching of our family history, which I'd long scorned as a pathetic waste of time. As I say, I'd had my fill of my family. But now, for my Project's sake, I felt obliged to open things up, not shut them into storage in the shadows.

Another narrative crack opened, with a jolt.

On the document issued by the Palestinian Mandate on his entry in the early 1930s, my father was identified as "Heinrich Federmann." Federmann was his mother's maiden name.

"That's how he was known then!" I'd croaked to Prunella. "So weird . . ."

"Why so weird?"

Why? Because neither he nor my mother had ever seen fit to mention this little fact. Weird because where was the baroque grandeur of "Wolfgang Heinrich Joachim Yourgrau," the name by which I'd known him every day of my life, until this moment? Who was this stranger, this plain "Heinrich Federmann?"

What else was coming down the pike?

I'd gritted my teeth tighter and now got in the loop with my older half-sister, Maya, my father's daughter from his first marriage. Maya lives in Israel and London. And unfortunately, through no fault of her own, to my eyes she is physically and gesturally a shocking apparition of my old man—as if he'd risen Poe-style from the dead, wearing braids. I'd kept our meetings to less than a handful.

Thanks to her I learned that my father suffered well and truly from the same condition of pseudologica fantastica that Freud ascribed to his cousin Moritz, the rug dealer.

"*He made it all up!*" I sputtered to Prunella.

"Don't squeak!" she ordered. "Stop waving those papers in my face!"

I'd interrupted her afternoon's work readying her own book project by rushing over. We sat on the couch. I rattled one of the astounding documents I'd just received—my father's birth information from Katowice.

"Family name? *Jurgrau*. German first name? *Heinrich*. Hebrew first name . . . ready? *Tzvi!*"

But the biggest shocker: "Not only was his father, *Josef Jurgrau*, listed as—"

"Calm down!"

"—listed as a Jew, *not* a Catholic, guess where *Josef* was from? Brussels? Or at least Belgium—as I'd been given to understand every moment of my life? No! Ready? *Grozny, Chechnya!*"

Prunella gasped.

"You're a Tat! That's so cool!"

"Huh? What I'm saying is I knew he exaggerated but—"

"*A Tat!*" cried Prunella. "You're a Mountain Jew from the Caucasus!"

She leapt to her feet, ran to a closet, and rushed back with a gray astrakhan fur hat the size of a winter melon.

"Put it on, *oh please please?*" Her eyes were feverish with glee.

"Okay, okay," I grumbled, "no need for hysteria!"

Sheepishly I tried on the big heavy furry haberdashery pill-boxy thing—emblem of my new heritage. I grinned crookedly into the oval mirror above the inlaid Indian table.

A goofball in a costume party hat grinned back.

"I always *said* you looked Asiatic!" Prunella burbled.

Prunella with her imperialist Iron Curtain childhood, retained a girlish romantic passion about all things orientalist.

My unearthed Mountain Jew background lasted all of a night. On calmer examination of the documents next day, I saw that Josef's father, Litman Jurgrau, my paternal great-grandfather, hailed from the shtetl lands of southern Ukraine. Ashkenazi country. The Mountain Jews were Sephardic, supposedly from Persia. Josef's mother had been from Grozny, but her family name, Orentlicher, didn't sound Sephardic.

But what did I know . . . me suddenly with a brand new ancestry?

I knew this: *my old man had been a veritable gushing fountain of invention.* Josef Jurgrau, said the documents, had indeed lived in Brussels—only starting when he was thirty-two, in 1914, the same year my six-year-old father arrived in Berlin. He married a Belgian Catholic woman in 1926 but was considered a Jew by the authorities, despite his pleading during World War II. He was never granted Belgian citizenship; he remained ever a stateless "Russian refugee." His name was variously Belgified by local officials in their paperwork as "Jourgrau," "Jourgrai" or even, yes, "Yourgrau." Or "Yourgrai."

As for profession, nothing about being a research chemist—a wealthy one, as my father touted him to us. Instead, variously: "coal worker," "hotelier," "professionless."

He died in Brussels the year before I was born. I read the death certificate.

■   ■   ■

Right before leaving for our four-month travels, I sat one afternoon pondering again the incriminating documents . . . and thought what a measly bureaucratic detritus they were. Archival crumbs from a life—from lives—scraping through such tragic, evil times.

I felt sudden shame at my self-important shock, my voyeuristic poring and sniffing for "the truth" behind my old man's revisions and fabrications. Who was I, there in my (much improved) sludge hole with things I couldn't bear to face stuffed away—who was I to sit in judgment of how my father negotiated the chaos of his mid-century life?

And then a gust blew me the other way. My God, the documents showed a man who'd never let on how he'd officially changed his name in 1938 in Palestine, age thirty—from Heinrich Federmann to Wolfgang Yourgrau. (Whence the "Wolfgang"? From Mozart? Goethe?)

After more than half a century of being gulled, misdirected, kept clueless, fed a fable, deliberately misinformed, I'd finally learned my true family name. For decades, when people asked, "Yourgrau, that's *different*, where's it from?" I'd inform them, "Belgian, originally." And now? What did I say now? "It's, um, Ukrainian, so I've just learned. By way of Chechnya."

Jurgrau.

It was a fairly common name, apparently, in the Bukovina region of southern Ukraine and northern Romania.

It was fairly common even in Queens.

There was a Jurgrau living two blocks from me in Jackson Heights.

■   ■   ■

BACKGROUND TO AN ARCHEOLOGY: IMMEDIATE HISTORY

And so, upon our return to New York from the long months away, a truly disturbing task of my Project's family archeology loomed. I don't mean contacting my neighbor Robert Jurgrau. I don't even mean disentombing the "W.Y." boxes supposedly under the piano.

I mean finally listening to the interview my father gave in 1975 to an American Jewish Committee project on Holocaust survivors. This despite his insistence that he never considered himself a Jew as such. Tug had shipped me all eight CDs of it. They were buried in my filing cabinet.

"I just *can't*," I bleated to Prunella. "Hearing his voice would be the very grave opening up!"

"How long ago did he die?"

"Over thirty years, I guess."

"Over thirty years and you're *still* . . ."

"The psyche doesn't look at the calendar."

She pressed my hand. "Maybe it should?" she suggested simply.

■　　■　　■

I stalled.

I sighed in my bedroom, hefting the lone book of my father's I had out. Fittingly, it was *The Surprising Adventures of Baron Münchausen*, those tall-tale whoppers of a globe-galloping soldier-adventurer. At first, the handsome volume was jagged with his aura—his signature of ownership, "W. Yourgrau," sank its claws into two pages, not one. Then time softened W. Yourgrau's presence in my handsome *Münchausen* . . . faded it like a too-intense color left for years in the sun. Now I regarded the book's aura as my own, pretty much . . . *formerly* my father's. An inheritance.

I felt the same way about the little silvery pocketknife he'd given me. It sat docilely on display on a dusty shelf in my studio area.

But the actual sound of his voice?

Out of the blue my younger brother, Palle, wrote from Cambridge saying he'd be in New York for a week.

"I've got an idea," I announced to Prunella.

■   ■   ■

My doorbell rang.

My younger brother and his friend, Mary.

"Oh," said Mary. "I thought there'd be goat paths."

My dining table was fully tidied to receive them, albeit the books and papers that had been on the table now sat in (neat) piles on the floor. I recalled Nadya's remark, how having visitors propelled her to clean.

"All looks pretty normal to me," shrugged Palle, glancing around.

He was thinner than when I'd seen him last, a year before. He'd had health problems.

"You think so?" I cried, beaming. "I *have* decluttered a fair amount. But what about this dust?" I drew him over a step to the gray-filmed built-in display shelves.

He snorted. "You should see my dust since I stopped the maid coming."

The first part of my plan was realized, then: to have him and Mary into my lair to comment—from the viewing point of the dining area, that is, no further. My father's boxes still lay hidden away.

Now for the harder part.

I smiled weakly at Palle. He returned the same. Both of us just a few years younger now than our old man was when he sat for the interview. Gray hair wisped on my kid brother's bald head. Gray fringed mine.

I pressed Start.

"Who's *that?*" said Palle.

The voice, unheard by us for more than thirty years, was higher than in memory, the German accent and manner much more pronounced. There was a slight tremble still from the long depression and addiction he'd gone through after his first heart attack, a slough of despond from which he'd then only recently emerged.

"I was born in Berlin in 19—" he began.

"Liar!" I cried. I stabbed Pause. "He was born in Katowice—which is now in Poland."

I re-pressed Play.

"My mother was a German Jew, my father was a Belgian Cath—"

"*Liar!*" I squawked, re-stabbing Pause. "His father was a Jew from Chechnya!"

"Can we maybe listen without all the interrupting?" Mary murmured to Palle. Mary is a Montessori schoolteacher.

I refrained from further outbursts until we left for dinner at Prunella's. Unimpeded, our old man Münchausened away about being born in Berlin (sic) because his pregnant mother couldn't travel to Brussels (?!). How growing up he always felt more Belgian than German (?!). How his Belgian Catholic father (sic!) was a wealthy chemist (sic!!) who took his Ph.D. at the University of Liège (?!) and was a captain in the Belgian army in World War I (?!). Blarney, all of it.

At Prunella's table, along with her mom, Palle and Prunella talked piano. A big fan of Glenn Gould, he was thrilled to learn that Nadya had attended one of Gould's legendary Iron Curtain concerts back in the 1950s.

It warmed my heart, having him here like this.

Our last New York encounter occurred in 1989. I'd been shocked to spot him on a subway platform. I had no idea he lived in the city, was teaching at Barnard. I was temporarily back from L.A., lost in the misery of my breakup. Given my palpable woe,

Palle grudgingly agreed to a coffee—despite being, as he informed me, "allergic to family." Meaning not just the old man, but us over-bearing older twins. He acceded to a second meeting. Then he stopped answering my calls.

For years again we weren't in touch, as we hadn't been before. It pained me. Then slowly, just every now and then, there'd be contact. Then more of it, usually by email, sometimes by phone; very occasionally in person; always initiated by me.

And now here he was at Prunella's table. With a further amazement.

"I never read a book before college," Palle was saying to her. Palle, the Harry Wolfson Professor of Philosophy at Brandeis. "If I wanted to know about something I'd just ask Dad and he'd give a beautifully succinct in-depth answer."

Could this be? My younger brother, whom I'd always admired for his early and open contempt for the old man's authoritarian ped-agogic bluster—was he complimenting our father intellectually?

My Project archeology was turning up all sorts of revisions of my family certainties.

And while I seethed with outraged betrayal at our father's Belgian-and-beyond baloney, Palle, whom I thought plain hated Dad, simply grinned and shrugged and shook his head.

"Because Palle has *separated* from your father," Prunella declared, after our guests had left.

"You sound like Dr. Equis," I told her.

I'd taken up with my Lacanian shrink again. Our sessions—our archeologizing—were at the mercy of my comings and goings.

Dr. Equis shrugged too. "People reinvent themselves. Especially people from those years in Europe." She added that I sounded like a disappointed hero-worshipper, furious that my hero had flaws.

■   ■   ■

I listened to more of my father's voice, alone at my dining table. I wouldn't have imagined such a thing possible. But the strangeness of his tones had a distancing effect. Or perhaps the passage of time was at work. Time, that "ultimate home remedy," as the indispensable journalist Janet Malcolm puts it.

It was oddly companionable, sitting there hooting at my old man's frauds and boastful yarns, highlighted by his hoary chestnut—true? half-true? phony? it thrilled me as a boy—about his rumble in a Berlin café in 1933, him against twelve (count 'em) Brownshirts. By "sheer luck," he yarned, he was rescued by an old girlfriend passing in her chauffeured auto—an old flame who'd become a Hitler-following gynecologist and who now hid him in her abortion sanatorium. For weeks there he played the piano to convalescing Nazi mistresses, until his injuries healed. And he could escape from Germany into wandering anti-Fascist exile, and then Palestine.

On my boom box I heard my father carrying on about finding a home at long weary last in Denver, in the first house he'd ever owned. I scoffed at his familiar self-dramatizing. Then I thought:

His life, too, was one of mostly constant moving around.

But his voice ate up the hours. The New York Public Library's Dorot Jewish division held a transcript of the interview. I quick-flipped through the big old-fashioned typewritten pages—across the hall from where I'd squinted at microfilm about the Collyer brothers. And came to his boastful references to his Einstein Medal.

Dad had received that medal in 1970 in Switzerland while a visiting professor there. It was for his achievements in general relativity—work which was indeed substantial. The medal lay now proudly in his archives in Denver. His archives bio and festschrift bio featured it: the "prestigious" Einstein Medal from the International Society of General Relativity and Gravitation in 1970.

Except Tug had discovered that the society didn't exist until

1971. The secretary of the society had found no record of Dad ever receiving the prestigious award.

My grimaces were drawing the attention of the Dorot librarian. I rattled through the rest of the interview and left.

■   ■   ■

AN ARCHEOLOGY, RESUMED

Gingerly now, without bringing the counter down, I wrangle out the first "W.Y." box.

Anxiety and agitation start to churn, as expected. But as ever, I have my distancing camera doings. And again, I've chosen a soundtrack to make a curated performance out of the operation. More exactly, I've chosen a movie to screen on my iPad—the magical 1943 German film adaptation, in glorious color, of *Münchausen*.

On my iPad Münchausen lounges in a gondola down the Grand Canal in Venice, clasping a princess he's rescued from a harem. Me, I grasp a Gallo wine box tagged appropriately "W.Y.— Einstein Etc." Carefully—obsessively, ritually, ceremonially—I remove its protective entrails of old newspapers. And gaze down at my father's two big volumes of Einstein's biography. More carefully still, I examine a special boxed publication celebrating Einstein's birth centennial, to which my father contributed an essay of personal reminiscence—for example, how he filled in on piano in the late 1920s at a couple of Berlin chamber music sessions with the father of relativity, who was an ardent amateur violinist.

What with the *Münchausen* for company—and what with all the accumulated miles of my Project—my emotions stay cool enough.

But then comes my father's massive tome of photographs of death masks. I peek askance at a few morbid visages of departed great men. The familiar leaden gloom associated with my old man falls almost mechanically on me. I shove the book from sight.

Almost mechanically I find myself at my laptop, googling the debonair actor playing Münchausen.

Distraction, my loyal bugaboo, has me again.

With a curse I haul myself back to the opened box. I find a third Einstein volume there which I decide to keep out, as opposed to just burying back away. A real first for me.

I grapple out a second box: "W.Y.—Poetry Etc." And from it I challenge myself to keep out a slim volume of poems by my old man's mentor, Erwin Schrödinger, one of the giants of physics— who knew he wrote poetry?—and a German volume of naughty vignettes with marvelous art nouveau-style illustrations. And then a book I remember so well: an 1895 first edition of Oscar Wilde's *Ballad of Reading Gaol* which sat in the lower bookshelves in our Denver living room.

Jumping to my laptop, I learn that the Wilde first edition is worth somewhere between a couple hundred and a couple thousand dollars! I learn that the script for *Münchausen* was written, under a pseudonym, by Erich Kästner, the beloved German author of children's books, most famously *Emil and the Detectives*, which I own. Kästner was anti-Nazi, a pacifist who nevertheless stayed in Germany during—

Another curse, another psychodramatic wrenching away by a guy grappling alone with family clutter.

On a gust of agitated adrenaline I stretch under the counter for a box I'd planned to avoid. It contains no objects from my father.

It holds things from my mother. Her last days.

a bamboo-shaped glass for her evening gin
an ice bucket, much-tarnished now
the faded checkered throw blanket she knitted, which
    she wrapped herself in on the couch in the living
    room

And the cut-glass hand bell? Not here, somewhere else . . . where, I don't know.

Strange to say I feel tenderness at these exposed relics of hers, not wrenching anguish. The raw tears of trauma have calmed to sadness . . . the grass has grown over things, with Dr. Equis's help. I should throw some of these away, I think; but next time, with proper ceremony. I find one small clump of newspaper wrapping I haven't yet unraveled.

My father's little red rubber fish falls out.

I hold it up, smiling. Hard to believe I'm not swaddling it right back into hiding. It's so charged with his presence.

Caught between my fingertips, the fish runs about three inches long, dull ruby in color, flat-sided like the penknife, with one proud fin, round eyes, and large lips pursed to blow a bubble. Its scales have partly rubbed away from handling. Stamped on its side: Aquatoy.

My father liked to produce this little Aquatoy from his pocket in academic settings, as a witty gambit during debates.

And I almost see him now, arriving home in Denver from the university. He's in one of his mellow moods, relaxed and wry. He wears a jaunty Panama hat and a gray-green slightly rumpled elegant suit—a Pickwickian figure with a worldly, even dashing air. And always a man for suits, my father, never jacket and slacks. Since we have guests coming for dinner, ahead of the international colloquium extravaganza he's organized, my father doesn't change out of his suit. Just stows his Panama and loosens his tie. And with his pink gin he leads me out to the summer table on our rear balcony. The Rockies rise above our back fence in the mile-high smog. My old man takes out the little red fish and grins his version of a debonair grin, cheesy but sometimes, like at this moment now, just right. He boasts, in good humor, how he "scored quite a triumph" during a tedious committee argument that afternoon by brandishing his Aquatoy at the exact strategic moment, to admiring laughter. Winning his point by demanding the likelihood of him having, say, *a fish in his pocket?*

"So you see, my boy," he says, "your old man still has a few tricks up his sleeve. Are you proud of him?"

Honestly, right there on the balcony, how can I not be? Maybe it's hero worship. Or maybe, just for the moment, it's love.

■   ■   ■

"Oh cute!" cried Prunella that evening as I showed her the red fish.

"I'd like to keep it here a while," I informed her. "To charge it with *your* presence."

She looked amused. Supportive. "Sure," she said.

I took it from her and placed it ceremonially on the coffee table by the couch.

It wasn't there next morning.

"No idea," said Prunella, glancing around with a shrug.

"What do you mean? You saw me put it down here! It's important to me, please help me find it!"

"If it's so important, why'd you put it by all the newspapers on the coffee table, where it can be knocked off?" she grumbled. "You and all your ambiences and presence-chargings and whatever."

She found it under the couch. I placed it in a bowl with some ornaments on a different table, to soak up karma more safely. After its journey across the decades and miles.

■   ■   ■

My archeology with the "W.Y." boxes was softening me, to my surprise, toward my old man. Maybe it was the red fish effect. Maybe his feet of clay and his fabrications had wounded him; lessened his larger-than-life force, as hero and its opposite, monster, on the kid that still lived in me. I was able to appreciate some of his books as admirable and approachable objects—as opposed to being clots of radioactivity.

And I realized something else. Freud, who started his statuary collection in the wake of his father's dying, called the death of the father "the most important loss" of a man's life. Every year I noted the day of my mother's death. But not my father's. I never thought of it. July 18, 1979.

"All these years," said Dr. Equis, "I don't think you've really laid your father to rest. Never said your farewells and mourned him."

■   ■   ■

There was a small hand sink area in my father's bedroom at home in Denver. My mother found him slumped on the floor there. He was wearing only his wraparound plaid towel and his slippers, the outfit he liked to change into when he came home. He mumbled to her dazedly his last words, "Thella, we're not in the Black Forest anymore." They'd just returned from a trip to Germany, where as usual he'd recklessly ignored his diet restrictions for his heart condition. It was his third heart attack. My mother called an ambulance, but it was too late.

Now back among the boxes of his, it dawned on me that I'd buried his things away not just to keep his presence at bay, but because I couldn't bear that he'd died. I wanted to hang on to him. I couldn't let my father go.

There now, among his boxes, I quietly wept for him.

■   ■   ■

In her book *The Secret Lives of Objects*, the English psychoanalyst and art-and-design instructor Jane Graves wrote thoughtfully about clutter; among other things, about the close relationship between clutter and memory. "Clutter always deals with memory . . ." wrote Graves.

For some people, clutter represents "the parts of themselves they cannot bear to think about."

Some objects are held onto out of hatred rather than love (echoing what Dr. Equis once observed). Hanging on prevents people from converting their deeper emotional ambivalences into "the ambiguity of love and hate"—the creative holding on to two feelings at once.

"These objects, which are loaded only with negative feelings," noted Graves, "are often stashed away."

Well, I was now unstashing my objects from the man I'd known as Wolfgang Yourgrau, working to convert my ambivalence to ambiguity.

Then I overreached. I read a couple of his old letters to me. They were rich in his brimstone and bombast, his cutting scowling asides about my lack of employment—mixed up with sentimentality. My father was a sentimental authoritarian.

The letters were wrinkled, from being crumpled instantly and flung to the floor.

I clenched my jaw—back in hating mode. And yes, I stashed the letters away again.

But every night at Prunella's I glimpsed the little fish.

Really, how could you only hate a man who kept a red fish in his pocket?

14

Gordon's Knot

It had been almost two years since my Project began. That long, thanks to all my travels with Prunella, my researches, my distractions and procrastinations. But at last I'd started across the hurdle of my family boxes. I could, carefully, begin to bear the pain and sorrow they aroused, and the anger. I could engage with them. Their scale of impact had changed.

I realized what a lurking oppression I'd always felt from having them sealed away like that. The anxiety that they brought into my lair. My root cellar of the undead.

But now, the last stretch of decluttering was dragging. I oscillated between estimations of my place. It was *almost* fine or just about; but if I looked close . . . or semi-close . . . Final-phase decisions, details, obsessional subtleties of what should go where, confounded me like a manifold Gordian Knot. My Project's everlasting tactical demands added their snags.

What I needed was some N-PD: Non-Project Decluttering. De-obsessionalized.

And something else Darian Leader, the London psychoanalyst, said to me resounded again: that a deep truth of life was that you could truly want something and yet not want it. Want to purge, in my case, and not want to at the same time.

What I really needed yet again was to heed the advice of everyone from Ron the Disaster Master to Randy Frost. Decluttering solo was a daunting and foolhardy undertaking. But I'd come up with no workable alternative. It didn't feel appropriate asking elderly Nadya to accompany me. But no one else seemed to answer my demanding privateness about that intimate role.

No angle then on the big Gordian Knot.

I didn't even want to think of my outstanding dinner obligation.

I found one of my last stray empty boxes, and leaving my ever-ready camera out of the picture, stolidly hacked it apart, tossed it. I put on my dust mask and cast a weary glance at the green pack of costly Swiffer dusters Prunella had pushed on me. I eyed the long counters along the wall, their pretty slushes still virtually untouched. It was 7:30 p.m., end of a long day.

My doorbell buzzed.

I felt my stomach clench. I took a very long, very deep breath of premonition.

I opened the door.

"*Surprised?*"

Her eyes sparkled, a little nervously. She held up a loaded plastic shopping bag. "I've brought you an Indian dinner from Patel Brothers supermarket. Happy to see me?"

I stepped back—me in my dust mask around my neck and torn cleaning outfit.

Heart thudding, I bade Cosima–Medea–Prunella enter.

■　　■　　■

She put the bag down on the dining table. She pulled off her coat and shoes, and glanced about distractedly. She looked smart and lovely in a black cardigan over a purple dress with a frilly neck. She'd dressed up for the visit?

Vulnerable, bravely grinning over my mask under my chin, I awaited her comments.

Whereupon she marched right around past me—heading for the piano.

Slowly she lifted the keyboard lid. The sound of Chopin in a melancholy key filled my apartment.

And kept on filling it, despite her wincing at the erratic tuning.

I wandered over, bewildered, ignored.

"My piano, my beautiful piano," she said. "The dust! What have you done to my Steinway?" She stopped, then started again in a sunnier key.

"The dust is unbelievable," I exclaimed defensively over Schubert. "I just cleaned it recently!" I looked on, admiring—she'd trained at Juilliard—but nonplussed.

"Okay, please stop now, the neighbors will complain."

"My piano, my poor beautiful piano," said Prunella, shaking her head, repeating chords, stroking the yellowed ivory keys.

"Stop! The neighbors!" I cried. *"And you haven't said anything about my place!"*

Tone: half-wounded, half-outraged.

She stopped.

"I'm here to visit my Steinway, too, which I haven't touched in years." She spoke very quietly. "It used to be my whole life, I miss it!" Her lips were trembling, as they do when she's about to cry.

I gaped at her.

"It's a big emotional moment for me," I wanly declared. "Having you here."

There was a pause.

Her first visit in two years seemed on the verge of a perverse, astounding collapse.

The difficult craft of a relationship. Item: how to handle being blindsided, finding out your intimate intensities aren't the sole ones.

I took another deep breath and said, "I guess it's a big emotional moment for both of us."

There was another pause. She looked down at the keyboard and played a couple of chords. She stepped around past me.

"The piano top doesn't look bad," she said tightly, about the cluttered Edgar Allan Poe stripes.

"Yeah? *Think* so?"

I followed her into the bedroom.

"Wow," she said, recovering herself; she has a tenacious ability for that. "The bedroom looks awesome!"

"You *think* so?"

I trailed her blue socks into the bathroom. The shower curtain she found "cute!"

I explained about the blue stain and restrained her from climbing in to inspect it.

"I've never seen a stove top so massively clean!" she gave a cry in the kitchen.

"Don't look in the oven!" I retorted. I was beaming. "*Or the cupboards!*"

■   ■   ■

Cheer restored, Prunella microwaved up the Indian frozen dishes she'd brought, while I set the table with hastily scrubbed glasses and plates, my lone proper fork for her, a plastic one for me. With my white and clunky corkscrew from the Hotel Ritz, Madrid, I opened the Chianti she'd also supplied. We clinked and drank, and started on the vegetable biryani and roasted eggplant with tomato and onion sauce.

It was just like long-ago times. I recalled again that very first evening I'd seen this dining area, almost two decades before. It was right after a February blizzard. The apple-green wall had just been painted. We sat at her long, folklorically decorated table, which moved with her to her new apartment, and ate slices of the smoked mozzarella I'd brought for wooing. There were no heaped boxes, no paper-drifted surfaces. And then—because Prunella laughed from the kitchen that the tuna she was going to cook had spoiled—we'd gone to an Indian restaurant. The first of our many many many restaurants together.

"So my place has a certain aesthetic charm, no?" I cooed, gesturing with my contented picnicky fork. "Hey, what's wrong?"

She looked glum again.

"I miss my piano." She gazed gloomily past me. "And it's depressing."

"What is?"

"Your house."

"*What? Why?*"

"That long cluttered counter by the piano. Makes the place look hoarderly."

"*Hoarderly?* Not messy? But I've thrown out so much! I confronted my old man's stuff from under the counter."

"Hoarderly."

I was crestfallen.

"But no no, it's fine," she temporized, seeing my face. "It's mainly that counter top, really. And these shelves here—the *dust!* How can you live like this?" She grimaced at the knickknack display nearby, which Palle had said reminded him of his apartment.

"Christ, *okay*," I protested. "I'll clean it up, it's just one small set of shelves!"

"All right, I've decided," she announced.

She'd decided that my place was "almost there"—and that now she was going to help me.

I stared at her. I swallowed. I felt trepidation and a glow of gratitude.

"I accept your gracious offer," I declared. We clinked glasses. I picked up my fork again.

Prunella didn't. She fidgeted. "I can't look at it, I'm sorry," she muttered. She jumped up and headed to the counter. "Give me a small box."

"But we're celebrating!" I exclaimed, mouth full of dawdler's biryani.

"Give me a couple boxes and a bag for rubbish."

"Ah, *Christ.*" Grumbling, I found a pair of nice shallow shoe-boxes for her. I brought a bag.

Postcards, brochures, notebooks, tickets—she began assailing my touristic slush, snatching items up and laying them in the boxes.

"Don't crumple things!"

"You don't need this brochure from the Guggenheim."

"Why not, I love it!"

"You don't need it."

"No!" I saved it.

"Some of these postcards are still in bags."

"That's how I *want* them!"

"You don't need this crap bag from an Istanbul bookstore!"

With a hard sigh, I pointed out "for the record" that her manner was violating practically all expert advice on how to aid someone in my position.

"What position? You always say you're not a *hoarder*—so where's the problem?"

Another sigh. "Okay, toss—why are you *crumpling* that napkin from the Florida Garden in Buenos Aires! *It was one of Borges' favorite cafes!*" I grabbed it from her.

"I'm dumping this tourist Seville map."

"No! Put it in a box!"

Here it was, then, what I'd opened myself to: my time for the brass tacks of sorting, for anxious haggling with a collaborator. I thought of the old client in his blue sweater on the Disaster Masters job ("Keep? Toss?"), of Richard Wallace dickering with Andy Honey.

As a strategic gesture I relinquished one of my two old front pages of *L'Équipe*, the French sporting newspaper, in exchange for keeping some important Roman papal ephemera. I also let her toss old Italian train tickets, Paris tabac receipts, Moscow and Amsterdam tram cards.

It wasn't easy: not just the decisions, the goodbye to things—travel chaff that were tiny souvenirs—but also losing the scenic presence of the slush. I was fond of my old "leaf-pile" look.

But deciding and purposefully acting were bracing.

Just like that, for the first time in years, I could behold the pink-and-green paisley surface of the Uzbek fabric on the counter. My winnowed mementos sat in two red Century 21 shoeboxes. Cosima draped them with tea towels she'd given me a while before as a reminder-present. Note: we both liked to drape things.

There was a last flare-up over her commandeering my prize pink scarf from Italy's Palermo soccer club, to cover the tidied pile of notebooks—she tried to take one; I refused—on the counter end. Grudgingly I allowed this "temporarily."

"See the difference now!" she cooed, back at the dinner table, impressed. Adding, with childish boastfulness, "And all thanks to me."

Ignoring my riposte, she announced the following:

That I could store some plastic bins of my stuff in the basement of her building.

"Yes—*storage!*" I exclaimed happily. "Like Sandra Felton advised me."

"Who's Sandra Feldman?"

Who's Sandra Felton?

I explained hurriedly that she was the octogenarian founder of Messies Anonymous, perhaps *the* original clutterbug support group, long predating Randy Frost. In my phone interview some time back she'd suggested storage to me—"'Cause your place is cleared and you're living with dignity." Which I'd resisted then, as a Project purist.

Once again, how my decluttering Project seemed to interfere with my decluttering.

"*Whatever*," said Prunella, with that glazed look that often came over her during my explanations.

She had a further announcement: she and Nadya had decided to buy me new bookshelves. Oh, and she'd drop by again periodically to inspect and help.

And of course I'd host her and Nadya to dinner.

I clutched my head and assented gratefully to all.

"I salute you," I said sincerely, seeing her out. "You helped cut the Gordian Knot."

"Who's Gordon?" she asked.

Once the door closed behind her I returned the pink Palermo scarf to its proper place of display, on my pile of soccer scarves.

■   ■   ■

Things picked up momentum. Now that Gordon's Knot had been untied.

Next day I cleaned up the much-maligned dusty display shelves in my dining area. It took me an hour—one hour perched on years of inertia.

Cleaned and edited, the shelves were fairly crowded still—but *cheerfully*.

But now I experienced additional consequences of Prunella's benevolent participation. Urgent cell phone calls from her from the street about "great" pieces of furniture on the sidewalk. Once I even rushed out mid-cleaning to inspect a "really useful" desk that would "be snapped up any sec!"

"It was an *awful hospital desk!*" I rebuked her, stamping back to my place. "And I don't need more things—we're *decluttering*, remember?"

Undaunted, she was at my door again several evenings later bearing a batch of plastic trays in Scandinavian primary colors.

With them we went at the years'-worth of mush on the small table between the dining area and the greatly improved counter. The table's merry red-checkered tablecloth grew visible to the naked eye.

Excited, I broke off a moment to share with Prunella my latest marvelous research find—that Moritz Freud, supplier of Sigmund's couch rug and compulsive liar, had resided in Berlin within *four blocks* of where my father, a.k.a. Heinrich Federmann, was at the time attending high school.

The two fabricators must have passed each other fairly frequently on the street!

"*And?* So? *Who cares?* Here, more old tickets, can I throw?" After my sulky grunt, she gazed about and then exclaimed, "Bravo, sweets, you're making stupendous progress. Well done!"

I told her that her fake compliments didn't excuse her pickled mushroom of a brain's inability to grasp the richness of the coincidence with Moritz Freud and my old man—as well as most other coincidences of my Project research—and that I knew her for what she was: a self-congratulatory, pushy, despotic loudmouth. A mini-Ron the Disaster Master in over-chic eyeglasses.

She tittered happily.

■   ■   ■

And then they arrived: my great thirty-gallon plastic storage bins in an enormous shipping box. Which then sat unopened like a tranquilized hippo while I couldn't resist tracking down and calling on an amiable New York psychologist and collector named Dr.

Barry Lubetkin, who'd just discovered he owned part of a grandfather clock from the Collyers' mansion. Alas, the piece of clock was in storage now and unavailable for viewing. But we talked clutter. He'd seen a rise not so much in hoarders among his patients, Lubetkin told me, as in people engulfed in clutter. "The difference is, hoarders can't let go," he declared, "but clutterers can."

"But it's not easy," I told him.

A week later the big box was open and four baby hippo tubs finally sat loaded up on my studio floor. Cargo: the most oppressive of the "W.Y." boxes; quantities of old LP records, unplayed in several decades but still dear to me; sacks and sacks of tax receipts over twenty years.

Then the tubs sat around for another week, in limbo, a herd I had to edge through to reach my writing table. Oswaldo, the super at Prunella's building, who was envoy to the storage area, had gone on vacation.

Then he was back. I borrowed a flat trolley from him. The trolley was slight; the tubs were *massively* heavy. Cut to one man's cursing, hernia-risk homage to Laurel and Hardy hauling a piano.

In Prunella's basement Oswaldo helped me grapple the tubs onto the storage racks. Then he waited, amused, while, panting, I snapped their picture. There amid the shadowy rows of luggage, of other people's plastic bins.

A wistful joke Randy Frost made to me came bubbling up. He said he realized he'd made a major mistake in his life after starting his hoarding research in the nineties. "I should have invested in storage units," he told me, "storage of all kinds. 'Cause ever since 1990 that industry has taken off. But, alas, I didn't."

It occurred to me to ask Oswaldo a question: Were there any (I lowered my voice) hoarders in Prunella's building? Did he know what hoarding was?

Of course, he replied. There were several in the building. "I worked at apartment complexes all around this neighborhood. Every one has some hoarders in it. You wouldn't believe what you see when you go inside!"

I said actually I would.

■   ■   ■

I met my decluttering collaborator next day at a furniture store on Northern Boulevard.

"I like the wood-colored ones," I decided.

"Bookshelves," corrected Prunella, "should be white."

■   ■   ■

"You were right!" I cried joyously, on the phone to her from my dining area. My new bookshelves gleamed, towering and alabaster and transforming against the wall, where formerly a flimsy, draped side table hid my boxed records and other crammed whatnot. I almost didn't want to move the books on my floor into my glorious shelves.

"Told you!" Prunella chirped. "And tomorrow Mom and I come do *subbotnik* at your house."

■   ■   ■

My doorbell rang.

It was my own subbotnik crew!

Subbotnik, from "Saturday"—for the old Iron Curtain custom in which groups of citizens devoted part of a weekend to cleaning up the neighborhood.

Delighted, and nervous too, a little rattled by the additional participant to monitor, I put Nadya to work in the bedroom, dusting the books and shelves there. And *only that*. She'd brought a drugstore dust mask, as I'd suggested, and her own spray bottle of cleaner, lavender-scented.

"Mom, the lavender stinks!" complained Prunella, passing by. She coughed. "And the *dust*."

And now a new complication.

"My mom," Prunella announced, "doesn't like being called Nadya anymore for your Project."

"Huh?"

"Yes," admitted her mom in the bedroom. She too wanted a name from "beloved" *Fawlty Towers*. "Can I be Polly?"

"Polly, *the maid*? Gee, okay . . ."

Nadya–Polly kept toddling out to the dining area with books to fill my white shelves. Books I didn't want *there*, I wanted in the *bedroom*. I carried them back, muttering.

But I felt a warm heady glow as the subbotnik crew bustled on my premises. My lair felt connected once again to domesticity, to a shared peopled warmth, instead of sitting as a solitary's withdrawn addled nest. I grinned emotionally, in disbelief. Prunella scrubbed away at the bathtub. Blue-green stain notwithstanding, it shone.

Then she had me join her to attack the slush pile on the other long counter, the one under the green wall. She began snapping—"Dump? Keep?"—through another quasi-curated rubble of yet more museum brochures, postcards, folded old newspapers, hotel shopping bags, and hotel shoeshine kits. I felt my agitation mount as she rushed us along. We had a harangue over nubs of crumbly lava rock from our first trip to Iceland. She kept coughing, mask down at her neck, waving at dust.

Then she grabbed at an old 2010 calendar propped carefully against the green wall.

And our subbotnik blew up.

"*What are you doing?*" I cried.

"It's rubbish, dump it!"

"*Says who?*" I squawked. I grabbed it back. "It's an Italian cara-binieri subscription calendar! You're like your goddam Soviet cleaning lady, Zinaida! *WHO ARE YOU TO JUST PRONOUNCE WHAT IS AND ISN'T RUBBISH?*"

I was shouting uncontrollably.

A scene right out of a hoarding reality show.

She blinked at me.

"Fine, good luck cleaning, Barry," she said coolly, and went for her coat.

And she was gone.

I stood there, woeful and distraught, shaking.

"I don't pay attention when she gets like this," Polly said, emerging in her dust mask with yet more books. "The important thing with her is: never apologize first."

■   ■   ■

Within two days Prunella was bedridden, running a 102-degree fever, slumped amid pills and cough syrups. "It's your vile dust, it's given me Legionnaires' disease!" she moaned. She blew groggily into a tissue. "I looked up the symptoms! You'll have to make up for it with an *amazing* dinner for us next Sunday—if I don't die!"

Next Sunday being the date I'd yielded to as my D (for dinner) Day.

"Maybe you'll die from my cooking," I murmured. I'd followed Polly's advice and resisted apologizing.

"An *amazing* meal," she repeated.

Then a truly alarming cough racked her, no joke.

I lay awake that night in a cold sweat. What if it was true? What if my apartment had poisoned my girlfriend?

■   ■   ■

Dread: an emotion aroused by the looming advent of certain particular demanding persnickety guests.

Especially if you'll be hosting in an apartment-in-recovery that
remains a showcase of possibly lethal New York dust—featuring a
barebones kitchen barely in proper use for a decade.

A frantic dust-paranoid declutterer in mask and latex gloves
with a girlfriend he conceivably poisoned goes vacuuming maniacally. Then he uses his girlfriend's costly Swiffer dusters. Then,
with a squeak of distress, he flings open the cupboard over the
kitchen sink—revealing an ancient tomb-world of dust, crumbs, a
sad semi-cracked sugar bowl, and various shadowy bottles. Struck
by the pictorial impact of it all, he immortalizes this tomb-world
with his you-know-what. He climbs up on a chair, to bag and
throw out the sugar bowl and oddments, to unpeel and bundle up
and bag and throw out the sticky paper covering the shelves. Still
on a chair, he goes barging about inside with his vacuum, before
wiping all with a sponge. Phew, at least it isn't an obvious health
hazard now.

He opens the narrow vertical cupboard alongside the fridge,
and tosses *everything* out.

He gets back on a chair. He goes at the cupboard above the
fridge, which is more dignified than the lower one, but still houses
unused plastic tubs and unused drinking glasses that look as if
fashioned from powdered charcoal. Out with them.

A savage mopping of the kitchen floor follows. As a sentimental gesture to his South African boyhood, he shoots a dose
of Dettol into the mopping water—to wild excess. His would-be
gourmet kitchen now stinks of disinfectant. Desperately he soaks
a paper towel in eau-de-cologne and hangs it from a cupboard
doorknob.

Somehow all this uses up more than several days. He begs for
and receives a grudging postponement of the dinner until Mon-
day. His girlfriend's temperature has moderated, mercifully.

Now for the unmerciful part.

He can't cook, first of all—other than the one crude spa-ghetti he made a couple of times for his girlfriend during their early furtive-lovers days, when romance made everything tasty. What's more, he is a terrible shopper, lacking common sense and proportion. He's decided on a proper pasta as a main course: "Penne with Country Ragu" (from the *Bon Appetit* website, hecti-cally researched). The recipe calls for a quarter pound of sausage. From Jackson Heights's grossly expensive new green market he comes back with a grossly expensive artisanal pork sausage the length of a baby python, and bunches of gossamer, sandy arugula that will require hours of soaking. Then from the delis he trudges back, brain-weary from decisions, lugging, among other burdens, a grossly expensive half-cinderblock of Pecorino Romano cheese, a vat of organic chicken stock, and vast bundles of celery and carrots of which he'll need but a small portion.

D Day dawns. In his kitchen he ties on his smart black apron, a memento of a "Gastronomica Catalunya" trip with his girlfriend. He begins mincing vegetables by the sink on a hand-me-down yel-low chopping board, trying not to get the fruit of his labors all over his apron and the floor. He cuts off the small hunk of the sausage python required, thinking uneasily of how easily sausage can spoil. Then his heart sinks as he realizes he read the cooking instructions inattentively—*distractedly*. As always so, with any instructions. They call for a complicated sequence of simmerings—some brief, some really *long*, which he'll have to time with a cute little kitchen timer he bought, cheaply. Which seems in practice not to possess an audible ringer. Then he realizes further, on the brink of the first long simmer of everything, that the fine red nonstick frying pan he intends to use—a hopeful gift some time ago from his girlfriend— is too small. He'll have to transfer everything, mid-cooking, to the big hand-me-down frying pan he cleaned up for display but has never used, because it's not nonstick and because it heats spottily.

It is at this point that he almost breaks down in tears of despair. That he almost picks up the phone and tells his guests the whole disastrous thing is off. *Why* is he being forced into the role of host, anyway, when he isn't a cook and his apartment is his *studio—for Christ's sake!* He'll bring extra carnations galore to repay all their hospitality—promise!

Decluttering is challenge enough!

But he restrains himself.

After more than an hour, he tries the ragu.

"My God, it's not bad," he blurts.

He sets the table with knives and forks borrowed from his girl-friend's mother. Then a last-minute shoving of stray items into the hall closet, and a grappling draping of the bare boxes remaining under the dusted piano with a big handsome ocher beach wrap from Turkey. Then setting out the antipasto of pedigreed Italian olives and braided bocconcini (homage to the smoked mozzarella of yore).

His doorbell rings.

■　　■　　■

"Wow," said Prunella, stepping across the threshold, still pale after her illness. "It's so clean!"

"Wow! So clean!" echoed Polly.

"Yum! The smell!" exclaimed my James Beard Award–winner.

Meaning: what I'd been cooking. *The smell of my own cooking that was filling my apartment.*

My heart swelled to bursting under my hostly black apron.

We sat, lit the candles—began on the appetizers. Prunella was touched by the bocconcini gesture. We raised our glasses— Amarone (Prunella and I), grossly expensive pomegranate juice (Polly).

"To this cozy, comfortable, and charming apartment," toasted

Polly. "Like a Matisse painting!" (Polly is a docent at a major Manhattan museum.)

"And to the transformational power of bookshelves," added Prunella, admiring them gleaming grand and white beside us. "Imagine if I'd let you choose the other hideous ones. Those hoarderly counters," she added, gazing beyond me, "that's what poisoned your life." She nodded in satisfaction. "Aren't you happy I helped you?"

Who was I to argue?

Who was I not to go and bring the great bowl of penne with peasant ragu out to the table?

As she reached for thirds, Polly murmured something to Prunella in their tongue. Prunella looked scandalized.

"What?" I asked.

"Mom says your pasta is much better than mine!"

Who was I not to beam my head off?

There was one unexpected jarring consequence of all this, though.

"We always cook for you," said Polly. "Now you can cook for us."

"We love it here," said Prunella. "Invite us once a month."

"But I'm not a *cook*," I protested. "This is a one-off. This is my writing studio."

"Barry's Pasta Mondays," said Polly.

"Here's to a new tradition," Prunella proposed, twirling her Amarone.

We raised our glasses once more.

I gave a grin of happiness. A crooked one.

■   ■   ■

I showed a picture of me and my guests, self-taken at table, to Dr. Equis in her little windowless office.

"That's your apartment now?" she said. "Wow."

I showed her a picture Prunella had snapped of me at the stove.

"That's your kitchen? It looks normal!"

I told her how my girlfriend and her mother expected me to cook for them once a month.

Dr. Equis smiled quietly and said, "*Your obligations will liberate you.*"

"Which is a curious thing, now, isn't it?" I replied.

. . . And left it at that.

Postscript

It's another three months later. I wake up with the sun glinting behind the blinds. I maneuver out of bed, carefully lest I waken Prunella, who needs all the sleep she can get these days. Her sleeping mask has a luridly tropical motif, so it always seems a Mardi Gras reveler has crashed on the pillow beside me. I shuffle out to the kitchen and start the coffee going. I yawn and get the milk from the fridge. A typical morning snapshot from the domestic scrapbook . . . other than it's occurring in my kitchen.

At my apartment.

We returned from a week of Miami seafood to face the aftermath at Prunella's place of an upstairs neighbor's burst pipe. It's left her semi-homeless, for ten days now and counting. Her bedroom ceiling looks post-Katrina; bits of plaster still come clinking down. The sodden mattress had to be thrown out. The closet where half her clothes were ruined reeks of mold.

So Prunella has turned for nightly succor to me—me and my lair. She continues to grumble and sniff about the dust (though I borrowed Nadya's outrageously expensive deep-cleaning water-based vacuum and went gurgling at my bed's dust mites). And she clucks about all my "silly tourist rubbish." But she prefers my place to her mom's, because Polly's apartment is "totally cluttered." And she always slept well on this bed. She says it's like old times, us here together. In response to which, I show her an ancient pillowcase of hers I saved all these years: a polar bear cub on a snowy pale blue background.

Prunella (immediately): "Eek, throw that disgusting rag out!"

Me (sighing and lying): "Okay, I will. Shortly."

But then, as gesture, as an exercise of letting-go muscle, I do it. Because why do I need this tender emblem of her when she's here herself? I take a photo first, of course. And tear up the pillowcase. I'm still that way about possessions.

Most nights we've gone down to Polly's for supper. Or we picnic on Indian microwavables at my ever-tidy dining table, beside the glowing white bookshelves, which hold more and more of my books. The dining area is my pride, my anchoring Hurdle. Before Miami, I redusted its recessed display shelves.

I've even hosted a follow-up pasta evening for mother and daughter. I went nostalgic and made fusilli with broccoli, my old standby when hosting Prunella in early days. My current version, with red pepper flakes, unincinerated garlic, and less frenziedly swamped in olive oil, is much improved. Polly, however, preferred the sausage pasta from last time.

I take a deep satisfaction in this unexpected role of my apartment as a site of nurturing. Before my Project began, the previous sentence would have been a dark oxymoron. Though I still feel a nervous twinge every time Prunella enters after burning the afternoon with insurance agents and adjusters. Because my Project remains, will remain, an ongoing process. One of the front hall closets is still a jammed jumble. The closets in the bedroom hold too many nostalgia-only clothes. The kitchen needs repainting badly. And the winnowing and sorting of the papery mishmash on the piano has barely begun. Prunella is too worn out from her day to get involved.

On the other hand, I had the super, Tod, in a week ago, without fuss, to fix the window behind the piano which was now well and truly broken after years of semi-broken neglect—years of fear that repair would be costly and get me afoul of the Bubonic Weasel. I'm now again in the flow of the world, not a skulker behind his anxious door. I have to say I've never missed my piles of boxes or bags—which gave me pause about my pet thesis of the comforting presence of clutter. But I realize my bookshelves are company; my counters, too, with their colored trays from Prunella to hold postcards and brochures. A more orderly company.

Am I, then, "cured" of cluttering?

I would answer that I've tidied up. That the atmosphere of mess and disorder no longer smothers my life. But I'm still fond of souvenirs and mementos, the "tears of things" from travels with Prunella, those ephemeral trophies nabbed from hotel rooms which I bring back to show off to myself. I possess a sensitivity—or hypersensitivity—to objects, their resonances, their powers as bearers of memory and igniters of mood (the *smile* of things as well as the tears). I'm a sentimentalist, at heart, with a maximalist streak.

Thanks to my Project, I've grown more aware and accepting of this. So has Prunella; it was she who handed me the hotel-giveaway postcard of downtown Miami's scintillating new skyline, which sits on display now in a white bookshelf. As for my precarious finances, I've sold my chronicle as a book; though I still rely, too much, on my credit cards.

Yes, I've gone kvetching at times about my Project impeding my decluttering. But I shudder to think where I'd have been without it.

What I continue to hoard are coincidences. This morning, while idling at my grand bookshelves, I spotted the volume from Prunella containing Walter Benjamin's essay "Unpacking My Library," which I perused at the start of my Project. I gave it a brief reminiscent browse . . . and came upon a line:

"To this day, Balzac's *Peau de chagrin* stands out . . . in my library as a memento of my most exciting experience at an auction."

Peau de chagrin is the French title of *The Magic Skin*—that very last book Freud was reading before he died, the novel with its narratively hoarded description of the dust-filmed trove at an antique store. Benjamin's special regard for Balzac's book in this case was not for its contents, but as a souvenir of his dramatic luck at snaring the prize old volume at a sale. He cited "the spring tide of memories which surges toward any collector as he contemplates his collection." Or his quasi-collection, I'd add myself.

I noticed Benjamin's essay was published in 1931. My coincidence sensors whirred further. In the fall of 1930 Benjamin moved into an apartment sublet in Berlin; that was where he opened his crates of long-stored books which sparked the essay. The apartment was at 66 Prinzregentenstrasse.

My father was also in Berlin then. His home stood less than a mile away from Benjamin's sublet.

So conceivably, my old man, then twenty-two years old and going by the name Heinrich Federmann, could have been walking past 66 Prinzregentenstrasse on the very night when Walter Benjamin unpacked his library!

The passionate middle-aged book collector Benjamin, whose life the swastika would soon throw into nomadic chaos, there six stories up, and my father, a young book collector whose life the swastika would soon throw into nomadic chaos, hurrying along down below, perhaps with some newly purchased volumes under his arm, perhaps late for dinner with his mother because of his book-buying.

My thoughts turning back to my old man and his possessions, I emailed Palle. Several months ago, I'd decided to give him the Bertrand Russell portrait that Tug gave me in Boston. It was to be a significant gesture, seizing on Palle's "gotcha" quip on seeing the drawing when he came here to my place. "I'm the one to whom Russell's philosophical work means a lot," he said, "so really *I* should be the one to have it." At first I was taken aback; then after he returned to Cambridge I thought, he's right. He should have the portrait. Besides, the drawing was not sitting comfortably with me. Too many memories, too many associations with Dad and his ponderous world.

So now this afternoon, months later, I wrote him to confirm my promise. His birthday is coming up. Polly will make me a high-quality Xerox at her museum; I won't lose the drawing altogether. I'll make my fine gesture.

Except I just had this reply:

"Not sure anymore if you should send the portrait. I think it may be best for you to keep it. You're the one named for him."

So now I'm stuck with the Russell drawing. And Palle, who took all of nothing from our Denver house after my parents died, still has nothing. The portrait stays for the time being where it is, up on a white bookshelf, hidden behind a flyer for James Brown's funeral in Georgia (a souvenir I'd requested from a journalist friend). It turns out my namesake's pencil-drawn visage is just a photograph of the original; but the dedication is the genuine article:

> *To Professor Yourgrau*
> *with good wishes from*
> *Bertrand Russell.*

Maybe I'll get used to it there. Or I'll stash it carefully in a plastic tub bound for Prunella's basement. A Russell signature is probably worth some money, should one be thinking that way.

■　　■　　■

"You and your family," says Prunella, shaking her head come evening. Then she goes into the bedroom for a short nap.

And then we head down to her mother's for dinner.

Acknowledgments

My agent, Susan Golomb, helped shape the vision for this book, and then found the ideal home for it. I'm abidingly grateful for her wisdom and commitment. Salutes to Jill Bialosky, my editor, for her faith in this project, trust in its writing, and knowing where lay the true heart of things—all an author could ask for. W. W. Norton has been marvelous to work with: Erin Sinesky Lovett, Angie Shih, Francine Kass, Laura Goldin, Esq., Nancy Palmquist, William Rusin, Louise Mattarelliano, Meredith McGinnis, Steve Colca, and my fine copyeditor, Allegra Huston. Salutes to Jamie Keenan's wonderful cover.

In the world that I encountered on my pilgrim's way, I'm indebted foremost to the insights, intellectual generosity, and empathetic patience of Dr. Randy Frost. My gratitude as well to his coauthor, Dr. Gail Steketee, and to Dr. Fugen Neziroglu, Dr. Sanjaya Saxena, Dr. Carolyn Rodriguez, Dr. Barry Lubetkin, and Dr. Teresa Castro-Lopez.

Similarly, in the UK, to Dr. Darian Leader, Dr. Ashley Nordsletten, and Sophie Holmes, CPsychol. Also, in the Netherlands, to Dr. Danielle Cath; in Vienna, to Dr. Elisabeth Vykoulka; and in Istanbul, to Fatma Torun Reid, M.A.

I raise my cap, high, to Ron Alford and Melissa Hladek Alford of Disaster Masters.

My thanks, for thoughtful counsel, to Lee Shuer, Rebecca Falkoff, Michael Connolly, and Sandra Felton.

My gratitude to Mag. Inge Scholz-Strasser, formerly of the Freud House Museum, Vienna, and Dawn Kemp, formerly of the Freud Museum, London; and Dr. Christfried Toegel of the Sigmund-Freud-Zentrums, Magdeburg, Germany. Also to Corinne May Botz and Dominique Nabokov; and to Nicholas Lowery of Swann Galleries, Matt Wrbican of the Andy Warhol Museum, and Ralph Gleis of the Wien Museum, Vienna.

Appreciations to Professor Edward Mendelson and William Bryk, Esq., for permission to quote from our correspondence.

I salute Mr. Richard Wallace, Mr. Andy Honey, and Mr. Christian Trumble.

Regarding the power of objects, I learned much from the perspectives of Zach Kahn, Anissa Helou, Doug Wright, Sean O'Neal, and the late Johannes van Dam.

I'm indebted to Scott Moyers and Kate Sekules, Peter Canby, Ursula and Jonas Hegewisch, Mert Erogul, Steve Fagin, and Knight and Jennifer Landesman (as ever) for their friendship and manifold kindnesses. The same goes in Istanbul to Cemre and Emre Narin, Sabiha Apaydin, and Bahar Karaca.

For far-flung hospitality (and a desk to work on), I thank my old friends Engin Akin in Istanbul and Lisa Abend in Copenhagen, and newer friends Andrew and Emma Miller and family in London.

My appreciations to Prunella Scales for sharing a memory and permission to quote it. My thanks to Vena Dacent of Conway van Gelder Grant Ltd., London.

To Dr. Equis and Dr. Nandy, as they're known in these pages, I express my very personal gratitude. To everyone I encountered in my experiences: you have my deepest respect. To which I add admiration, for the courage of my fellow sufferers with whom I shared various groups.

My twin, Tug, and his wife, Beth, and my brother Palle and his friend Mary Sullivan, I embrace. Likewise my sister, Maya Berger, to whom I'm indebted for the genealogical researches of Yossi Yagur, which were invaluable.

To all who know her, Nadya (later Polly) is a personage beloved and esteemed. This doesn't half express how I feel. I count my Nadya blessings.

As for Cosima (as I'll just call her), this book, as must be blindingly obvious, would not exist at all without her acuity and special dynamism. Nor would my Project. She was instrumental at every step. I express my gratitude, my wonderment, and all my tender love. Thank you for being the joy of my life, under any name you choose.